CHAPTER 1

IMMORTA

Today is August 11, 2010. I am in bed. It has taken me nearly a year to make up my mind about writing this story. I have hesitated in doing so for various banal reasons. However, on this auspicious day, my decision to put pen to paper is now absolute. I will be brave and share my spiritual experiences with you Reader.

So often I have asked myself the question "Who am I, how and why do I exist?" and have not been satisfied with trite, mundane answers. For the most part, I have brushed aside for the majority of my life answers that involve what my limited five senses could not perceive. But at last, I understand now that there are no accidents in this world or the next all the way to the lightest part of Infinity. There are only probabilities of occurrences; and if we should listen to the purity within, we will discover what the vast majority of us have forgotten—the essence of our true Light Self, that we exist now and will always exist—**no exception**, no debate about it. How we exist is another story. It is therefore a huge mistake, a complete utter insanity to believe even for a fraction of a second that this solid, physical world is all there is. We are not biological beings! When we buy into this pointless, limited and **foolish** view of infinite possibility of existence, then we limit ourselves of what is naturally a part of us. When this happens, then we not only give our power and positive energy away to what I call negative forces, but imprison our Light Selves deep inside our physical, solid bodies with fear, confusion of what we really are beyond time, space, and all that is naturally and literally part of the undying Ensemble.

There is an immortal love within and beyond this physical dimension and it cannot die. Like it or not, believe it or not, it is not a gift. It cannot die. It cannot be "created." It can only have positive or negative experiences in each level of consciousness. Suffering is the worst thing that can happen to a soul residing and interfacing with the condensed, solid body. Death of the physical body is merely a separation of the heavy vehicle from the infinitely light body or the soul.

Most Light Beings enter this consciousness initially more aware. With the passing of time, constant societal, worldly and inter-dimensional manipulations and assaults, and what we feed our physical bodies and minds, our soul's global awareness diminishes. However, a piece of Infinity cannot be fooled forever. Sooner or later the dormant piece of God within the solid body must be awakened.

As I put pen to paper, I can only imagine the possible ridicule that lies ahead by those whose souls are deeply asleep within their human bodies. Unfortunately, we live in a world where the *insane* person thinks the *sane* person is crazy simply because the former is unaware. No matter how smart or educated a person is, he or she can still be very unaware of his or her true nature of existence. In fact, it seems to me that the more *formally* indoctrinated a person is, the more likely it is that his or her soul exists in a dormant state. This is because formal education, at all levels, as it is now has been set up to worship the intellect, which is *the mind*. As a person becomes more and more indoctrinated through the process of a mostly false religion we call science, the awareness of his or her true Light Self

A GLIMPSE OF WHO WE ARE

AGBE BEN EPOU

Contact: P.O. BOX 1136,
             Spring Valley, New York 10977, U.S.A.

For information about special discounts for bulk purchases,
        please contact Agbe Ben Epou at the
        above address or the website below:

www.agbeepou.com

Library of Congress Control Number: 0000TXU0017615940101

ISBN: 9780985274207

ACKNOWLEDGMENTS

To all those souls in this dimension and beyond who are helping to raise the consciousness of our world; to my father's unfaltering love; to Mother Earth and Mother Ayahuasca for their spiritual healing; to Marlene Moss for editing this book, and for her encouragements to go all the way, and not to hold back; and foremost, to my brother Essevi for his tenacious, incredible, mind boggling love, and his unrelenting dedication to keep me alive to see my life's mission through:

I thank you from the purest part of my soul.

CONTENTS

becomes more inhibited or blocked. And I absolutely know now that this is no accident.

I write to be brave, to be free, to seek freedom beyond this physical world. I am trying to be brave, because for so long, I have lived in fear, fear of what lies ahead after the death of the physical body, in fear of going against established traditions, cultures, religions, and science; but mostly, I must say that I have lived in fear of what others might say or think. Perchance, they would think that I am different, weird, or even "have lost my marbles." But, I am trying to surpass all that in order to get in touch with the inner core of that part of us that is not afraid, that is beautiful, infinite, and that embraces pure love, the luminosity of Infinity. And so, I am pushing aside all these obstacles to describe pure beauty that goes to Infinity.

I am also writing for those across the world who are practicing negativity, either physically or through the use of the dark arts. There is no neutrality about using Black Magic to hurt your fellow soul mates. **None!** Governments across the world, stop creating negative energy by sending our young men and women to fight in wars under the pretext of serving your countries. Negativity is literally harmful for you. In the very long term, you cannot and will not get away with any such things, even if it takes five or ten thousand years. Whether you like it or not, believe me or not, you are eternal and your soul cannot die despite how many people you hurt or kill. You can only suffer. And suffer you will if you do not stop such practices. And when you eventually begin to suffer beyond your wildest imagination, you will see that there are worse things in the universe than physical death. When this happens, do not blame God. It was not Infinity's fault. It was your fault for not listening to your intuition, and for not having taken the time to consider and research the basic questions of existence outside of what is considered the norm. It was your fault for not listening to the literal piece of God within your physical vehicle. This is one of the ultimate lessons to be relearned—obey the purity within yourself that is pushing you to reach the Most High, the Most Positive, no matter the obstacles or fears. If you can do that, what awaits you in each dimension of consciousness is beyond the human imagination.

This story is so fantastic that if one's awareness is blocked or not open enough, I can only imagine some people brandishing it as fiction. But, it is not. Satan or the Devil has nothing on us. **A MILLION SUPERMAN PUT TOGETHER HAS ABSOLUTELY NOTHING ON ONE SOUL.** Superman's super human powers are extremely primitive compared to the literal weapons inside each individual soul.

This is not an easy story for me to write. Despite this difficulty, I feel my inner essence pushing me on to accomplish the task. I feel my strength increasing each day, and despite whatever negativity some of my fellow soul mates may have in store for me, either via ridicule or categorization or black magic as I have recently physically witnessed, I will dispense waves of positive energy toward them. I will be strong, light, and resist some of the dimly aware-person's theories and rationalizations of me and themselves. Yes, too many people do this. Too many people are forever limiting themselves. This, I will no longer overlook or accept, because it creates intangible negative energy and holds us in a state of slavery. Having had a glimpse of my soul is not a result of being Black, American, African, a male, a catholic, or any other mundane and superficial reasons some people may make up to brush aside my experiences.

To do justice to my superheroes' courage and unconditional love, I must commence the story from my childhood. Perhaps even more importantly, I must share with you Reader my strengths and weaknesses, my thoughts and reflections, even the emotions that I experienced while writing this book. And if I can do all this, then I am already brave. Pure love transcends all ephemeral things.

CHAPTER 2:

MY CHILDHOOD

Only a handful of beings have affected me so profoundly in this world. When I think about my current state of consciousness, I recall my paternal grandmother, my father, my mother, my ram, and most of all you Essevi, my brother. I want you to know that I love you beyond time, space, and to the stillness of all things, where there is only the now and time exists not. I love you beyond our competitive nature. I love you beyond that day when we both wanted so much to be right about the paragraph thing. I love you for rushing to me that day in the kitchen, going past me. I was not brave then. I could have prevented the pain you suffered—*maybe*. But yet, I just seized his hands merely saying, "Can't you see he's hurt?" I am crying now as I write these words. I have been trying so hard to follow a chronological order as I write this book, but emotions run deep. It looks like I am failing miserably...

Alright, I am feeling better now, less emotional, less crying. Why do I weep so? After all, you are here now. Images of that night—you recall, November 6, 2009, flashed before my mind's eye, you fighting for me again. Perhaps, it is not all because I miss you. Perhaps, part of the tears is because I really feel loved by you.

You and I did everything together: climbing trees, fishing, eating certain types of insects, playing soccer, and swimming. That day at the lake! Images just rushed into my mind. The sun was shining beautifully, and we were in the sandy area, on dry land. My eyes wandered from left to right. There was no one around but you, me, and one of the village children who was drowning. That day, do you remember when you saved him? Do you remember that I was afraid of the water when we were children? I still am. I cannot swim to save my soul.

You jumped into the water, without hesitation. You brought him out. I stood on the rocks by the bamboos to the right. You pumped his stomach and water came out of his mouth. He breathed with a cough. Do you remember the stillness of the river? You, as you stood there! That would be one of my greatest memories. Even now, I can still hear the placidity of the music of the river. I remember the look of you. A life saved!

We would return home that evening with the silence of that day's accomplishment, but no one would ever know except us. This would be only one of our great adventures together.

Oh, the Ghanaian guy! Do you remember him? We were selling food for our wicked grandmother in the street in front of our house. We were standing up. Do you recall, mon cher frère? A Ghanaian man approached us from across the street.

"Are you twins?"

"Yes!" I nodded with my head jubilantly. Do you recall him giving us some money because he believed twins brought good luck? It was a lie, though it was a nod of the head. He wanted good luck and I gave it to him.

Do you also remember that auspicious day when you destroyed some of the mounted earth you erected with your agricultural tool? We were at the farm. Our grandmother

Amano said something that upset you. She was whining without appreciating the work that we had done. I remember the way you walked away. We were in the middle of the field in Kusuntu. There was a surprised look on her face. I wish you would have ruined more of the mounted earth. I should have left with you, but I stayed with her in that smoldering heat until the evening. Do you recall her punishment? So many times we went to bed hungry because she refused to feed us. Ha! Oh, what about the time she refused me food for three days? You must recall how I handled it. As I think about this now, my mind is again full of images. I was in front of the kitchen. I had some cookware in my hand, which I bought with my own money from fishing. I uttered a few words to my grandmother, and left the house. I went to the backyard, the field right behind the house.

There was a lemon tree there, which is now gone. Under this tree were heavy rocks, piled up one against another. I put my cook wares underneath it. You did not come with me Essevi, but do you remember that I too attempted to be brave? That first evening, I only had a shirt, which I took off to use as a sheet. I folded it, and placed it on the thick, heavy rocks, and slept on it. The rocks did a number to my back, but my determination was renewed when I woke up that morning thinking about how this woman really did not care about me.

I made a fire by gathering a few rocks and some sticks. I cannot recall if I had matches. In any case, as I cooked my yams, the smoke of the fire rose above the sky. Several women passed, curiously looking at my direction. My grandfather must have known by this point that I was outside, but I do not recall seeing his face in the yard. My grandmother was in charge, controlling things. Such a short, little person! She was not even five-foot tall, but yet willed so much power in that household. How? I would learn the answer only when I became an adult.

I walked to the left, toward the big bread oven, right next to the entrance of the house. I saw no one. I thought about going inside, but then remembered the firm words I proffered to my grandmother.

Day two came now, and I was starting to become accustomed to my new life. I was either ten or eleven years old. I do not recall precisely, but I do remember that it was not long before I went to the United States of America.

Smoke filled the morning sunny sky, and as usual, women passed through the backyard, heading to the market. Unpleasant words would be uttered about my grandmother. I would not hear them all but would understand their general meaning.

Day three came and went. I slept under the tree again. I planted some root vegetables. I was beginning to take pleasure in my new life when I began to hear talk around town. My return to the house was imminent. People in the village were complaining about how poorly my grandmother Amano was treating me. Once the whole village started talking, it was a done deal. During the entire time I resided in the backyard, my grandmother did not once come to check on me. She simply did not care. Only embarrassment would render her to her knees. And that was exactly what transpired. She was summoned to appear before the king of Kusuntu. The king spoke about the accusation against her. She was compelled to kneel before him, and in that position she remained for hours.

Upon returning from the king's house, she asked me to come back to the house. However, I would not go right away. Do you remember all this, Essevi? Well, you see, I can be as brave as you *now*.

More mental pictures just rushed into my head. There was an evening when a lot of people in the village would talk about. There was a party somewhere in Kpalimé, which you attended all alone. It was very late at night. I was impressed because you were only about eight years old but so audacious. I thought at that time that you were different, bolder. Unlike you, I was ordinary and unadventurous. So, I admired you that morning when everybody in the village was talking about it.

The spring seasons were the most memorable for us. We hunted delicacies together. We gathered little editable insects. Do you remember? The ones with wings! We roasted them on the open charcoal or wood fire and they were succulent. I know you remember! We would take the little wings off and then roast them until they were brown, delicious. Ha, ha! Our grandmother was not able to starve us in those days. She complained and complained, saying that the whole thing was disgusting. But, they were so appetizing and tasty. There was a certain delicious oily taste about the insects. No matter how much she complained, we went out and got more under rocks. Sometimes, we went as far as Kpalimé, the next village. I am smiling now.

When I was not spending quality time with my brother, I was with my special friend, to whom I owe much of my spiritual growth today.

I was about eight or nine old when he came into my life. I was there when his mother gave birth to him. I used to feed him everyday. I recalled many magical moments together where he showed me love. One of those times was on a Saturday morning. I passed my cousin Kudjo's room to the right, and opened the first door, walked through the narrow corridor and reached the final door to the rams. After closing the main door, I saw them at the entrance of their den. All four of them were sitting with their legs tucked in between their stomachs. So calm—they appeared as they chewed and rocked back and forth. They stirred slightly, rose and approached me. I swept my eyes across the room to acknowledge them all. Then, I intently settled my eyes upon the one. Standing in the narrow corridor, not knowing why I had let him out, I glanced at the animal. He stared back and waited patiently and calmly for my next move. I walked to the last door, opened it, and motioned forward for him to follow. No words were uttered. I opened the door and he followed me out. His forelegs bent slightly in every time he took a step. My brother Essevi ran past me. Kudjo pursued him.

We exited through the back of the house, across from which there was a large opening where I normally played. I looked around, walked toward the fence of the neighbors. They seemed to be absent. I heard no voice or sound emanating from there. The ram did not approach. He stood at a distance, watching me as I solemnly stared at the fence. I was feeling a little sad, thinking about my father. I sat down on the ground, leaning my back against the semi-grey brick wall. The ram was still observing me. Then he came to me. He bent his head, lowering it toward the earth. His head was in the palm of my hand now. I raised my knees and pulled my hand away. My head was now between my knees. It was not long before I felt a nudge. The ram was gently nudging me with his horns. I did not move. Still, he nudged me harder. I raised my head to look at my friend, who presently had his head on my thighs, with his eyes gazing upward at me. I was not surprised at this. I had always known that this creature's inner essence was special, smart, but now as he stared at me, there was something distinct, eternal, and human about him. He lowered his head and averted his eyes downward.

I observed his head and stroked it. My hand descended to his awesome, strong horns. Beautiful! I sat there repeating this motion with calm and he laid there receiving it peacefully. Time passed, but we had no notion of how long we had been there. I was completely comfortable, worry free. I was with my friend. At some point, we both became motionless. We stayed like this for about an hour or so undisturbed, both dozing off. I felt a connection with him, but the moment's deep signification would only reach me in 2009 when I would begin to awake spiritually.

Presently, a woman with a big bowl on her head was returning from the market. She recognized me as she seized me with her vivid brown eyes. Her heavy sandals made a slapping sound as she walked. Startled, the ram raised himself up promptly. I dug my hand into my pocket for my flute. I put it to my lips and began blowing not knowing exactly how to play it. The ram looked at me curiously, wondering what I was doing. I stopped to figure out how to produce a more harmonious sound. I placed a finger on every other hole and began to blow again. No! That was not it. I did not know how to play. However, as the big ram started hopping about me, I decided it did not matter how well I played. I blew and blew with my might. The unharmonious sound excited him, and he hopped joyfully about me. "Look!" I thought, he was dancing.

As I played, it did not take me long before I learned how to manipulate the flute and cause the ram to move to action. I blew the flute in intervals of harmonious sound and then paused. Each time I did this, my friend marched about. It was exciting and above all fun for him. It was a march, a harmonious march. His hind and forelegs marched. They actually marched! And each time I paused he paused rhythmically. *This cannot be!* Surprised, I ceased playing and took out the flute from my mouth. A minute or so passed where I did not play it. The ram stood still, observing and staring at me. I put the flute back in my mouth and recommenced. And once again, he danced. His hind legs, forelegs, march! Forelegs, hind legs, march! Pause!

Essevi ran pass us. Kudjo was still chasing him. They must have taken a break at one point. Essevi probably came back from somewhere and Kudjo started on him again. My friend and I went inside the house. He held Essevi with his left hand while striking him with his t-shirt with his right hand. He delighted in hitting him harder with the t-shirt.

"What did he do to you?" I demanded of *fo*[1] Kudjo.

"He has no respect for anyone."

By this, he really meant that Essevi always spoke up for himself. The lamb was curiously watching as he stood beside me.

"Let him go!" I shouted.

"Mind your own business!"

"You're hitting my brother!" I shouted at him.

He turned to hit me as Essevi stepped away from harm's way.

"Stop! Kudjo, stop!" I pleaded.

The ram took a few slow steps toward fo Kudjo, looking at him intently and beastly.

"Let go of my arm!" I shouted, "Fo Kudjo!"
The ram advanced decisively toward him.

"Let go of my arm!" I shouted again. I yanked my arm about, but I knew fo Kudjo was not going to stop. What was I to do? I thought about kicking him in the foot, but decided not to do so because he was older and bigger than me. I knew that if I employed force, he would have returned it two-fold. However, I needed not have worried because I had a loyal friend. What happened next was a

---

[1] This is the polite form of saying mister or señor in English and Spanish respectively. It is used before a male's first name. Da or davi is the equivalence for a girl or a woman.

demonstration of love that would compel me to glimpse at the soul of all living creatures much later in life.

The ram raised his forelegs and brought them down with a powerful stump. The rise was awesome; the airborne hold seemed infinite. The fall was immense and thunderous. He curved his head forward with fury and passion and consequently pushing his two horns forward wildly. The fall of his forelegs jolted his body slightly backwards and then forward again. His eyes intently met Kudjo's and did not waver. Kudjo understood the meaning of this and ceased his infliction of violence upon me. But it was too late. My friend moved forward a couple of inches. He lowered his head and pushed his horns fiercely. Kudjo took off running, heading toward the front door near the street. "Call him off!" he yelled as he ran out with the ram on his tail.

A few weeks after my ram saved me from Kudjo's beating, I walked into the kitchen one early Saturday afternoon and heard grinding of rocks. I passed the kitchen, to the other side where the pepper-grinding stone was. Fo Kudjo was passionately grinding something. I went closer. I saw red chili peppers. Still, I was curious. I walked even closer. There was something on the flat stone with the peppers. The whole place smelled of some sort of burned hair of an animal. Finally, there it was, staring at me—the head of a big lizard. I stepped back, stupefied. So, that was the smell I was sensing. Fo Kudjo had smoked the lizard, and was now about to grind it with the peppers. On the fire was cassava boiling. I did not say anything to him. I simply observed in amazement. He seemed to be in a jovial mood. It was evident that his good mood was in the anticipation of his meal. As he walked over to the boiling pot, he smiled and said:

"It's going to be really good."

14

The cassava was apparently ready, for he drained the water from the pot. He took the lid off the pot so as to let the food cool, and returned to the grinding stone. I walked toward the shower, which had large stones and rocks where we put the hot water-bucket to wash ourselves. I looked around for an edible rotten, just hoping, knowing well that there was very little chance that I would find a headless large rat. If there had been one, I was sure that fo Kudjo would have beaten me to the punch. Occasionally, we children found headless rats near the grinding stone. Essevi and I were well fed in such opportune times. We would gut the rat and season it with salt, black pepper, and ground chili peppers. Then we would roast it on the open fire. We usually ate it with cassava or yams. Boy, was it good!

I turned to leave. Fo Kudjo was already eating. He offered me some, extending his plate. I stared at him, half fascinated and half disgusted. I remained absolutely silent for a moment, then walked away to find something fun to do.

One of the few entertainments that our village Kusuntu offered was the lagoon. Essevi, my younger cousin Koku and I often went to swim there. The lagoon on this Saturday afternoon was filled with the village children. I was on top of the big, oversized rock, which was elevated above the water. We used to jump into the water from this rock. Presently, I was on top of the rocks when I saw several adults approaching us. Some of them went to the lower level of the lagoon where I was and asked us to leave. The others walked to the larger section to secure the perimeters. All the children obeyed, and they thought the place was safe from intruders. They had guards stationed at the entrances, but had neglected the area behind the bamboo trees. It was there that I was hiding, waiting to see why they had kicked us out of the place.

It was not yet five o'clock in the afternoon. The sun was waning. They were talking. Gingerly now, I walked closer to the bamboos. A smile etched on my face. I held the bamboos. I was about to see the whole thing from its inception to its end. The adults walked into the water, the shallow part. One of the men placed himself in the center of the water. The water digested a good sixty percent of his body. The group positioned itself in somewhat of a circular structure. The only woman among them was directly in front of me. I could see her back. The group chanted words, repeating certain expressions over and over. I watched and listened acutely, understanding most of their words, but some escaping me. The tall guy closer to the elevated rock was in charge. He was calling something, talking to an invisible being. I do not recall his exact words, but it was clear what he was asking for. A couple of them lathered African style sponges with soap until they were foamy, then they began to give the guy in the center a bath. They washed and rinsed him. Then came the request from the tall man.

"Marry him!"

I tried to understand what this man was asking, and above all, *whom was he asking the man in the center to marry?*

A few seconds after I posed this question, my answer literally appeared. A woman rose from the depths of the water—with a huge, long tail of a fish. My mouth dropped, and would remain ajar for a long while. I tightened my hold on the bamboos. My eyes widened. I blinked. The woman who just rose from the water had arms and a face like that of a human being. She was smiling and grabbing onto the man who was supposed to marry her. The mermaid pulled the guy toward the bottom of the water. The others fought against this. Water splashed every which way. The mermaid fought harder. Her excitement was palpable. She had accepted their request for the marriage and wanted to take her husband down underneath the waters. The others, I supposed, did not want the guy to drown. Well, at least, that was what I thought. Perhaps, the mermaid had a solution to this. After all, she existed! Then, my logical mind kicked in. *Is there life underneath the waters?* My mind was filled with questions. This was the first and the last time I would ever see a mermaid.

The group managed to prevent the mermaid from taking their companion with her. She disappeared underneath the water. The group talked among themselves. It was clear to me that it was time to go. I had to get out of there before they saw me. Thus, I rushed out of there as fast as I could. Years later, because of my formal educational training, I would rationalize this incident as scientifically impossible until 2009 when the invisible became visible and I would completely accept it as real. But, for now, I would tuck this memory away, to be understood later.

I returned home. My grandfather asked me to kill a chicken to be cooked for dinner. *Yeah!* I heard myself say inside my head. It was my first time. That meant that he thought I was old enough to do an adult's task. He handed me the flapping chicken, and I seized it by both of his wings, and he left. Not only did he give me the job, he also trusted me enough not to supervise or bear over me... I was only a few feet away from the relatively small, detached brick house which was located near the principal door of the main entrance to the house. Inside this shed-like house was Togbui Sikpui, which literally means "grandfather" in Ewe. I heard adults describe it as a chair, representing the spirit of the Epou family. My grandfather prayed in front of the door once in a while. The prayer was always more or less the same. "Grandfathers, great, great grandfathers, and ancestors, Epou...protect the family, your family."

I averted my eyes from Togbui Sikpui and returned my attention to the chicken that I had just killed. I cleaned up the blood on the ground. My grandmother put it in a pot and poured boiling water onto it. This allowed the feathers to soften for the plucking. I removed the feathers. Then, I cut the chicken into pieces. Not even the feet, the entrails, or the intestines would be wasted. I recall very well the intestines being quite good in fufu soup. For the life of me, I cannot recall what we ate that evening. I do not remember if it was fufu or akple. I cannot be sure, but I definitely know that the chicken I had killed was part of this delicious meal. I recall my stomach being particularly stuffed that evening.

The next living creature's life I would take was a snake. One weekend, I went to my elementary school to kill time. I walked around the school. I was presently under several huge mango trees. I looked up at the mangos. *Should I throw a rock or a stick up?* No, I was not really hungry. I walked to the classroom buildings, where the upper grades were located. I looked up, pondering whether or not to climb. I was on the ground level—the soil. From where I was standing, one had to climb up using the cement stairs which was a meter or so above. *Well, maybe I should go home.* I heard chalk striking a blackboard. *Someone must be studying on the weekend.*

I was on the verge of turning around to go home when a snake appeared out of nowhere. I did not budge. The cobra was a mere yard or so away from me. We were face to face. It started hissing, staring at me intently. I pondered the little creature. My soul was calm inside my body. The snake must have sensed this, or perhaps not. I stood there waiting for it to make a move. The guy studying must have heard the hissing noise, for he came out. He was above us on top of the stairs. I looked up at him. I did not know him. He stood there at the elevated position, looking down at the cobra and I, waiting to see what I was going to do. I picked up a stick on the ground. The cobra elevated its head and body, curving its head. It was tall, very tall, hissing. It seemed taller than me now. It was a formidable sight to experience.

My countenance remained the same—cool, poised to battle. I advanced toward the creature. I struck it without fear. Strike after strike, its body receded. Finally, it lied on the ground still, motionless. It was lifeless now, dead.

"Here!" I heard from above.

"You are very brave!" he said, throwing a penny at me. I picked it up, not uttering a word. I walked toward the cobra, observed it. Not long ago it was so full of animation. What animated its body? I asked myself silently. Even back then I was curious about the nature of existence. I wondered if the cobra would still exist in some shape or form. *What just happened? It's dead! It was going to attack me.* I turned and walked away with calm. At that time, I did not feel any remorse, but in hindsight, I know that the snake did not have to die. I could have simply walked away once I knew it was ready to attack me. Contrary to the older boy's declaration, I was not brave. I stopped the cobra's earthly experience prematurely and unnecessarily. *Why did you challenge me with your hissing? You must have known that there was no way I would have backed down. Wherever your soul is now, I apologize for what I did to you twenty years ago, though it was not entirely my fault. I could have simply walked away, but I did not. It is only now that I feel the sorrow for having ended your life before its natural end. I am sorry.* May the powers of the Universe hear me. May you hear me now. I am truly sorry.

Not long after ending the cobra's life, my curiosity to explore the unseen world would cause me physical pain. I was home with Akpené, Essevi and others whose name I do not recall. My cousin Akpené had suggested that we explore the forbidden shed-like little house. She wanted to go inside. I do not remember where she found the key. She must have taken it from my grandfather's room. I hesitated going in because I did not want to be caught. They were already inside. I followed along. They stopped where the light met the darkness. I looked around, waiting to see something mysterious. Maybe I was going to see spirits or ghosts. I went farther inside the room. I was alone now. My fellow crime mates were far away. My curiosity propelled my feet forward. Still, I did not see anything. I turned to the right. There it was—a very small chair. This was the "Togbui sikpui." It was just a little wooden chair that one could grab with one hand. There were not any spirits. I did not feel or see any such thing. I was calm, unafraid. I could no longer hear my fellow crime mates's voices, but could hear their feet scuffling away from the room. I began walking toward the door without haste.

"They're coming!" someone shouted out. By the time I reached the door, my seven-foot tall, slender grandfather was there to seize me. As he grabbed me, I saw my cousin Kudjo running after the rest of the children. He did not catch any of them. They all ran out of the house. Togbui pulled me toward the kitchen as he and Kudjo discussed how to punish me. Kudjo went into the kitchen and came back with small hot red chilling peppers. They peppered my eyes, and I screamed and tried to fight them off with my hands and arms, but it was too late. I could not see. Every time I tried opening my eyes, they stung so strongly that the pain was intolerable. Despite this, every once in a while I had to open them to guide me to water. Eventually, I succeeded, but the water was of very little use.

Hours passed, but I still did not feel any better. It would not be until the next morning when I would be able to see. I did not think the punishment was just. I was particularly unhappy with fo Kudjo who seemed to have enjoyed administering the punishment. That was fine, for his day to experience physical would soon come. And so it was during the early evening when I exited the kitchen to the right, where Kudjo's room was. Reader, please do not ask me what possessed me to go hang out with him. All I can say is that children can sometimes forget and forgive bad things done to them rather quickly. I heard a discussion between my grandmother and my younger aunt's husband about some stolen food—sardines. The husband was insisting that it was fo Kudjo who had stolen the food.

"He didn't do it," my grandmother protested vehemently. Refusing to believe my grandmother, he walked into Kudjo's room. He stared at Kudjo with a look of anger for two or three seconds, and then took off his shoes, and let one of them descend upon Kudjo's face, slapping him so hard that one would have thought that he were merely an object of no value. When the guy was tired of striking him with his shoe, he put it down and slapped his face with his hand so hard that I literally uttered "Oh!" meekly. The husband stopped for a brief second. Kudjo uttered no cries, no sound. He received the hits with no emotions. Blood dripped from his face. I had never seen a human being receive such brutal, crude physical strikes upon his body and not utter a single wail.

"Where is it?" the husband demanded.

"I don't know," Kudjo responded the first few times, then after that he was silent. It would soon be obvious that Kudjo was lying. The guy was now apparently tired. He searched the room, and found the sardines very close to where he was beating him. I was completely speechless. I could not stand looking at the cuts and blood on Kudjo's face, so I exited the room.

The husband was so brutal that I would never dare go near him again as long as I was in that household. I mean, he savagely beat Kudjo so intensely that I was beginning to doubt if he had any compassion left in him.

It is true that Kudjo was a strange soul. A few years after I went to America, I learned that he had returned to Kpélé, his native town, where my grandmother was also from. I was told that he became crazy and died soon after.

Besides my brother, Koku, and my ram friend, I also spent a lot of time with my aunt's husband's oldest daughter from his first marriage. She was always teaching Essevi and I life lessons. If I recalled correctly, she was two or three years older than us. Essevi and I spent a lot of time with her.

On one particular weekend, I recalled her life being in danger. We were passing through Sokpoyo's farm; we had to in order to get to the other side. This was the route we usually took. We were merely a few yards away from traversing to the other side when we saw Sokpoyo. He had a machete in his hand. I was concerned because the village people considered him crazy. I looked at his face. His eyes looked full of desire, envy, and steadiness. He stood there with wondrous, anticipatory eyes. He threw his arms around my cousin, squeezing tightly. She made a disagreeable moaning noise. He kept going; she insisted that he stop, citing her father's name. It was completely clear to me that he was going to kill her without really meaning it. The desire in him was immense and intense. He hugged her so tightly, as if he were never going to let go. She told him that her father was on the way. He stopped. Saying her father's name had worked. We passed him and were gone. When we were far away and could no longer see him, she talked to me about her father. Apparently he was the only person in the village of whom Sokpoyo was afraid. He had beaten him up fairly well at one point. He was about average height: about five foot seven or eight inches tall.

Not long after the Sokpoyo incident, a few of the children in the neighborhood informed me that something strange was happening at my aunt's house. I immediately rushed to go see the spectacle. Upon arriving, I had to fight a crowd of people to see the real action. In front of the bedroom door was my aunt's husband palpitating on a wooden chair. He was shivering uncontrollably. Neighbors from different parts of the village had gathered around to see what was transpiring. My cousin-friend, his oldest daughter, was there. Even Amano was there. I looked at him pitifully. His feet were in the grey, silver bucket, in the hot water. My aunt went to the kitchen, which was to the left of the bedroom. She returned with more hot water and a washcloth. She changed the water, and soothed his face with the washcloth. Nevertheless, he shivered in agony. It looked as if his whole body was going to give in at any second. My aunt applied the towel to his forehead. This seemed to go on for an eternity. I honestly thought that he was going to die. Several thoughts went through my mind. First, I thought that perhaps he had a real physical sickness. Then I considered Black Magic. That was what a lot of people were saying in town—that he was involved in it. A couple of people went up to where he was and started praying for him in Ewe. Mawu's name (i.e., God) was evoked. It seemed we had been there for an eternity. Finally, he was getting better. The shivering had decreased tremendously.

Several months passed. My cousin left us forever. I think she went to live with her mother. I have not seen her since then. My aunt Lisa, pronounced with a z sound, was pregnant again. I guessed this because she was constantly spitting. She and her husband only lived a few minutes away, and so she often came to our house to see us, to talk to her mother, our very wicked grandmother. It seemed they got along. My grandmother knew how to conceal her wickedness extremely well. The depth of her negativity came in different guises, shapes, and forms, and her facet of negativity was a bottomless pit.

One day, ashamed from having done something shameful, I sought to hide myself from the world. I took some food from my grandmother's pannier without asking for permission because I was extremely hungry. I hid myself in the chest box in the living room and tried to remain as still as possible.

My grandmother came into the room, followed by a stranger. I knew now that I could not get out. If I did, I would be caught. The guy and Amano talked and talked for hours. From an opening, I was able to see both my grandmother and the man. They were very deep into the conversation. She was so excited.

"Do you know that they can put a person's soul in an animal, kill the animal and the person in turn would die?..."

The guy listened attentively and seemed to be enjoying the conversion. I, on the other hand, created pictures in my head as she spoke. Directly behind me in the other room was the living quarter of my rams. A picture of my favorite emanated in my head, and I imagined how a person could be turned into an animal and then murdered. A part of my brain pondered this seriously, while the other part brandished it as fantasy. *She was just talking.* However, I would learn twenty years later that the dark arts is no joke, and my grandmother had a good understanding of it. One could kill people without physical weapons. Later, I would understand that once the animal is killed, the witches would cook and eat the meat. It is part of their ritual. Such people knew secrets. They have their own owls, owls they use to travel, fly at night. They would leave their bodies, enter the body of the owl and fly to whatever destination they wanted at night, to do whatever wickedness or negativity they chose.

I was able to escape without them ever finding out. I left as soon as they left the room.

About a month later, my grandmother made a most interesting pronouncement. I was standing near our renter's place, which was several yards away. She was in good spirit. She stood near the kitchen. I was looking directly at her from the other side of the house. She was talking to one of my aunts. I understood that she had gone somewhere and was reporting back what she had learned. She turned slightly to her left and said the most interesting thing.

"One of Yema's three boys will do something great for the country."

I maintained a steady lock on her face as I considered her words. She was serious. Given this observation, I began considering which one of us three boys would do this. I eliminated myself and settled upon my brother Essevi because he was the most daring and adventurous. Then I asked myself what he would do. This again would be one of those things that I would tuck away for years to come.

A few months later, my grandmother announced that she was going to find and bring home all of my father's children. She found Elomevi and Afefa at the capital city. Elomvi was supposedly one of the two. He was about two and a half years younger than I was. Elomevi had a slick personality and it showed especially when he ate with others. It was normal in those days for children and adults to eat from the same bowl. Elomevi and I often ate together. Whenever this occurred, the food did not last. He had a peculiar way of hiding most of the food that he took with his hand. Take rice for example, he would join his fingers of his right hand into a pointed circle. When he did this, only a little bit of the food showed up on the top, pointed finger area. This allowed most of the food to be hidden in his lower palm area. When he took his hand to his mouth, the majority of the food in his hand was therefore concealed.

Afefa, also had a distinct and interesting personality. I was only a year older than her. She had a lot to teach me about women, if only I applied those lessons to my future relationships, especially the last girl who broke my heart, about whom I have not written. To me, Afefa would have made a superb actress. She was an outgoing person and I liked spending time with her. She was joyous and was very expressive emotionally. Unless you knew her well, she could be insincere or untruthful and you would have totally believed her.

Once, my grandfather was smoking a whole fish on a portable charcoal grill oven in the left, open area of the house when he suddenly realized that he had to go do an errand. To the right of the grill was one of the people renting a room from him. When my grandfather returned, he was upset to see the grill empty. I guess he thought that it would still be there when he came back. Ha! Someone had taken the fish. He asked Essevi and I if we did it, and we answered no. The look on his face indicated that he did not believe us. I waited for Afefa to confess. She did not. In fact, she started swearing to God with her fingers that she did not do it, and had tears to show for it. Even the intonation and the eco in her voice all seemed sincere. To complete a stranger it would have seemed that she was telling the truth.

I stood near the kitchen door watching my sister's extraordinary gift of lying. She cried profusely, and begged my grandfather to believe her. Seeing this *audacious* Oscar performance, I knew that a third party had to come to our rescue. I turned my eyes to the guy renting the room from us. I stared at him intently. I definitely saw him look at me. I waited for him to say something. Before I knew it, he turned to my grandfather and told him that he saw Afefa take the smoked fish. Despite this, my sister persisted with her lie. Fortunately, it was now clear from his face that my grandfather no longer believed her.

I think the major lesson I was supposed to learn here was that no matter how nice or loving someone appears to be, he or she may not be strong enough to demonstrate his or her inner bright purity.

Several months later, we received a guest one inauspicious evening. She had recently travelled abroad where my father was supposed to be hiding from the government. I am very sure it was the Ivory Coast. Chairs were brought out for her and the adults to sit. They were placed under the avocado tree that was in the center of the house. A kerosene was also brought out. Our guest seemed to be in her early forties, a little bit on the plus-sized and light skinned. She was wearing a white shirt and a dress and was very pretty. She reported that she was with my father before he died.

Shortly after I obtained news of my father's death, some of my interests waned. One of such things was the ridiculous formal education system. This was the excuse I needed to skip school. I did not like going to school at all. I was not learning anything, and besides, we were constantly beaten in the hand and in the buttocks. My first grade teacher did not teach. He spoke Ewe the majority of the time. Since I really did not feel that I was learning, one

27

Wednesday morning, I decided to skip school and go fishing. Besides, I needed the money a lot more than this futile education I was being given. Thus, on that morning, I decided to have fun. I went to Loméme. There was not a single person at the river. I fished all morning, but was only able to catch one cat fish. Given that my fellow students would be returning home soon, I left the river as quickly as I could. As I approached the central place where the village obtains drinking water, I held my breath, being nervous that one of my classmates or schoolmates might see me. That was precisely what happened. Agbessi, one of the boys in the village with the same first name saw me and reported me to the teacher. That same afternoon, I already understood that this same Agbessi was spreading the rumor that he actually saw me fishing. He was lying, of course.

Fear of being beaten took over me and I refused to go to school the ensuing day. Given these rumors, I feared that my buttocks would be swollen by beatings if I were to return to school. The short first grade teacher had a small wooden baton which he had over the years. He even christened it as "Togbui Kpui," which translates as "short grandfather." The image of Togbui Kpui dancing around my buttocks swiftly weighed heavily upon my mind.

I stood in the front portion of our house that day as two school students passed the main road. One of them was quite nice to report to me the danger I was going to be in if I were brave enough to return to school.

"Agbessi told the teacher that you skipped school to go fishing. The teacher said that he is going to give you a good ass-whopping when you return."

The second student displayed a serious countenance in agreement of the first. I studied his visage cautiously. Upon such serious observation, I understood that I could never return to school again. No, it was not safe to go back. The teacher delighted in whipping us children. He used to do it as he chewed cola nuts right in the classroom.

Friday came and I still did not return to school. By Monday afternoon, my grandmother had understood what was transpiring. She understood that I would never go back to that school. I had decided that taking the physical abuse was not worth obtaining a formal education. Having understood this, she went to talk to my first grade teacher. She came back in the evening with a smile to report her success. I still vividly recall her gait as she entered from the left entrance of the house. I looked at her inquisitively as I waited for her report.

"You can go back to school now."

"No, not happening."

"He's not going to beat you anymore."

She did not explain why my teacher would no longer beat me, and I did not ask her. Yet, all I knew was that I could not trust her. I did not go to school the next day either. I stayed home doing absolutely nothing. I did not worry much about obtaining a formal education, but I also did not have a plan for making it as an adult. I went outside to the street, right in front of our house. This was a paved road that separated the village into two. To get to the other side, I climbed the hollow ground. On the other side were big rock seats where young people and adults alike hung out, usually at night when women were selling food. I sat on a rock seat. Usually the place was bustling with energy, but given the time of day its dullness was understandable. Most of the children were at school, and the adults were off working.

As I sat there, as I would numerous other times, I watched cars passed. Some sped by really fast, while other went by slowly. Thoughts of my father entered my mind. *You're never returning again? Never? How did they kill you?* I wondered how school was going. Togbui Kpui! *Were you beaten in the street like the lady said? Beaten to death!*

That must have been very painful. Eyadema! How could he have done this? I saw a tall man on the ground. A couple of soldiers with riffles were standing over him. One of them struck my father in the face with intensity. A tooth gave out. He could barely breathe. Dark blood filled his mouth. He could not move. You could not tell whether or not his eyes were closed. The thick bruises of his brows obscured them. A car zoomed by so fast that it shook me out of my reverie. I was suddenly feeling downcasted, depressed. I looked toward the west, the direction of Kpalimé. The car was now far away at a distance. I brought my eyes back to the center, to our house. As I did this, more images of my father came to me. I was on the steps near the living room. He was below. He was teaching me how to shoot a plastic toy gun. The bullet was elastic. He pulled the trigger, thus launching the bullet in the air. I watched with a smile and excitement. I went to recover the bullet. My father joined me. He put it into the plastic gun again and handed it to me. I shot it. I loved the noise the gun made as the bullet ascended and travelled in the air. He smiled at me. Another car would pass and I would leave this memory.

Some of the students were returning from school now. A few of them passed and waved to me. They were a few yards away from me, but I could still hear their conversation. It was about me. They said that I was not going to school because my father's death was taking a toll on me. I brooded over their words for a few seconds. Why were they saying this? Yes, it was true that the whole village knew about my father's death, but why would these students be saying that this was the reason for my absence from school? I purposely skipped school to go fishing, and one of my classmates had told on me, and that was the real reason why I refused to attend. It did not make any sense. *Amano!* That was it. My grandmother had told my teacher that I was sad because of my father's death. I understood now. It was safe to go back to school. I walked toward the village's water pump in order to hear more. I did not hear anything else.

I returned home. I looked for my school uniform, which consisted of a light brown short and a short-sleeved shirt. I checked to see if it were clean and put it in a safe place in the room. When I went back to school finally, my teacher was actually very kind and considerate to me. He made a comment early in the class that morning about how hard things were for me because of my father's death. *Yeah, absolutely, my grandmother had used my father's death to smooth things out with him.* He did not beat me that day or ever again. In fact, he would take a certain liking to my mother. He was not shy about this. He was bold enough to ask her to marry him, despite knowing full well that she was married and was overseas. My mother immediately told him no. She did not particularly care for his teeth, which were severely discolored and very stained from the cola nuts he constantly chewed. These were reddish little seeds-like nuts, that when you chew and swallow the juice, you would receive a lot of energy. However, the toll that it took on the inside of your mouth was tremendous

Shortly after passing the first grade, my mother returned to Togo to take Essevi and I to California, the United States of America. Our soon to be stepfather Avon, who was originally from Chicago, came with her. I recalled going from place to place in order to make the necessary preparations for our departure. One of such trips took us to Lomé, the capital. We walked down the somewhat-red dirt road. My mother, my stepfather and I were at a clinic, to do some medical exams as part of the requirements for my departure. We were now at a clinic. I was close to the entrance of the door. My mother pulled down my drawers.

The guy approached me with his oversized needle. I remembered the immensity of the needle as it approached my buttocks. I pulled back. Futile! My mother pushed me forward. The needle approached closer and closer. Then, it penetrated my left buttocks. I felt a chill, my buttocks and legs went numb. I could not walk. I had to be carried out of there.

My mother was going to do it, but my stepfather beat her to the punch. He carried me on his back for a long while, it seemed. When we were able to, we took a cab back to Kpalimé.

The next important thing that I would remember about my stepfather was the few expressions in English that I would acquire before going to California. I recalled the scene vividly as if it were yesterday. Dada (i.e., mom) was on the other side of the main section of the house, in the open area, cooking with charcoal. She was fanning the fire with a hand-made plant fan. I approached her. Red sparks of light flutter every which way upward. She ceased her fanning activity and looked at me. I sensed a request coming.

"Go tell Avon that I need some ketchup," she said in Ewe. She repeated her request in English, "I need some ketchup." I repeated these words as I walked toward the room where my stepfather was. I repeated it so many times that by the time I reached him, I was able to make myself understood. He handed me the ketchup. I walked quickly back to my mother, feeling triumphant. I was speaking English. I now knew how to say, "*Yes, no* and *could you please pass me the ketchup?*"

I was one day away from turning twelve years old when we departed for California, the United States of America. My mother had woken us up very early in the middle of the night. I was not sure of the time, but I do remember that it was quite late. She gave us a sponge bath using a bucket full of hot water.

Fo Bernard came with us to the airport. Avon and Dada placed the baggage on the conveyor belt. I remember the look on fo Bernard's face, and how I watched him. He began chanting a song that I would forever remember.

"Nous sommes peu, nous arrivons. Nous sommes peu, nous le ferons-ons-ons-ons; peu, peu, avec courage-e, on va arriver avec ce qu'on veut..." I do not recall the rest of the lyrics, but what caught my attention was the last couple of lines that I have not written, which goes like this:

"Would you leave your friends? Never!" This verse repeated several times. I heard him clearly. I was not going to forget my friends or experiences in Togo. I was leaving the only place I had ever known, but it had not yet dawned on me. Usually, major life changes do not dawn on me until after the changes have passed.

CHAPTER 3

LIFE IN AMERICA

The plane ride to America was awesome. I have always loved the sound an airplane makes when it takes off and when it lands. I love the feeling of flying. Perhaps that is why I fly a lot in my dreams.

We arrived in the evening. Essevi and I were dead tired. One of our parents, Avon, I believe, opened the door. I vividly recalled the sun setting on our house—its reddish, soft color. It and everything around was beautiful. The exterior of the house was well kept, there were flowers on each side of the steps leading to the front door. It was evident that my mother kept a very clean house.

As soon as we entered the house, we began taking off our shoes. That was how my mother liked it, even in Togo. Avon did not waste a single second before laying down the rules with a very stern, frowning face. Essevi and I were sitting on the foot of the first two stairs. We were facing the front door, whose upper region was made of some sort of glass. To our left was a big fish tank with a variety of fish. This was where the living room was. It was extremely clean and was off limits to us children. To the left wall was a multicolor sofa.

Essevi and I did not understand what Avon was saying, but his facial expressions were helpful. Besides, my mother was doing her best to translate the English words into Ewe for us. I was definitely not getting a good feeling about our new stepfather. He told us that same day not to call him dad or papa. We were to call him by his first name. For the ensuing five years that we would live with him, Avon would never have a friend over the house nor go visit anyone. As far as we knew, he did not have any friends. The two major things in his life were the family and work, and he failed miserably at the former. When he was not beating us with the electrical cord, he was downstairs in his office working on his computer program. We really did not know much about him. I did not dare be direct with him by asking questions because I feared he would whip me. In terms of his brother, he once said:

"It would not surprise me if he were in prison or dead." Essevi and I were in his office when he said this. He did not give any explanations. There were so many questions that I wanted to ask him. I so wanted to ask him about his childhood and what happened between him and his brother. I also wanted to know why his first wife left him. I thought this particular question was inappropriate to ask, but if I were to ask, I could have phrased it so that it was appropriate. I recalled him saying that she left one day without saying anything. *Good for her* I had thought when I learned about this. Perhaps she had seen bad signs. If I knew her name, I would have searched for her.

We also did not know anything about his parents. *Maybe they were dead.*

After Avon's long speech and translations of the household rules, my mother asked us boys if we wanted to eat or to go to sleep. We opted for sleep because we were exhausted. She took us to the computer room. She had two beds already prepared for us with nice pillows and bed sheets and covers neatly tucked in.

We slept all the way through the evening and the night. Morning found us rejuvenated. We showered and ate breakfast with our mother. She made pancakes. I hated

35

pancakes in those days. They were so thick and difficult to swallow. My throat suffered, suffocated. Often, I had to drink an awful lot of Vitamin D milk to wash it down. My mother gave us so much of it. Breakfast seemed to last forever. It was a complete torture. If we did not clean the plate, then we were threatened with "a butt whopping" by Avon. His infamous line for why we had to eat everything on the plate was:

"There are children starving in Africa."

At first, I did not understand what that meant, but after a few mornings of repeating the same thing, I needed no translation. He seemed to take delight in the fact that Essevi and I had difficulty adjusting to the new food.

After breakfast, my mother showed us the inside and exterior of the house. The interior was as nice as the exterior. There were five bedrooms, three full-baths, a living room, a family room equipped with a television. The kitchen was a little elevated vis-à-vis the family room. The kitchen had two sections, and was near the dining room. On the first floor to the left was the computer room where we slept the first night. Our bedroom was to the right of the computer room. Next to the right of our room was our bathroom, which directly faced the stairs—a few yards away was Avon and my mother's master bedroom. Their room was immense, in my eyes at least. Deep in the back to the right in the corner was a television, which sat on top of a small table with a VCR. It was an old television, but it worked well. Their bed was near the door. It was a nice bed, twice the size of our beds. The head of the bed was high, had a tall mirror and dressers on each side. Avon slept on the side closest to the door. In one of these drawers was a handgun. He would show me one day. He said the gun was to protect the family. I was not sure about this. We did not live in a violent neighborhood. On the first floor, next to the family room was another full bathroom.

One day Avon called me into his bedroom to show me how to use the gun. We sat on the bed. He opened the drawer and took out the gun. The drawer was locked with a key. He showed me where to find it. He brought out the gun and a bullet.

"Be careful. I'll show you how to load it."

He was explaining to me how to use the gun, but I was too nervous to understand all of the instructions.

"Turn it and be careful. Once the bullets are in the holes, you aim and shoot. If you point, then you shoot. No hesitation! Understood?"

"Yes," I answered.

"Now, it's your turn. Do exactly as I say."

He had me load the gun a few times before letting me go free. It was a very uncomfortable time with him. I was happy to leave. The palms of my hands were sweating. I rubbed them against each other and against my clothes.

I held the gun with both hands and pointed it at the air…It was as if I were in a movie. In the movies, people with guns usually were tough. I did not feel tough. I was afraid inside. The shudder went through my body and maintained its hold around my heart, chest, and stomach areas all at the same time. Avon put the gun back into the dresser.

"Well, now you know where it is."

I was the only child to whom he showed the gun.

About three days after arriving in Sacramento, California, my language learning would begin. It started when I was in the garage doing something, when one of the neighborhood children on a skateboard road by. He asked me a question. I stared at him, trying to understand. It appeared to me that he could tell I did not understand what he was saying. Still, I wanted to say something, but could not muster a single comprehensible word. Recall the two words and a sentence that I learned in Kusuntu: "Yes," "no," and "Could you please pass me the ketchup?" I thought about using one of the first two, but I had absolutely no idea what my new neighbor was saying. As my new friend spoke, I focused on the awesome skateboard. I had seen one of them on television, and they looked really cool. The young people who were riding them knew awesome moves. Yet, I was sure I could not do all those flips and turns. Finally, he waved goodbye to me and disappeared to the right side of the house. I felt like I had a lot to learn language-wise.

The feeling of being lost increased when I went to school. I felt out of place inside myself. I was twelve years old in the fourth grade. I was not sure whether or not to cry or to feel sorry for myself. I was behind in school in Togo, but that was different. Most of the children were also behind in their studies, so I did not feel badly about this. In this Californian school, however, things were different. The majority of the students were the same age. They could read and write very well in their own language. I could read and write too in my own language, but I had the impression that they were better at it than I was in their own native language. For this reason, I kept my age to myself for the most part. Most of the children were three years younger than me. However, I was about their size physically. Some of them were even taller than me.

My main teacher was Mr. Jordan, a tall slender, quiet-spoken white man. I would say that our racial make-up was pretty good. There was a Native American girl in the class, some black children, as well as a good number of white children. I did not understand a thing in the classes. I focused on reading the teachers and my fellow classmates' physical expressions and emotions. This seemed to help. In addition, two girls and a boy adopted me as their mentee. The girls helped me with my history and English courses. My brunette friend made sure that I sat next to her, often explaining things to me with gestures. Elizabeth, the other girl, was skinny, blond, and a little taller than me. During lunch she directed me to her table. The boy showed me how to play during recess.

My mother's after school lessons also seemed to help, though I did not appreciate her abuse of the belt. She was a traditional African teacher with a whip in hand to make sure Essevi and I were taking our studies seriously.

Overall, I enjoyed my education for about the first two months before things began to take a turn for the worse at school. One of the fourth grade black students who had a different main teacher, discovered that I was from Africa. Everyday during recess he would run and snatch anything that was mine that he could seize. It was really annoying. Everyday when I returned home, my mother would ask me how school was. I gave her a routine answer:

"Everything was fine." That sometimes was not sufficient. She often dug deeper until she got something. Her advice to me about most things at school as well as the super active boy Andrew taking my jacket and other clothing possessions was:

"Tell him: 'Leave me alone!'"

This, I did for weeks. One would have thought that after the first week I would have tried a different approach. I did not. In the meantime the name calling and the jacket-grabbing continued. Andrew continued calling me "African buddy scratcher." I knew what it meant to scratch something, but I definitely did not know what the whole expression meant. In any case, I did not like it because I knew he was insulting me.

One day during recess, Andrew swooped by grabbing my jacket. Mr. Jordan was a few feet away seeing all this. I was close to his classroom. Andrew was at a distance, laughing at me.

"Give it back to me!" I yelled out.

The more I yelled, the more he seemed to snicker and amuse himself. In one intense moment of determination, I took off running after Andrew like a cougar. I ran after him faster than I could ever recall in my life. He ran off too. I chased him at an incredible speed. He tried veering at different directions. Each time his attempts were in vain. I caught up with him in no time. I seized him by the hand. I launched punches at him so fast that you would have thought I was a professional boxer. I threw punch after punch while posing the question.

"Are you going to do it again?"

Several punches later, he still did not answer.

"Are you? Speak up!" I shouted, thinking about Avon's daily commands to us at home. Soon, I realized that it was not that he did not want to answer: He was too busy suffering, for I was punching him very hard and fast. I ceased and snapped my jacket out of his hand. From that day on, Andrew never took anything of mine again. In fact, we became friends. Whenever he saw me at recess after that he was very polite and wanted to play with me. When I went home that afternoon, my mother asked me how school was. My answer was "It was good." She did not dig any deeper probably because of the big smile on my face.

It was not long before I started making friends at school. One of them was Jessica. She was tall and was half black and half white. She told me that the boy who came by the garage during the first few days of my arrival was her older brother. Jessica was a nice person. I sensed that she thought I was different, but not weird. She sometimes observed me.

Once at school during recess, I recalled my classmates running away from bees by the basketball court, which was behind our fourth grade class. I did not think it was necessary to run. There were only a few bees. One of them was flying in the air clumsily, for it had been smacked or hit by one of the children out of fear. I reached out my hand and let it fall in my reddish-like palm. I was looking at it to see if it was alright. After a while, I put him down on the ground and took my leave. Jessica was watching me at a distance.

"You were talking to it!" she exclaimed.

"Talking?" I asked puzzled. I did not recall saying anything out loud to the bee, but then it dawned on me that she was talking about a different kind of communication. Talking is not the only type of communication.

"You weren't afraid of it." She was making comments, and each time I sensed the sincerity in her words, but did not answer. I did not know what to tell her. I was simply being myself.

I had overcome my school bully and saved a bee. Life was great. I was being fed well at home, and was learning to read and write in English. I was even free to be my playful self around my mother. I recall walking home one day and simply being happy for no apparent reason. I do not recall why Essevi was not with me. I had a big book bag on and was in good spirits. Up ahead, just a few yards away was my mother. Her back was turned and she was in a crouching position, her garden implement ascending and descending with her hand upon the earth. I walked quietly and quickly. Almost there! Gingerly now, I was in position, right behind my mother. I wanted for her to stop digging.

"Hi!" I shouted as I seized her with both hands.

"Ah!" she screamed with much fright. She said hello and hugged me.

"You scared me."

She asked how school was, and I told her that it went ok, and that I had some homework to do.

About two and a half months after coming to America, my luck was about to change for the worse. I was quickly becoming aware of the fact that my stepfather was a very "special" soul in every aspect of the word. I felt that the freedom Essevi and I had experienced in West Africa was going to vanish.

Every morning when we children woke up, he also got up at the same time to check up on us. I supposed he wanted to make sure we were up on time. I found his morning ritual quite peculiar. He always walked into our room completely naked. At twelve years old, I found this bizarre, partially because he was not circumcised. Every morning was about the same.

"You're getting up too soon, like you're having a nightmare. Go back to sleep a little longer. Five more minutes. It's not good for your health to wake up that fast, in such a hurry."

He even came to check up on us sometimes at night, late into the night. Perchance, this was his way of showing he cared, but it did not make me feel better. To avoid him coming into the room, sometimes Essevi and I would fake sleeping by snoring loudly enough so that he would turn away. Sometimes he came into the room and would turn on the light and chat with us briefly. I did not mind the chatting, but for the love of God, why did a ten and twelve year-old boys have to see their naked stepfather every night before going to bed? If we were going to have nightmares, this would have been the cause of them. I mean, I had seen his penis so many times that even now as I write this book, the visuals of the genitals are unfortunately still easily accessible to my mind's eye.

The other thing that he did that was not at all to my liking was how he disturbed our bathing. We would be showering and BOOM! the shower curtain would be opened brusquely. He did it with such agility each time that we never knew when he had entered the bathroom. He would let the flowing water run through his hand, checking to see if we were using too much hot water.

"You should not use too much hot water," he would often say with a frown. He would turn the knob to the left so that the water became lukewarm, and often cold. That forced us to shower faster. In fact, I had developed a plan that would put an end to all this: I would shower really fast and be in my room before he got to the bathroom. This did not work.

One day, I had showered fast and was putting on lotion when he came into the bathroom.

"Did you shower already?"

"Yes."

He looked at me for a good second.

"You're not clean. Go back and take another one."

There was no winning with this guy. I was quickly understanding that Avon liked being in control. My mother was no exception for him.

Once I found I had to stay home because of a headache. We were on the second floor. My mother and Avon were near the bedroom door.

"How's your head?" he asked me.

"Ok."

He then asked me to go to him. He put his right hand to my forehead. "I don't think it's necessary for me to stay home." This was the third day that he was keeping me home unnecessarily for the headache. I felt well enough to return to school.

"I don't think it's a good idea for him to go to school. His head is still a little warm."

My mother had her work uniform on. She was working as a cashier at the supermarket. This was the third day Avon was obliging her to stay home with me. She touched my forehead and didn't say anything.

"You know what you have to do. His health is more important than working. You have to take care of your family above all else."

"What are you going to do?"

"I'll stay home with him, and go back to work tomorrow."

"I think you should seriously consider not working altogether."

I was twelve years old, but even I could figure out what my stepfather was doing. He was trying to control her. For a person to submit herself docilely to the other, it is always necessary for the other who is in control to find a weakness in the other person. The point must sufficiently and emotionally be strong enough so that the submissive person does not oppose too fast. In this case, my stepfather had found this vulnerable point: my mother's love for me. She submitted to his manipulation, his control, his domination. I am employing the word "domination" here because that is usually the underlying goal of control. If my mother did not work, she would have been obliged to do as he wished. Years later, my mother would expand on this.

"I was not able to continue taking my classes at the junior college because he told me to stop."

"Oh yeah? I always wondered why you stopped, but I didn't know that he told you to stop."

She only had a few more courses before completing her two-year degree. She never did.

I had only been in the country for a year but was in a complete despair. One day, when I was alone in the house, I walked to the window in my bedroom on the second floor. Various images and a few facts of Avon came to my mind. He was about five-foot and seven inches tall. Over the years, I would gather some information here and there about him. He wore glasses and hardly smiled. He was in the military for less than a year, and was discharged or let go of, but I would never learn the reason why. In terms of his first wife, he would not explain to any of us or my mother. Furthermore, I once saw a picture of his family. From the quantity of people, one could see that he came from a large family. With the exception of his sister on the phone, the rest of the family did not know where he was or how he was doing in life. Once he stood in the kitchen talking to his sister on the phone. The gestures with which he took small steps and his tone of voice inspired pity. He did not like his brother in particular. From time to time, his sister would call the house and speak to him, but she never came to visit. He seemed a wounded soul, and I wish I had known this sooner. Unfortunately, his negativity would reduce my positive energy.

My despair ran deep. One day, I looked out of the window with a heavy heart. There was the tree. Its branches reached the roof. The branches and leaves undulated in the breeze. They seemed peaceful. That was not my state of mind. As I watched the leaves and branches dance in silence, I kept asking myself "When is all this going to end?" It was a general question. I was not necessarily asking when I would no longer live in the household. I was asking myself how much longer I was going to endure this life. Then one day, relief came. Well, at least I thought.

It was in the evening about nine p.m. My mother and my stepfather had an argument. Avon had said something really hurtful to her. It had cut my mother so deeply that she called me from her bedroom with sorrow in her voice.

"Tell your brother to pack. We're leaving."

I was not sure what to feel. I certainly did not like living in the household with Avon, but where were we going to go? I did not think my mother knew anyone with whom we could stay permanently. I did not want to be homeless. I went to the room and related the decision to Essevi. It was about 10:30 a.m. We were packing. I packed very slowly because deep inside of me I knew that we were not going anywhere. I guessed this because as I walked away, Avon was softly caressing Dada and calling her "baby." His caresses were slow and appeared to be full of compassion. His voice was smooth and tender. This was not the Avon I knew. He was working his magic and it worked.

A few minutes later, she called us and said, "Unpack your things."

Nearly three years later, Avon and my mother made plans for us to return to Kusuntu to bring Messa, our youngest brother. We had been informed about this weeks beforehand. Presently, we were in the back seat of the car in the parking lot of a supermarket. Avon was in the driver's seat, while my mother was in the passenger's seat. She was telling us about the trip. Avon turned his head toward us like a soldier with a stiff, mechanical movement. He kept his frowning face upon us as my mother spoke. It was an intense, scary look with his neck jerked forward like a soldier who was ready to kill his enemies or to throw himself on a prey. We were his prey. If only he could have seen how silly he looked. This guy was too much.

"Are you listening to your mother?" he barked at us like a dog.

"Yes!" we answered right away.

"If she tells you to bark like a dog, you *bark* like a dog. If she tells you to jump, what do you do?"

"Jump?" I answered.

"No, you ask how high?"

He did not understand how ridiculous he was being. We weren't the type of children who purposely disobeyed their parents.

"And when she tells you to jump, what do you do?" he asked, reviewing his directives with us.

"We bark," I answered.

"Now, get out of the car."

He certainly didn't have to ask me twice. We quickly got out of there, and went to the supermarket.

We went to Togo and returned a few weeks later. We returned with Messa. I turned fifteen about a month later. Everything was the same at our household—constant scolding and physical beatings. There was one occasion that I do not believe that I would ever forget.

I was fifteen years old, and had been in the States for three years—an eternity, especially living with my terrorist stepfather. If he could not be called a terrorist, then I did not know who could. It was about six o'clock in the evening. Shortly after he came home, he asked me if I had finished doing my homework. He did not look happy. He seemed irritated by something.

"Not all of it. I don't really understand the geometry homework."

"What don't you understand?" he asked with a serious menacing air about him. He had not even seen the homework, but yet he was upset at me for not understanding it.

"Go bring it."

I went upstairs to get it. I handed Avon the piece of paper, which he looked at for a few seconds.

"It's not difficult. You're being lazy."

I definitely was not being lazy—I really did not understand how to solve the problem. I had read and examined the math exercise several times. There were diagrams on the paper and I was to say what kind of a triangle they were and why. We had studied all sorts of shapes such as parallelograms and trapezoids. This particular question was about trapezoids, but I do not recall the latter part of the question.

"I am going to work out. When I return, I want it done."

It was futile, I thought. He was definitely going to whip me that night because the only way to get out of that problem was to lie, and I had never lied to him up to that point, despite all that he had done.

I was upstairs in my room when he returned. Avon called me from the kitchen. I brought the homework because I knew he was going to ask for it. I handed it to him.

"Did you understand when I explained it to you?"

"I think so but I am not sure.'

Avon must have sensed that I was trying to appease him, for he gave me a frown.

"Go get the whip!"

It was not an ordinary whip. It was a thick brown electrical cord that he folded. My hand opened the closet door, afraid to take the whip from the wall, but yet knew sooner or later I had to do it. Many thoughts ran through my mind as I stood there. I imagined the sharp pain in my feet and buttocks. A voice augmented the fear of my immediate future.

"Hurry up!" Avon shouted at me.

I reached for the whip, hesitating. I seized it, the brutal weapon, and with a reluctant painful hesitation, handed it to my master. Whoever was being beaten was the one who usually retrieved the whip from the closet. This was the worst part of the physical abuse experience. I wondered if he had calculated this as part of his terrorist activity.

"Go to the computer room, undress yourself and wait for me. I'll be there soon."

I wondered if his parents always beat him without any clothes on. With the exception of my white underwear, I was practically naked. I became anxious as I waited. As I heard him mount the stairs, my heart beat faster. The stairs seemed to creak ever faster as he climbed. It was as if the acceleration of each step were calculated. I felt like a prey who was recoiling with each step. Maybe it was the Devil himself who was coming after me. And just maybe, he was delighting in the thought that my fear could be felt. Finally, he stood in front of me, armed with the whip.

"Now explain to me what you don't understand."

"Uh, uh, I don't know. I don't know anymore. I want to understand. Let me try again."

"What? Are you dumb or what? It's been two hours since you have been working on the same problem."

He whipped my buttocks, each strike with more force. He could not slow down. It seemed as if he did even for a fraction of a second, he would be depriving himself of some twisted pleasure. He whipped me hard and fast. He was sweating, really sweating. Still, he would not obey the law of fatigue. He was breathing deeply. Finally, he stopped to ask me questions.

"Why are you lying?"

Try as I might I could not give him satisfactory answers.

"Stop saying stupid things,"

Once again, he was whipping me.

"Why are you lying?'

He whipped me all over: on my back, my hands, etc. The whip even reached my genitals. That was the most sharp and penetrating feeling of the night. When he was really tired, he stopped again—to give me a moral lesson.

"You know, lying is not good. Why did you lie?"

"I was confused." I was trying to answer his question in a way that would suit him. I had to answer quickly for my previous strategy of being truthful was not working.

"I am sorry. I don't know."

"Say it! Say that you understood the problem and were pretending not to understand!"

Was he insane? He could not possibly have thought that I was pretending. He was insane! We were quiet for what appeared an eternity. I was thinking about when I would be allowed to go to bed. It was getting late, and my butt and the back of my feet were bruised. The left top corner of my back was bleeding.

"Answer me when I talk to you!" he launched at me with full force. He took me by the neck and threw me on the floor.

"Do you hear me!"

He slapped me and spread my body on the white carpet floor with force. Then he put his knees on my feet and shook my body violently. I lied there with him on top. He held down my two hands crossed above my head.

"Answer me when I talk to you! Do you understand me?"

"Yes"'

His eyes and face were upon mine. I felt his breath and saliva. He spat all over my face, including my lips as he hurled comments at me. It was disgusting. Some saliva had slipped in between my lips. I brought my lips together as tightly as I possibly could in order to prevent further damage. My greatest wish at that point was to rinse my mouth with Listerine. I was tired of this so-called mockery of discipline. This guy was mad! I no longer held in the pain. I cried out louder as he hurt me.

My mother could no longer pretend that she could not hear a thing. She was upstairs in her room. I saw her come out near her door a couple of times, but she did not come into the room to stop Avon. She grabbed him with her right hand and begged him to stop. Sweat was dripping profusely from his entire face—nose, ears, jaws. One would have thought he had just won the marathon. She finally came. What took her so long? What was she afraid of? Her son was being beaten like an animal, and she hesitated to rescue him. I did not care about the hesitation. I was happy she had decided to come. Avon looked at her.

"He's pretending not to understand."

"What don't you understand?" my mother asked me.

She had posed a silly question. She was aware of the conversation between Avon and I the entire time, but to humor them both, I answered her.

"I don't' understand why…"

"Do you see what you've done? He is going to start lying all over again," he said, cutting me off.

"Read the problem to me," my mother said calmly. I started reading the exercise, but Avon grabbed the paper from my hand, and started whipping me all over again. The paper ripped. My mother begged him to stop, and he did. However, he was angry. What happened next was *utterly* mind-boggling.

"Don't you see that he is lying? Are you going to stand there and let him lie? What will happen later if we don't correct him now? This is the critical moment in his life. Here, take the whip."

"No!"

"You're saying no? Take care of your responsibility. We have to be in agreement on this. Take it!"

He pushed the whip toward her. She did not budge. Her facial contortions indicated that there was a battle going on inside her.

"Take it! I said!"

My mother took the whip and whipped me. During the entire time that my stepfather beat me, I cried. I cried because of physical pain. But now, what I felt was more emotional. I wanted to cry because I was sad, heart-broken at her betrayal. I did not struggle or resist her. She had succumbed to the whip. Figuratively speaking, she was whipped. Tears would not come from me. I capitulated to the betrayal. I felt as if someone had taken a needle and pierced it through my heart. I was surprised, stunned, flabbergasted. The first strike of the whip did nothing to me. I was looking at her in amazement. I was not angry, just shocked. The needle had penetrated my naked heart like an electrical current. The whip was the electrical current and the needle holder was my mother. My tears were drained like an empty well.

When she was done, she remained quiet. Avon did all the talking.

"Sit down," he said, a little calmer.

I sat to the left of the door in the threshold. He was still drenched with sweat. He also seemed tired. This did not surprise me because he had finished exercising. Maybe he would not go to the gym the next day I thought.

"Do you know why what you did wasn't good?"

This guy was a real a-hole, and I must have been insane like my mother for tolerating such living environment. He did not even know how to solve the math problem himself. I knew he was faking it. He went as far as algebra in high school.

I stared at him, trying to feign an expression of shame. I was tired. I wanted to go to bed, and the only way to do that was to lie and play along with his manipulation. He was comporting like a father who was obliged to make tough decisions despite the costs.

"I won't do it again. I am really sorry."
I was really sorry to be a part of the family. I was sorry for not being strong enough to fight him back physically despite the consequences. What was the worst thing that could have happened? He would have broken my jaw or something like that. In hindsight, this would have been a good thing, for if someone noticed it at school I would have been taken away from the family. I really did not know what held me back. Perhaps, it was my mother's fear that "they" would take me away from her if I talked. Well, that night, I could not have been farther away from her emotionally. She was teaching me how our loved ones can betray us, while Avon was teaching me how to lie to myself.

Avon was still talking. He spoke about the importance of following a good path in life, leading an honest life. He never did understand that under no circumstances would I lie to myself and actually believe all the crap he was feeding me. My mouth may have been saying one thing, but deep inside, I knew the truth and would not waver.

"I am sorry for having lied. I lied to avoid punishment, but now I know that it wasn't the right thing to do."

Oh là là! As the French would say, I could not believe the words that were coming out of my own mouth. I was getting good. Avon was turning me into a liar, a "bull-shitter." I was lying so well that I was convinced that he was buying the crap. He seemed to be soothed by my words. His tone changed to calm and understanding. In hindsight, I understand that this guy needed a lot more than prison. He needed some sort of intense psychiatric help from someone like Dr. Brian Weiss.

"Is there someone who you really respect?" Avon asked me.

"Yes."

"Who?"

"Mr. Jordan."

Reader, recall that this was my fourth grade teacher.

"Why do you like him?"

"I don't know. He's nice."

"Think a little. Does Mr. Jordan lie?"

"I don't think so."

"That's what you have to be."

"You're right. It's not good to lie."

"Before lying next time, think about him. Ask yourself if Mr. Jordan would lie. Use him as a model to guide you. Do you understand what I am saying?"

"Yes."

"I want you to succeed in life. Can I trust that next time you will not lie?"

"Yes, I have learned a lot tonight. Next time I won't try to avoid punishment by lying."

He stood up and signaled with his hands for me to get up. I stood up, and he hugged me. This was extremely emotionally uncomfortable. I wondered what was going on in his mind. Instead of hugging me, he should have been begging me for forgiveness.

I went to the bathroom, washed my face with soap, brushed my teeth, and went to my room. I had to get into bed cautiously. The top left side of my back was bruised, my buttocks were very sore and did not support contact with the bed sheets. I could not sleep on my back. I had to sleep on my stomach, which was fine because I hardly slept on my back anyway. I went to bed that night without saying anything to my brothers. The next morning was even tougher. I could not sit on a chair. The pain was deep. When I sat down, I felt a tear, the skin separating.

Up to then, I had not outwardly resisted or expressed my grievance against Avon's tyranny. This changed one day when we were returning home one weekend after shopping at Sunrise Mall. We had gone to big department stores such as Weinstocks, JC-Pennies, and Sears. While we were at a red light, Avon posed a geographical question.

"How many continents are there?"

"Well, seven!" I said with excitement.

"What did you say?" he asked, appearing upset apparently because of my use of the word "well."

"I said there are seven."

He also did not like the way I answered his second question.

"Watch your mouth!" I decided to be quiet.

"You're not going to say anything?"

I knew what he wanted me to do. He wanted me to apologize. I was not going to do it. I really did not know what overcame me that day, but I was not going to apologize. Perchance it was the weather. It was 104 degrees Fahrenheit. I had enough of his dictatorship.

"I should never have accepted to live with you!" I said crystal clear.

Avon turned his head really fast like a military general who wanted to reproach a soldier.

"Your mother is doing the best she can for you and you dare insult her? Repeat what you just said."

This was a dare. I knew I had crossed the line. As soon as he was able to, he pulled to the side of the road. He nearly yanked me out of the car.

"There's nothing preventing me from whipping you right here in the middle of the road naked. Do you want me to do it?"

Actually there was, but I remained quiet.

"Do you want me to do it?" he shouted at me again, "If I've told you once, I've told you a thousand times. Haven't I told you to always respect your mother?"

"Yes," I answered with a frown.

"Get your butt in the car!"

When we arrived home, Avon ordered me to get the whip.

"Take off your clothes."

I did it hesitantly, with a mixture of anger and fear. He whipped me next to the kitchen, in the dining room. When he was finished, he folded the whip and told me to bring him a piece of paper with a pencil.

"Go apologize to your mother first."

I went to mother and said:

"I am sorry. I was just angry. I didn't really mean to say it."

"It's ok," she answered. I returned to Avon.

"Now write what I say: What I said was stupid, and I am sorry. I will always respect my mother. Write it three hundred times. Show it to me when you finish."

I do not recall exactly how long I was in my room, but I was sure that I had been writing for several hours. When I finished, I descended the stairs to show Avon my finished product.

"Here it is. I finished."

"Good, did you understand why what you did was wrong?"

"Yes, I'm sorry."

"It's not me you have to apologize to."

I turned to Dada to offer my apologies again.

"I'm sorry."

"It's alright, you've already told me."

For a brief second, I thought I was clear and free.

"Now, follow me," Avon said.

I mounted up the stairs with him. I had no idea what he was up to. When we reached the top of the stairs, he opened the closet door to the left.

"Get inside!"

I was puzzled.

"Stay inside for an hour. Do not turn the light on. Stay in the dark, and let the darkness make you think a little."

An hour and a half later I thought I had been in there for three. What was this? Maybe I was in prison, in the hole. It was clear to me that Avon was trying to break my spirit. He did not know how to do it. He may do a thousand of such similar things, but he could never reach what was inside. Despite the pain, I absolutely knew that I was in the right. I went toward the door to listen. Maybe he had forgotten me. Another half an hour would pass before he came for me. He opened the door and turned on the light. I opened my eyes only to close them immediately, for the light was blinding. When I opened them again, he was looking at me with a menacing frown. He seized me with his right hand and nearly threw me out of the room.

"Get out of my face!"

I obeyed with pleasure. I went to my room and closed the door.

The next morning was a typical day. It was about 10:30 a.m. Essevi and I were preparing breakfast in the kitchen while Dada and Avon were upstairs, supposedly sleeping.

"Agbessi, come here!" he called out from the top of the stairs. He was holding the ramp, which was to the right of the stairs—completely naked. He was always naked in the morning. I don't think I have ever seen any man shown his nudity more than my stepfather. I studied his penis with my peripheral vision as he spoke to me. It was medium.

"You didn't hear me calling you the first time?"

"No, I didn't hear you."

"Are you going to lie again?"

"No, I swear I didn't hear you."

I was confused. I did not understand why he was always convinced that we were ignoring him. There was not much noise coming from the kitchen. I was sure that if he had called me, I would have heard him. He was probably lying about it.

"I don't want to hear any more lies."

" I was not…um...Ok." I knew I needed to shut up.

"Ok what?"

"Next time I'll answer right away."

"Next time I'll whip you!"

He went back to his room, and I to the kitchen. Essevi heard the whole conversation.

"I didn't hear him call you."

After eating the pancakes and eggs that we made, I went upstairs to ask for permission to go out.

"Could we go out to play basketball?"

"You, you're not going anywhere. You're staying to clean all the toilets in the house. Tell your brothers they can go out. They must be back by 5 p.m. What are you waiting for?"

I looked forward to Saturdays. This was the only time I had to escape his household.

"Well, go!"

I went to the kitchen to deliver the message. Essevi was already putting his shoes on.

"I'll be ready in a few seconds."

"Yeah, have fun."

"Why are you saying that?"

"Because Avon doesn't want me to go," I answered sadly, "He wants me to clean all the toilets. He said to come back at 5 o'clock."

I worked nearly until 5 p.m.

"I finished!" I said joyously to Avon.

"Let's go see. He checked all the toilettes.

"The toilettes downstairs are not well done."

I did them again. By this time, Essevi had returned to the house, and another day ended.

In addition to the physical violence at home, Avon also limited my sport activities, with the exception of one. I was sixteen years old and had gotten into wresting. I joined the school's wrestling team during my sophomore year and was practicing nearly everyday. It was a very physically demanding sport. We practiced for hours, sweating and throwing each other around on the matt with different wrestling moves. It was not only for amusement, for it was an activity that allowed me to see less of Avon. It was during this particular time that things were not going well at the house. One day due to an error on my part, this activity also came to an end.

It was a Friday afternoon, and I was out with my wrestling club. We were competing against other high schools. This was my first partaking in a match, and I was excited. The first guy I wrestled had a lot of experience. He claimed to have been competing since he was seven years old. To be honest, I was a little disappointed because I almost won. Well, at least that was how I felt. It was a mere back error. I had turned part of my back at the wrong time. That day I thought that I would have another chance to win, but our group did not find the next location on time.

Night was falling upon us. We were hungry, so we went to a fast-food restaurant to eat. It was either McDonald's or Burger King. I do not remember which. By 8:27 p.m. I was beginning to worry. I should have already called my parents. I told Tion's parents that I needed to call home.

"Your parents are strict?" his mother asked me.

"Yes, I need to call."

I called from a pay phone. Avon picked up the telephone. He did not seem upset, but when I went home, it was another story.

"Why didn't you call us sooner?"

"I didn't remember. We were late."

"How's that?"

"We had a hard time finding the place."

"So why didn't you call?"

"We were eating."

"You need to learn to respect the rules. You can't call only when you feel like it. It's not acceptable."

That was the end of my high school wrestling experience. I continued practicing, but my enthusiasm had decreased. It was not the same as when there were competitions.

I was not the only one to be deprived of his favorite sport. Essevi had asked several times if he could play American football on a team when he was a freshman in high school. My mother was against it. I vividly recall her protest.

"He could get hurt."

She said that she did not have the health care money, and that if he were to get hurt, she would not have been able to take care of him financially, and besides, he could get paralyzed playing football. She was in the kitchen discussing the issue with my stepfather.

Essevi protested by saying that all the kids were going to play next year, and that their parents had signed the permission form. Since Avon was in agreement with Dada, Essevi would never play football.

As time passed, it is now obvious to me that Avon was less interested in using the whip to strike us. He now preferred his hands. This was about a year later.

We were at Lake Tahoe, in California…I recalled fond memories there years passed because we children shared a room and were free to watch television to our eye's content.

The beds were very comfortable, and most of all, I could lock the door. That meant that I knew who was able to come in and who was not. My stepfather could not surprise us. Besides, the lock was metal. The check-in at the entrance was fast and efficient. Avon gave me a key to our room. There were two beds and a television. I took the bed near the window, while Messa and Essevi took the one near the bathroom, the entrance. Our door was still open when my mother and Avon came. They wanted to see how the room was. Besides the television, there was also very clean and white carpeting that covered the entire floor, an air conditioner, and a telephone.

"There are two beds. Agbessi, you take that one there. Essevi share this one with your brother," Avon said, not knowing that we had already decided.

We stayed at the hotel for three days. While in our room the ensuing morning, Messa and I heard two voices, one was a little disagreeable, while the other was calm.

"Shoo! Shoo! Do you hear that? It sounds like Avon," I said to Messa, checking to see if the door was locked. It was. Essevi was the last one to leave the breakfast table and had not returned yet. He was still with Avon and Dada when Messa and I left. This was because he was the last one to shower and so he came later. Avon's voice became louder and louder. From what I could hear, he was angry.

"I hear them, but I can't understand what they are saying."

I was definitely sure now that Avon was upset with Essevi again. There was not anybody in the corridor with them. I did not understand why Dada was not with them. Perhaps she was still eating, or perhaps she stayed on the first floor to take care of something.

"I am going to sneak a look through the peephole."

"What do you see? Let me see!" Messa said. I did not move. Instead, in a low voice, I said:

"I see Avon and Essevi."

"Yeah, but what are they doing?"

"Why don't you ever listen?

"What?"

"No, no, not you. That's what Avon is saying.

Messa took my right hand.

"Let me see! I want to see!"

"No, wait a little!

I was silent for a few seconds, then said:

"Impossible! He's slapping him. He slapped him. Again! He has Essevi's head in both of his hands. He hits his head against the wall."

"Let me see!"

"Go ahead! I don't want to see anymore."

Messa took my place.

"They are coming to our room!" Messa said, and quickly ran away from the door. He turned on the television, and we pretended to be watching it when they entered.

"What are you doing?" Avon asked suspiciously.

"We're watching TV." Messa answered.

When Avon left, I approached Essevi.

"What happened?"

"I don't want to talk about it," he said, frowning.

He was silent for a few seconds and then said:

"I don't understand why he can't pick on someone his own size. It's always us. We take it like idiots. What is that? An adult who's always beating kids, what is that!"

"Lower your voice. He'll hear you and come back to hit you again," I warned him.

"I don't care! If he needs to release stress, then why doesn't he go workout? He's a coward!" Essevi said furiously in his bed.

"I know, but keep your voice down." I was afraid that Avon would hear us.

"He's always showing his authority."

Avon was in a bad mood for the rest of the vacation. I did not catch him smiling even once. I was not particularly surprised because this was the way he normally comported himself. I did not like going on vacations with him: I did not even Disneyland. We children preferred to stay home alone. Heaven for us was when he and my mother went on a vacation all alone, and left us at the house. We had so much fun at the house. We would listen to music as loud as we wanted to, watched television until one or two o'clock in the morning, and played video games like Super-Mario Brothers, Link, etc. Vacation with him was definitely hell. I even preferred to do homework than to go with them.

Messa was no exception to the abuse that Essevi and I experienced. Once, the turntable of the microwave turn was burned. Messa had apparently heated up his food a few minutes too long. He seemed really afraid, for he could sense that the whip was a-coming. The first thing he did when he arrived at the house was to go to the microwave. Messa had been in the kitchen, but went to his room before Avon arrived. The wait was always the most painful part of the abuse process.

Upon arriving, Avon immediately went to inspect the microwave.

"What happened?" he asked me.

"I don't really know. I suppose he tried to warm up something in the microwave. When I arrived, I saw that he was trying to put out the fire."

"Did you give him permission to use the microwave?"

"No, I didn't."

Messa was not allowed to use the microwave without permission because Avon said he was too young.

"Messa, get your butt over here!" Avon commanded.

He came down the stairs and hesitated entering the kitchen. Avon was looking at him as if he were going to devour him whole.

"Haven't I told you never to use the microwave without permission?"

"I just wanted to heat up a little bit of the food," he squeaked out like a little mouse.

Avon took the whip from the kitchen closet and let it dance around Messa's butt in the dining room for a few minutes. Messa screamed and Avon kept saying: "When I tell you to do something, you do it!"

As I write this now, clarity seizes me, and I think I partially understand the words he was saying to Messa. Avon had heard these words from somewhere before. They did not originate from his mind. He appropriated them from his past; perhaps from one of his abusive parental figures. I say this for I am now able to put many of my spiritual experiences together.

"Do you understand?" he shouted at him as he tightened his teeth.

"I am going to work out. When I return I don't want to hear anything from you. Is that understood? Get out of my face."

Messa ran to his room as fast as he could. I thought to myself that perhaps he was thinking: I was lucky. It only lasted five minutes. Perhaps, that was what he was thinking but he had no idea what would ensue. As he usually did, Avon had planned to go to the gym soon after coming home, but that would not be a typical day. He searched the refrigerator for something to eat, and somehow he found himself by the microwave again. His facial expression altered as he observed the microwave. Perhaps, I should not have been laughing, but the look on his face was too much. He was exaggerating the nature of the disaster.

"Messa! Come here! I don't think you've had enough. Go bring me the whip."

He tried whipping Messa in the butt again, but Messa was trying unsuccessfully to block the strikes with his hands. Avon turned him about.

"Why don't you ever listen when I tell you something? Huh? Answer me!"

"I am sorry."

"I'll show you sorry."

He hit him some more, and then let him go.

"Get out of here!"

Messa practically ran out of there back to his room upstairs. Avon ate his peanut butter sandwich and drank his protein powder drink and went to work out at the gym. He returned about an hour and a half later to the kitchen. I was standing by the big tall counter between the actual kitchen and the eating table. The right side of my face was parallel to the kitchen door. The telephone was to my left, and I was leaning against the wall a little. Avon came into the kitchen and went to have another look at the microwave. This was the third time. A most hilarious frown was depicted on his face. I struggled to contain my laughter. I tightened my stomach and grinned my teeth. I knew that my success at not laughing was dire, for I did not want to be whipped. I averted my eyes away from him.

"Messa, get your butt over here! I'm not done with you yet."

He grabbed Messa by the hand.

"I don't think you've had enough!" he said to Messa.

So again, Messa was whipped for a few more minutes.

Despite the difficulties we were having at home with Avon, every once in a while I try to think about the positive aspects of him. I thought it was nice of him to take on such a big responsibility for children who were not his. Financially, we were fine. After all, we lived in a beautiful blue house thanks to him. The grass to the right of the house was well maintained. There was a nice green tree on the grass, near the edge of the side to the right of the house if one were facing toward the street. Even the street was indicative of the quality of life. It was always clean. It was definitely no ghetto.

These thoughts were overcome by another set of thoughts. I told myself that he was always mistreating us without due cause. If he hated us so much, he could have let us stay in Africa.

Years later after I had completed my college degree, I would understand the man a little better. My mother would confide in me the story of how he first met Avon. It was a fatal attraction, I thought. He followed her to her lodging. After hearing the story, it was clear to me that she knew that there was something mentally or psychological off about the guy. He displayed a clear sign for his inclination for violence. Yet, I am convinced my mother took the chance to try out the relationship because of us. I believe she had convinced herself that it was worth it. Her children were in West Africa without a father or a mother. They were living with a grandmother who hated her children and who practiced the dark arts. She wanted to get us out of there. And so that was her best option: so she thought. She was twenty eight years old. In my mind, she was still very young. She definitely wanted to become a U.S. citizen in order to help us. She initially came to the United States with an American couple. She was their maid. Their two daughters were born in Togo, and she took care of them at the capital. This was part of the reason why we hardly saw our mother when we were children.

Now, I believe that Avon and my mother's meeting was not by chance. The cards were drawn out before their births.

What decision they would make once they met would be entirely up to them. Every step of their near decade relationship would be filled with choices. How they would treat each other would not be forced by "God." They were free beings. We learn through different types of relationship: as couples, sons and fathers, mothers and daughters, as siblings, colleagues, associated coworkers, and as friends. Each day is an opportunity to become more aware about love through positive energy. Each day is a chance to demonstrate the good intentions we as souls "came" here to manifest. Some of us falter more than others. Avon was faltering big time. As you will see, his fall would be formidable.

It began one day when Dada came to pick us up from school in her car. Our very tall friend Rance was in the car with us. He and my brother were seating in the back. I was in the front passenger's seat.

"Are you coming to the dance on Friday night?" Rance asked us both.

"I don't know. Dada, can we go?"

"Is that how you ask a question? Ask nicely and maybe you can go," my mother said.

Apparently, I had not said "please," and my mother was obviously being a little picky. Essevi on the other hand was a little annoyed.

"That's how she usually is," he said to Rance.

"What did you say?"

"I said it's ok. That's all."

"No, there was something else, say it! If you don't say it, I'll tell Avon when he gets home and you'll see. You know he won't be nice. So talk!"

The threat did not have any effect on Essevi, who remained silent all the way home. He was absolutely not going to say anything. My mother was frustrated and angry.

She dropped Rance home and a few minutes later we were home. As we pulled into the garage, she said:

"You are very stubborn, aren't you?"

When we entered the family room, she pointed to the corner, commanding:

"Kneel over there."

He resisted a little, but my mother forced him down. My mother forced him to kneel on the floor and to put his hands in the air until he was ready to apologize. She then went to the kitchen to start dinner. After a while, she went to the family room a couple of times to see if he would change his mind. She was not successful.

After a while, the house phone rang. It was Avon. He asked her how things were and she told him what was transpiring. After all, my mother may have rationalized that Avon would only punish him a little. That was all. He would not really hurt him. After all, we children had gotten our buttocks whipped before, and we lived. But, perhaps deep inside her she sensed that things were different this time, and was afraid. My mother tried to convince Essevi again to say that he was sorry and he could go to his room. Her gestures and facial expressions became wild and rapid. But, they were all in vain. This was the day that my brother would proclaim his independence through none participation to comply with my parents' commands and physical abuse. It was an act of liberation whose determination I would really understand only sixteen years later. He was a determined soul who was able to put fear aside much sooner than I was.

"Are you going to apologize?" she demanded with a mixture of fear and frustration. He did not say a word. He was holding his ground. He did not think he did anything wrong and this was obvious to me. I was watching sadly and was predicting the outcome of his refusal.

"He's coming home soon!" she said with fear, referring to Avon.

As we heard the garage door open, my mother shouted out:

"Do you see, he's coming! Go quickly to your room."

Avon opened the door and rushed inside the house. His face was full of rage. My mother said a few words to him. He told my brother to get up and to apologize. He was yelling at him, but still my brother would not budge a muscle. He did not utter a single sound. He remained on his knees. Avon became very violent. He grabbed Essevi by the hands and tried to drag him to his office. Essevi would not go. He seized the couch with all his might. I was getting worried and I went toward the eating table in the kitchen to have a better look. Avon, the all-powerful could not move a fourteen-year-old boy.

They struggled, battled for about two minutes. One was fighting for control, while the other was fighting against the pain that was coming, against being told what to do, blind obedience, against docility. It was the hour of resistance, of revolt, a revolt for change. Finally, only when Avon calmed down did Essevi walk into his office. However, the apparent calm displayed by Avon hid the rage he was about to manifest. He was talking to Essevi without much noise, so I thought. However, what transpired next was mind boggling.

The door was closed, but not locked. Avon was posing Essevi questions, but we could not understand what he was saying to him. I was in the kitchen attending to the food and the dishes. I opened the freezer door to get something when Essevi ran into the kitchen. Blood was dripping all over the floor. Essevi was trying to contain the bleeding with his hands. He was behind me now in the stove area. Avon was in front of me with a determined look upon his face. The blood and the pain upon my brother's face did not seem to evoke any sympathy from him. As the freezer door closed, Avon took resolute steps toward Essevi, with an angry facial expression. I was stupefied. He was going to continue beating him. The whip no longer did the trick for him. He wanted to feel the infliction of his violence through his flesh. My eyes were glued upon his in bewilderment at his lack of sympathy. I seized his right wrist in determination.

"Can't you see he's hurt?" I said.

I was surprised at myself. Grabbing him was spontaneous, and the words I uttered came out of nowhere. Perhaps, I felt a little guilty for my brother's cut forehead. After all, I was the one who started the conversation that brought this whole thing upon him. No, I didn't just feel a little guilty for Essevi; I was the cause of his pain. And…no! Avon was not going to get through that night. He stood there right in front of me, perhaps thinking: He's holding my arm or he is challenging me. Our eyes met and there we held them, reading each other's thoughts. In the end, he began to back away, and I let go of his arm. It seemed to me that he understood that I did not want to fight him, and that I merely wanted him to leave my brother alone. He went to his room upstairs, and I escorted Essevi to the garage. My mother called the police, and came out to the garage. Messa and Essevi were already in the car. She started the engine as I put my seat belt on. Just as we were about to drive off, Avon came to the garage.

"Do you think it's over? Life is not a soap opera. You'll see!" Was he predicting the future? My mother did not take his words seriously. I knew now that she kept hoping that things would change for the better. How about me? I heard those words, but was not brave enough to do something. Not that calling Child Protective Services did not cross my mind—I simply did not know what to do. I was not independent or brave like my brother to brace uncertainty. As I think back to that night as we drove to the hospital, I am fairly certain that if I had known what I know now about the nature of existence, I would have run away from home somehow. The only problem would have been my little brother Messa.

The hospital front desk staff put us in the waiting room. We waited and waited forever. No one was coming. We must have waited at least forty-five minutes before the doctor came. The desk clerk was not at all nice, nor did she seem to care about our plight. She merely said in a disagreeable voice:

"Sit there and wait!"

"Shouldn't this be taken care of right away?" I asked.

"Heads bleed easily. The doctor will be with him soon," she said as a matter of fact. I had my hand folded and wasfrowning. I had grown up fast that night. I was learning how uncaring people can be.

We returned home that night about half past midnight. Avon was not there, of course, because he was in jail. The police had picked him up that same evening after my mother called them. I guessed they took him because they probably saw the blood on the kitchen floor, which he did not clean. The next day, he was released. We saw him in the evening. What was interesting was that he called Essevi to his office to explain to him that what had happened was an accident, that his fist went up before he could think. That was all he said. Not a single "I am sorry." No, he only explained that it was an accident, but he could not apologize because he felt no sorrow for his act. Besides, if he had done so, that would have meant that he was wrong, and he was never and could never be wrong.

A few months after the hospital incident, our mother called us into the kitchen to help her make dinner. Avon was absent from the house. As I entered the kitchen, I knew she was preparing a fancy meal. She was always cooking things that would stick to the bottom of the pan. We used to complain among ourselves because we found it difficult scrubbing the pots to get every dark spot off. You do not understand Reader, it sometimes took us hours to scrub such pots clean. Nevertheless, I must say that she was an excellent cook.

Upon entering the kitchen, she assigned different roles to us. Some of us were cutting while others were peeling garlic. Suddenly, she posed a very serious question.

"What do you think about me having a baby?" We were quite surprised.

"What do you mean?" I asked.

"I just wanted to know what you think."

The way she asked the question made us think initially that she really only wanted to know what we thought. However, as the conversation continued, it was clear to me that she was already pregnant and had not informed us until then. None of us had suspected anything.

"I don't know," I finally answered her.

"Me neither," Essevi answered.

A month later, we were in the kitchen again talking about her having the baby. This time, she was going to be more direct. She started with the usual greeting.

"How was school today?"

"Good!" I answered.

"Not bad!" Essevi began, "Actually, my teachers were deadly boring. "I almost died," I said jokingly.

"What classes did you have today?" she asked.

We had the same course once every other day for ninety minutes. The days alternated between A and B days.

"Listen, I have something very important to tell you," she said, pausing for a moment as we died of anticipation.

"So, what is it?" I asked.

"I am pregnant."

"Is it really true?" Essevi asked.

"How long?" I inquired.

"About a month and some days"

So, I was right. I had suspected the day she asked us that hypothetical question.

"I see!" I remarked. This was one of my favorite phrases. I rarely say "I don't understand."

"So what do you think?"

"I don't know. It's surprising, but I guess it's good news," Messa said. I was thinking that my mother wanted a girl. She had all boys and had always talked about having one.

"And you, Essevi, what do you think?"
Essevi's reply was sharp and straight to the point.

"Allow me to tell you what I honestly think. It's not a good idea," he said as he mounted the stairs to get something from his room. He came back about thirty seconds later.

"Why do you think that it's not a good idea?

Essevi was standing up, his back leaned against the kitchen wall, near the kitchen entrance. His arms were crossed.

"Why would you want to have a baby for a crazy man?" he asked with excitement. He was serious, and his brows indicated it. My mother listened attentively.

"How are you going to raise a child with someone like that? He's nuts! You don't see how he treats us? That's the type of life you want for a new child? I don't think so," he said passionately

My mother was speechless, for deep inside she knew that Essevi had an excellent point. She continued preparing the food with calm. She sat on a chair and turned toward me, and waited for me to speak.

"The child has nothing to do with the father's stupidities. Not to have a child for this reason is a sort of punishment. We would be punishing the child before it has the chance to show the same physical and mental behaviors that his father has shown. It is true that it would be difficult for him or her with a father like that."

Was I hearing my own words? It seemed that I was philosophizing.

My mother had listened to us children, but I wondered what her husband thought about all this.

About a week later, I would have my answer as I descended the stairs. Avon was on the stairs that led to the living room. He was facing my mother when I walked by. I wanted to go to the family room, but given the look on his face, I decided to go to the kitchen instead. I walked slowly so that I could read both of their facial expressions. Avon's countenance was one of bitterness and distaste. My mother's was somewhere between sorrow and determination. She was silent. He spoke furiously.

"Didn't I tell you before getting married that I didn't want any children?" His words possessed a deep negative intensity. I do recall my mother finally saying something, but I do not recall what it was. It was probably something to appease him. I was already in the kitchen and could not hear much. I was a little afraid that he might have hit her. I honestly do not know what I would have done if he had hit her. Fate did not let me decide this. After all, I was afraid he would use the gun in the master bedroom.

I could still hear talking when I sat down and placed my food on the kitchen table. I listened furtively as I put peanut butter and jelly on my bread. I closed the lid slowly, for the conversation was getting sort of philosophical in a way of speaking.

"If it's a boy, are you going to have an abortion?"

"I don't know what I am going to do yet," she answered conservatively. He knew how to make her feel guilty, for that was exactly what she wanted: a girl. Another week passed and she told him that she was keeping the baby even if it were a boy.

Avon hated the idea of having a baby so much that we heard about it *every* morning when he drove Essevi and I to Center High School at 7:15 a.m. He came up with all sorts of reasons why my mother should not have the baby. One particular morning was brutal. He talked the entire time as he drove.

"At her age, it's really dangerous for a woman to have a baby. The risk for having a handicapped baby is very high. He could be deformed. He could have deformed hands, feet, and even worse, he could be retarded, incapable of thinking."

I knew that it was harder for a woman to have children in her thirties, but I thought it was still possible. I did not think that thirty-six years old was really that bad, then again I was not a doctor. I just wanted to go to school, not to hear him anymore.

When I had the chance, I reported this particular conversation to my mother.

"If you want my opinion, I think there is something under all those excuses he made up for not having the baby. He doesn't want to be a father. Do you know what I mean? He is already a father, but not really. But now, he is really going to be a father. He doesn't want to 'create' anything."

That same day after venting profusely I went home after school. I thought I would be home alone for at least four hours. Unfortunately, I was out of luck because Avon left work early that day. I was feeling joyous and tranquil inside when the garage door opened.

"Oh shit," I heard myself say aloud. I wanted to run upstairs to work on my homework in my room. However, by the time I gathered my things and was about to go upstairs, he had already entered the house. It was too late! He said hello to me, took the newspaper on the kitchen table and began reading as he stood up. A few seconds later, he put the newspaper on the table and spoke as he made his peanut butter and jelly sandwich with his protein power milk.

"I told your mother that it is not a good idea to have the baby, but she's not listening to me. She's very stubborn."

I showed a sympathetic face so that he would finish complaining so that I would be in peace, but it didn't seem to work. He knew very well that I needed to do my homework, but he did not seem to care. After an hour and a half, I was dying of fatigue. I should have stayed at school to do my homework. Only if I had known he was going to come home early!

After a few months, my stepfather stopped complaining about his desire for my mother to have an abortion, for it was too late.

Talk of divorce was the next element of our dysfunctional family household. My mother showered us with joy each time she spoke about getting it. It was something they kept talking about. They talked about it whenever they fought or had a big argument. Meanwhile, they also made plans to build a bigger house near the Folsom area. Each time, the divorce would be cancelled. My mother and I had a conversation the second to the last time they were supposedly going to get the divorce. My mother and I were in the laundry room which was to the left of the garage door. She was seven months pregnant.

"I have something to tell you," she said.

I already knew that she was going to cancel the divorce again, but I answered anyway:

"Ok."

"Avon and I are not going to get a divorce anymore."

"You're not?" I said in disappointment. I could tell that she was not pleased with my answer.

"Don't you know that it is difficult to raise three kids all alone? I am seven months pregnant."

Despite her decision to remain married to him, fate had its own path. There are moments in existence in the universe that compel souls to look beyond fear and to render decisions that are not based on financial stability, mortgage payments, pain, death, or above all, fear of the unknown. Such decisions are always in some shape or form based on pure love, a love that is stronger than the superficiality of stability of physical things or negative energy. My mother had made a decision that was not based on financial stability or fear, and I was deeply proud of her.

A few days later, my stepfather was out of the house. He moved into an apartment nearby. One afternoon after my summer school Algebra II class ended for the day, I asked her why he moved out. She was near the laundry room and was sad and disappointed.

"He gave me an ultimatum. He said he wanted Essevi to be put in a juvenile house for teenage delinquents. He said that he wanted you three to grow up to be responsible citizens."

"Really?" I asked as a matter of fact in Ewe. Essevi was not a delinquent. Yes, he challenged Avon only because he had physically abused us for years and years. He did not do drugs or stole from anyone.

"How was he planning to do this?" I asked.

"I don't know."

He could not put him in juvenile detention center without lying about Essevi's moral character. At the time I thought that it was because Essevi had refused to say hello to him when he saw him. However, I realized later that

Avon was upset at him because he felt he was responsible for my mother's final decision to separate and divorce him. In hindsight, I think my stepfather thought that my mother had no choice because she had three children and was pregnant with another. In his logic, she had nowhere else to turn. He therefore mistakenly assumed that she would never divorce him, and he could do whatever he wanted.

"How could I?" my mother said with strain on her face, "I could not. He's my son. He hasn't done anything," she said, referring to Essevi. He said it was either Essevi or him. I told him that I couldn't and he said he would leave." She uttered the words with heaviness and pain.

"I see," I said. There was in that answer of mine comprehension. Faced with love and fear, she chose love. Years later when I was in college, my mother would tell me that she tried to have Essevi stay with several of her close friends temporarily. These people were aware of what was happening in our household. None of them helped.

About a week after leaving the house, Avon made a final futile attempt to keep the family together. He had private conversations with each of us. Essevi was the first person to whom he talked. He drove him somewhere, while Messa and I waited at the house for our turns. When he returned, he spoke with Messa. Then, he called me into his room. I sat on the left foot of the bed, while he sat at the other end. He explained to me that he wanted to make things better. He asked me if I could forgive him for the past. It was a vague question. I did not understand how a person could ask for forgiveness for something so vague, something he could not admit. I was not comfortable with this, so I pressed him for clarification.

"For beating us all these years?"
"Yes."

"Are you sorry for what you did?"

"I am sorry for what happened..." He was dodging the question.

"So you regret beating us all these years?"

He sat there, quiet, and was looking at me gravely and calmly. He had some nerves. He wanted to be forgiven, yet he could not admit he was wrong.

"If you can't admit that you were wrong, then I can't forgive you." I did not quite know what to tell him.

"Maybe one day when you recognize what you've done, then I can reconsider."

For me, the issue was straight forward: you did something wrong, you recognize and apologize for it, and that was the end of the story. I have always done this when I sincerely felt I have erred. The inability to do this was serious. Unfortunately, I did not understand this before it was too late. I should have accepted Avon simply as he was. This, I would deeply regret.

After the conversation, Avon went to his apartment, I think. In any case, we were home alone. I called Rance to relate the conversation to him. He told me that I did well. Afterwards, I went to talk to Essevi, to find out what he told Avon.

"So, what did you tell him?"

"I didn't tell him anything. I only said that I will never forgive him. He was not happy, but he deserved it."

"Did he say he was sorry for beating us?"

"He's not sorry!" he said vehemently. I believed my brother. For me, this was another proof that Avon did not like to be wrong. Nevertheless, I was also beginning to see the difference between our personalities. Essevi was firm and not as forgiving as I was. He was also braver and more rebellious in terms of refusing abuse. That ultimate summer he also completely refused to even look at Avon when he passed him. I could only imagine what Avon was thinking. I sensed a hint of danger for him.

Two months later, September 24, 1993, my mother began to feel contractions. She said it was time to go, and wanted me to go with her. As she drove, she remarked how bright the moon was shining. It was nearly morning, 5 o'clock. She did not seem stressed or worried that her water might break as she drove. Instead, her mind was focused on the full moon.

"This is how it was when I had you in the morning," she said with a smile. About thirty-five minutes later my mother successfully checked into the hospital. She was dressed in hospital attire. I stayed with her for a while, long enough for the nurse to moisturize her ballooned stomach. Her water must have broken at that time, for she was in pain. She breathed out deeply. There were periods of calm and periods of suffering. During one of those periods of calm, I took my leave. I knew what was coming—blood! And a lot of it! I did not like blood, and did not want to see it. Blood invoked in me an unimaginable terror and disgust. I reached the door's threshold. I was out. *Good!* I thought. Just as I was about to head to the waiting room, there was Avon looking at me. He motioned for me to follow him. *Darn it!* We were going back to the delivery room again. He went to my mother's bedside, the side where her left hand was. He rubbed and caressed her shoulders and hands softly, and called her "baby."

Avon knew what I was thinking.

"Stay and watch!" he said. He was very serious. I found the whole thing bizarre. Why should I have stayed to watch my own mother give birth? If he had bothered to learn a little about my life before coming to America, he would have learned that I knew a lot about sex and women giving birth. No, he did not know that I used to care for rams who used to have sex in front of me. He also did not know that I had seen my aunt giving birth to my cousin Akukuma. Had he asked I would have told him that I had not enjoyed seeing the pool of blood that Akukuma was born *in* inthe house. I stayed to see the blood again. This time there was a lot less than I recalled in Kusuntu.

I did not remember the exact details of that day, but I do recall being in the car all alone with my stepfather who was being totally fake.

"Giving birth to a baby, to a human being is wonderful, isn't it?"

"Yes," I answered mechanically. He dropped me off home and returned to the hospital. He and my mother rang the first doorbell about two hours later. I opened the door and my mother brought the baby inside. Akofa was born. She was honestly one of the most beautiful people I had ever seen. I wondered how someone like him could have produced such a beautiful creature.

We spent the rest of the day getting accustomed to the baby. That is, Avon had bought some speakers that he was testing. He put it in the baby's crib and was trying out the walkie-talkie in different places of the house.

Everything seemed to be alright. Avon came by everyday to see Akofa, then returned to his apartment. This was the routine, so I did not assume that any life changing event was going to occur on that day. I mean after all, Avon would come to the house, say hello, and Essevi would ignore him as he had been doing for months. It was nothing new. And so I thought.

That particular evening, my mother had organized a birth celebration for Akofa. She invited all her African and American friends. The house was packed with people. There were people in the dining room, the family room as well as the stairways conversing in many languages. I was in the kitchen preparing more food for the guests. I had prepared some rice, with stove-fried mixed vegetables and hot sauce, for I knew Africans love spicy food. Everyone was having a great time. One of the guests congratulated me on the food with:

"I don't know what you put in the food, but it's really good. You have to give me the recipe."

"It's just something I threw together as I was cooking. I did not know how it was really going to turn out."

"You made this?" another person said, "It's really good." I turned to the food I was cooking. Avon came to the kitchen to test out the walkie-talkie again. The baby was upstairs in their bedroom. He occupied himself with this as the guests mingled among themselves. He hardly exchanged any words with them. He took his leave again, to go to another part of the house to test the walkie-talkie. People had begun leaving, and most of them had finished eating. Essevi came down to help me with the dishes. He sang as he dried the plates with a hand towel. He was singing a Snoop Dogg rap song. I did not hear him use any foul language. However, my stepfather disapproved. He came into the kitchen, stopped by the refrigerator.

"Stop singing that song!" he ordered. Essevi continued. Avon's face became very intense. He was enraged. His voice seemed to eco with rage.

"You will do exactly what I tell you as long as you live in my house."

"I'll sing what I want!" Essevi said and continued wiping the dishes. Avon just stood there immobile. Anger and surprise dominated him. This time his sense of authority was lost. He must have believed that Essevi was challenging him. As such, he remained there in front of the refrigerator with his mouth agape in astonishment. He did not know what to say. Seconds would pass before he would leave. I would not see him again that Sunday night.

That night was a special night because it was the premier of <u>Louis and Clark: the New Adventures of Superman</u>. Dada (i.e., mom) gave us permission to watch it in her bedroom. Dean Kane played superman. It was much anticipated. All three of us watched it peacefully. Little did I know that this would be the last time the three of us would be together. Essevi looked so peaceful, so calm. According to my mother, Avon left several hours ago. She told her that he wanted to do some grocery shopping and would return in an hour. Three hours passed and he did not return. He had another plan.

CHAPTER 4

FALL INTO DARKNESS

Most souls, no matter where they are from in the Universe, do not change easily. To rise, they often fall deeper into darkness. Only when the pain becomes unbearable do they rise.

On September 27, 1993, Avon's fall would be so great that he would drag the rest of the family down with him.

I had gone to bed at about midnight. As usual I locked my bedroom door downstairs. I set the house alarm before going to bed. At about 1:30 a.m., I heard a female voice, screaming! Avon had returned when everyone had gone to bed. As I try to recall the details, I am of the opinion that everything was meticulously executed. According to Messa, Avon went upstairs to tell him to take out the trash to the garage. That means that he went to their bedroom, quietly woke up Messa without disturbing Essevi, then waited for Messa to descend, and then planned the execution.

Despite the loudness of the house alarm, cries could be heard from upstairs. I put on my shorts and mounted the stairs with hesitation. My heart palpitated in my chest. The climb was arduous. A feeling of intense suffering within my heart enveloped and submerged and choked me with every hesitating step. A shadow descended upon me. Fear and anguish overtook me. I walked slowly up the stairs as I have had a thousand times rapidly. Tonight was different. A crease hallowed in my feet with every step. If that continued, I was going to have a heart attack before I reached the top of the stairs. *Can't rush!* My heart beat with each step. The abyss surrounded and tortured me. I was suffering physically and emotionally. I had never felt pain so deep within me before. No amount of Avon's beating compared to this none physical agony. I wanted it to end. Each breath of respiration devoured me. *Must go up the stairs, to see what happened.*

I was nauseous. I began to turn like a drunk man. *I need to regain control.* I climbed without ever reaching the top. But, I knew that I could not escape the anguish, the atrocity that awaited me. As I set my foot on the last step, I had the need to run away, to escape forever. My mother was to my left, with the baby in her arms. She was topless and utterly hysterical. She had gone mad.

"He killed my child! He killed my child!"

My mind tried to grasp the meaning of her words, all the while feeling her pain.

"He killed your brother. Your brother is gone forever!"

I did not want to hear those words. They penetrated me and hurt. I wanted her to be quiet, but I knew the futility of trying to tell her to remain calm. Besides, I was not calm inside. I turned away from her and headed toward Essevi and Messa's room.

"Why did he do it? My God, he could have hurt him and let him live. He could be alive now." Those were the words I heard my mother say as I entered the room.

Essevi was there, lying in bed, his head in the middle of the blood. He was there spread out, the sheet covering him up to the waist. Blood was running from his mouth to the sheet. There was an unsuspecting expression on his face, as if he did not know what was going to happen to him. Blood also dripped from the edge of the bed to the white carpet. It was as if it were a slow drip of blood from the ceiling to the floor, with each drop carefully calculated and measured. My brother was in the pool of red as if he were in a red swimming pool. I was staring at his dead body and was refusing to accept what my limited five senses were telling me.

Everything proceeded in an unreal manner. I experienced the air around me more intensely. My mother and my new born baby sister's hysterical crying seemed unreal. The expression of disbelief in my face was forever holding. Even the sound of my mother's cry and the din around was unreal. I saw all this in a surreal haze of imagery. Even more so, the actual reality unraveling before my eyes superseded a dream. My body shuddered in the surrealism of the disaster and my mind slowly spun with mental disturbance. I felt emptiness, unable to reason, for my mind was in a circle of confusion as I tried to understand: *Essevi is dead!*

My head began to hurt from the confusion. I closed my eyes hard and fast, and tried to pretend that the whole thing was a dream, from which I would soon awake. *No!* I shouted within myself.

My mind was filled with an absurd refusal to accept what was: *You are going to wake up from your sad sleep. I'll wait here for you. Wake up! Universal law of life and death doesn't apply here. It will experience a rupture, an exception this time. You are going to wake up and everything's going to be back to the way it was. If God really exists, now is the time that He show himself. Wake him up! Give him life again!* I waited, but no miracle came. None! *You are not superior to death. There is nothing, absolutely nothing that you can do for him. You are powerless. You only show your powerlessness...*

I left the room and found my mother in the corridor again. She was still hysterical.

"He killed my child!"

The police had arrived and were climbing up the stairs. I repeatedly told my mother to get dressed, but my words were in vain. I tried to escort her into her bedroom, but she just kept asking me why Avon killed him. One of the police officers said:

"Ma'am, please get dressed."

The Caucasian officers asked me to go outside. I protested.

"I have to get dressed first. My room is downstairs."

"I need you to go outside," he insisted.

I do not know why I listened to him. I think it was because he was in a position of authority. So was Avon at some point.

It was cold outside. The police officers, black and white, were gay, jovial. They cracked jokes and were laughing about their lives. I observed them. I was puzzled why they would let me stand there freezing when it would have taken less than a minute to get a shirt. I looked at them. The laughter became personal to me.

"This happens all the time. It's one of the family members who did it," one of the police officers said. Nearly an hour would pass before the ambulance took Essevi's body away.

Later during the same day, I learned that Avon had ran to the nearest gas station, which was next to the Seven-Eleven convenience store, called the police to turn himself in. I also learned that I had not heard the gun go off because he had used a silencer. The last piece of news came from my mother. After having shot Essevi, Avon came to her room to stare at her and the baby. My mother reported that his stare was "weird." She claimed that he killed Essevi because he had promised to take something very dear from her. Personally, I think what brought death upon my brother was his defiance. After all, in my stepfather's eyes, he was the cause of their separation, and finally would be the cause of their soon to be divorced.

The ensuing day, we went to spend the evening at a friend's house. There were a lot of Togolese and African people there. Some of my friends from the high school were also there. A guy came out of nowhere to talk to me. For the life of me, I could not remember everything that transpired that day, but I knew one thing for sure, this older Togolese man, who appeared to be in his mid-50s, annoyed me very much. God knows what he had said initially, but what I do recall were his latter words.

"You think you're suffering more than she is?"

My eyes widened in disbelief. I had not said a word to this guy. I was quiet, enjoying my misery when he pronounced those words. Still, I said nothing to him.

"She gave birth to him. She's his mother."

I turned my confused mind away from him. He was not important. He might have been correct in his statements, but they were unnecessary and uncaring, for I too was grieving in my own way, and he just brushed that aside.

That same evening, another older Togolese man came to talk to me. I do not think he knew my mother. I think he was just a friend of a friend of the family.

"Don't forget your language," he said to me in a calm and caring voice.

I studied the expression on his face, and did not say anything. Nevertheless, I would always remember his words, for they displayed a kindness that went beyond words. There were not many Ewe people in America with whom I would practice my native language. As a result, he must have figured that I would forget if I did not make an effort. From time to time when English would begin to dominate my head, I compelled myself to think in Ewe in my head. There were times when I did it daily. At other times, I did it weekly. That was the trick for remembering my native language.

I do not recall where we went that evening, but soon after, I found myself in my mother's so-called best friend's house. The man she married was an interesting West African fellow. He was extremely reticent and hardly showed much emotion. He was in the kitchen now, reading the newspaper—silent, hardly moving a muscle. He and I hardly exchanged more than a few words. I do not know why this particular image would remain with me, but try as I might I cannot rid my mind of the image of his back turned to me as he sat in the kitchen. He was almost immobile. I watched him out of the corner of my eye. I observed him as I myself was suffering inside. I was not comfortable within my skin. There was a sadness about this Ewe man that was reaching me across the room. I was extremely depressed, and did not need his sadness as well.

I tried to think about something else. I could not. I could not control my inexplicable suffering. I was not comfortable within my skin. Suddenly, I had it. I would focus on my immediate environment. The living room was rather small, but clean. I sat on the couch, where I would sleep that night. I closed my eyes. My skin and soul tormented me. I was depressed, agitated, uncomfortable, and perhaps most importantly was confused. Every so often images of my dead brother appeared before my mind's eye. My heart and chest area cringed in turmoil. All attempts to relieve the pain were only slightly successful.

I woke up the next morning in my shirt and underwear. Catherine, his wife, had already left. I did not know where my mother was, but what I did recall was that Catherine was not happy with her husband. He did not seem to be physically abusive. I felt the only thing he was guilty of was his inability to show his emotions. He seemed like someone who had been suffering inside for a long time.

Not long after his death, we went to see his body. It was just us—his family. I was sitting to the right of my mother who was repeating more or less the same thing she had said the night Essevi was murdered. I turned to my brother's face. His features seemed life-like, but yet he produced no words. The agency had done a good job embalming him. He looked clean. The wound was not showing. However, his facial expression was the same as that Sunday night. The more I gazed at his face, the sadder I became. I should not have been there longer than a minute or two. He was gone, and I was going through the ritual of creating negative energy.

Two weeks later, we moved to an apartment very close to school. My mother brought a lot of furniture from the house. As soon as one entered the apartment, to the left was the kitchen. The kitchen was nice, especially the silver color faucet. It would be in front of the faucet where my mother and I would have a verbal argument, where she would repeatedly stick her index finger to my nose and I shoving it off my face: nearly biting it. The kitchen floor had tiles. Directly in front of it was the living room. There weren't any doors between the kitchen and the living room. On the left side of the living room was a chimney which always seemed to be full of wood and debris. It would be nice now to have a chimney in my New York apartment. The couch was set near the front, closest to kitchen. Thus, the television was directly in front of the couch. It was directly across the bathroom. In the bathroom, there were a big white bathtub to the left, but the bathroom itself was narrow and tight. Unfortunately, there was only one toilet in the house. As a result, we were always fighting over it. To the left of the bathroom was my mother's bedroom. In the middle of the room, next to the wall in the back were a big night stand and a tall mirror. The night stand had make-up material, hair brushes, two hand mirrors, and several pictures of Essevi. By this time, my mother had made a shirt with his picture and the words: A Child Killer Should Not Live. This t-shirt was in the room. Another curious thing was the naked light-bulb in the middle of the ceiling. It shone too brightly.

Next to the left of the bathroom was our bedroom. Messa slept on the left side, while I slept on the right closest to the door. The window was on my side of the room. Next to this window was a dresser. This dresser was very significant, for I often drew and wrote on it. Overtime, I drew a very odd and ugly-looking man. He had short hair and had an abominable look upon his face. If one were to ask me today to describe or say whom I had drawn, I would not have a good answer. It was a mixture of emotions. The surface of Messa's dresser on the other hand was bare.

About a month and a half later, I was in my room starring at the drawing on my dresser when the phone rang. I was watching cartoons: The Tom and Jerry Show. I got up to answer the phone. I picked it off the ringer and headed toward my room.

"Hello? Who is it?"

"It's Avon's sister. I don't think we've ever had a chance to speak."

"Yeah, sounds about right, more or less. So, how may I help you?"

"Can I talk to Avon?"

What a question she just posed. That meant that he did not tell her. This was most interesting. I thought he was close to her. Perhaps he was ashamed of what he did.

"You want to talk to Avon? So you are not aware of what he did"

"Aware of what?

"Of, of…" The words exited my mouth painstakingly.

"Of the killing; he killed my brother!"

I paused thinking about the possible reason why he did not tell his sister about what he did. After all, she was the only person whom he called. She was his only confidant, his only real family. Despite all this, she never came by the house.

"No, I didn't know."

"Is there something else I can do for you?"

"Where is he?"

"In prison."

"Yes, but where."

"Listen, I just told you that your brother committed an atrocity, and you're so calm. It would seem that you don't care."

"Things happen in life."

What did she just say? My ears must have been deceiving me. I could not believe it. I was stunned, stupefied. She did not have a heart. Maybe it ran in the family.

"What did you just say?"

"Tell me where I can find him."

"What?" I said, and hung up the phone. Not a single "I'm sorry for you." I felt like ripping out her tongue so she would never say such mean and apathetic things again. Her voice was so calm as if "things like that" happened in her household everyday. What an idiot. I was angry! My heart was bruised again. I was sad and angry at the same time, as if blood had rushed to my head. I grinned my teeth and launched to the air, speaking aloud.

"Bitch! Bitch! Bitch!" May she and her brother go to hell, the two of them! Oh, how I would have loved to seize her in a choking position, to wring and shake her neck, to slap her with pleasure, to slap her endlessly.

I walked to the family room and turned on the television. I was still talking to myself, inside my head when I heard the key turn inside the lock.

"What are you doing there?" my mother asked.

"Nothing."

I turned off the television and headed toward my room. My mother turned it back on.

"I am going to do my homework," I told her.

I still could not stop thinking about Avon's sister. How did she get our phone number? We just moved into the apartment not too long ago. Our phone number was unlisted. I lied in my bed, looking up at the white ceiling. You know, if you stare at the ceiling long enough you could begin to see or create images. Weird images appeared before my mind's eyes: Faces of deformed people. I tilted my head and held the images to ponder their lack of existence. I was bored, and was not feeling well inside my skin. *Why was I here?* I wanted to get away from it all. I felt empty inside. I was tired of this daily worthless experience of existence. And why was I always thinking about things so obsessively? What control did I have over my own thoughts if I cannot make myself stop having them? What control did I have over my own life? Was I in control of my body, my being? People sometimes say that we are in control of our actions, behaviors, and what happens in our lives. To a great extent, this was unlikely. For instance, was Essevi in control of his life? Did he commit suicide? Of course not, he was murdered by Avon. In a way, one could say that Avon had control over Essevi's life. Essevi made a lot of his own decisions while he was alive. Avon was also free to act and make his own decisions. Nevertheless, it was Avon's freedom that reigned over Essevi's. If he had supposedly lost his life by acting the way he did, then that meant that he caused his own death. He would therefore have been responsible for the life he led, the decisions he made. Evidently, he was not responsible for Avon's actions. He could not control Avon, because Avon was also free to do as he wanted. The only way to have prevented Avon from interfering with Essevi's liberty would have been to take away Avon's liberty. All this led me to one conclusion: the dumb things that people say about being in control of oneself were false. We cannot totally control what happens in our lives, our actions, and to a certain extent our decisions are not totally ours.

Other people have a fair amount of control in our lives. They deprive us of our liberties. They control us because we cannot watch every minute of our lives.

Take the example of a person who is walking in the street, and suddenly finds himself on the ground, incapable of breathing because a crazy guy decides to shoot him. I do not think this person could be held responsible for being on the ground dying. I mean, how could we reproach him? Can he be blamed for having decided to go out when he did? Maybe if he had waited just five minutes longer, he would be alive. Was this person destined to die that day in one way or another? I don't think so. Our destinies depend on others as much as ourselves. Why was I thinking all this? All I really wanted was to run away, to be far, far away. But where was I going? It would not have really mattered. The important thing was to be far, far away from here; to be far away from these quotidian, familial and adolescent life problems. I did not even want to be on this planet we called Earth. This planet was devouring me alive. I did not want to exist. Existence bored me. I woke up each day and I did things, and at night I slept. So repetitive! Sometimes I realized that I existed and that scared me, not because I really didn't want to exist, but because life is ephemeral, fleeting; and soon I would simply cease to exist. The thought of this frightened me. I know that people say that life is a gift, but I was not convinced of this. I could only feel the pain, the suffering inflicted by others. It was other people who were in control who were making me suffer. It was other people—my parents, friends. Avon was a part of them. I so wanted to go to his jail cell and bang his head against the wall like he did to Essevi. I hope some guy literally screws him in prison.

I could not understand why I never revolted. Was I so peaceful? Was I alive because I did not tell him that I too would sing whatever song I wanted? Was I alive because each time he came to the house after the separation I greeted him? I said hello to him despite the fact that Essevi did not salute him. In hindsight, I see now that I greeted him simply out of politeness. I should have shown my true repressed feelings, kept inside for years. What does it mean to respect one's parents, anyway? One is punished for each little thing. He tells you not to do this or that and then he turns around and breaks all the rules. Children should not be the only ones to follow the rules. All I had to do was be brave. My true lack of freedom was due to the fact that I was afraid, afraid to say, "Give me liberty or give me death." I was afraid of death, and this fear would follow me for years to come. Liberty knew no age. The mere fact of having accepted and done what Avon wanted meant that I was really always free. We didn't sign a contract that obliged me to follow his unjust rules. I was a coward. I was a coward because I did not express what I was feeling. I was a coward because I almost beat him up one day when I was seventeen years old; but something stopped me from fighting him. I was a coward because I used to lock my door each night before going to bed just in case he would have thought about entering my room in the middle of the night. Such cowardliness! Why was I so weak?

I would have liked to have taken my brother's place. I would have wished that it were me that he had killed. Essevi was brave. I was not. He was brave because he was not afraid to tell Avon that he would never forgive him for all the physical abuse. If he were alive, he would have done great things. I wondered what was going on in Avon's head when he pulled the trigger. I wondered if he thought for even a second that what he was going to do was abominable and immoral. I doubt he seriously considered such things. For crying out loud, he was the same person who told me that life was priceless. After killing Essevi, he still wanted to see his baby daughter. Butwhy? If he is incapable of respecting life, then why should he merit the chance to see her?

My mind was filled with so many thoughts that if I continued I would never get any of my homework done. I had a lot of homework and book reports to write for Monday. I opened the shades and the window. I stuck my head out, my elbows on the edge. I did not see anybody, but zigzagging escalators—the fire escape. The parking lot was vacant. After a few minutes, a little black girl with long hair came into view. She was running after the ball. She seemed so happy. It's good for her to be happy, I thought to myself. I closed the window. I was not in the mood for doing homework, so I went back to the kitchen. There was nothing to eat. I went to the living room and sat next to my mother who was watching the news on television. There were images of a young Hispanic man being arrested, who had killed somebody.

"Look at that! He is smiling. He just killed a human being and he is smiling. He's proud! Killer! He is not ashamed at all. That's what's wrong with this country. You kill someone and smile," my mother said with frustration and anger. She sneaked a look at me, but I did not say anything.

My grief was great. I was depressed. It was as if I were becoming insane. One evening while at home alone, I opened the window and watched the rain. It relieved my heartache. Since my childhood, I have always appreciated its tranquility. It was pretty. The wind was knocking the rain drops off balance. They were not falling straight. I remained there contemplating the rain as I rested my elbows on the windowpanes. It was falling intermittently. I obeyed its music.

This rain, this violent rain, is beautiful. Turbulent! My state of mind was changing from calm to agitated. The rain was getting in the room. I wanted to be invaded by the rain. There, I would be in the middle of the inundation. I imagined this intensely. I had to join the rain, to become a part of it. I closed the window and went to the bathroom to look at myself in the mirror. Was that really me? I did not like what I saw or how I felt. I went back to my room to change clothes. It was now time to become one with the rain.

I was walking without an umbrella. The desire to find my brother again grew in me like a physical malady that was eating me inside with all of its force. I walked faster. Now and then I had the desire to scream, to see something break. I was a lion in a cage. The bars prevented me from getting out. The lion wanted to express its rage, but was blocked. My hands were its claws and I felt the intense feeling in them. Mental suffering was eating me inside like physical pain. What is physical pain if not just mental suffering that eats you inside, tearing your heart apart. The transformation is made when the brain interprets mental pain as physical pain. If the interpretation is not made, there would never be any pain. I was convinced that our neurotransmitters were responsible for this interpretation. The contrary, mental pain to physical pain could also occur. I felt the pang.

There was not a difference between physical and mental pain or suffering.

I wanted to stop the suffering, but I did not know how. I therefore resigned to its suffocation and continued walking in the rain. *My brother was more courageous. He resisted sooner. He escaped, leaving me behind.* What was I saying? *But he's dead!*

I stopped for a few seconds to survey my environment. I was literally lost. I kept walking straight ahead, hoping to recognize something. But, somehow my soul knew the way. I was across the street, in front of our old house. I walked closer. I saw lights inside the house. It must have been past eight o'clock in the evening now. Behind the window I saw two figures, which I imagined to be two brothers, for my convenience. They seemed happy horsing around in the guest living room where we were rarely permitted to step foot in. I could not watch this any longer. I turned away. Only a year ago this was our house. I turned toward the house again. *I need to get inside.* I thought about ringing the doorbell, but my hands would not respond. *I must be dreaming.* I turned away again, knowing that the house was no longer ours. I was desperate. I thought that maybe, just maybe my brother would be inside. I closed my eyes, wanting to think about something else other than this sadness. I opened them again. The rain was still pelting me.

A few meters of walking, I turned to look at the house one last time. It was no longer black. At the moment I had turned my head, lightening had struck, shining light upon it. Its true blue color appeared for a brief second. This blue was worse than the darkness of the night. The color brought back memories of yesterday. It inspired dislike in me. At that moment, if I had paint, I would have painted it right there and then in the rain. I crossed the street. A car was passing at an incredible velocity. Where was the driver going at that speed? Maybe he wanted to hurt himself. It could have been a woman. I struck my forehead with the palm of my right hand. This was supposed to yank me out of my reverie before a car really hit me.

I was on Zephyr Hills Way. I veered right. This was the only option available to me. This was the same street where I skateboarded so many times, where I played basketball, where I had driving lessons when I was seventeen years old. Somehow I felt like I was saying goodbye to the house, to the neighborhood. I wondered if this would be the last time I would step foot on this exact street.

By the time I arrived home, I was tired. I went to bed without taking a shower or brushing my teeth. I turned my head toward the drawing on my dresser. I turned off the light, and began thinking about a conversation I had with a high school friend. He supposedly knew how to get a gun for about sixty dollars. I was impressed, but a little skeptical. I imagined having the gun, becoming one with the gun. I considered the hole of the imaginary gun. Its circular image stared at my eyes. It was enormous. There, in that hole was where the bullet would exit. It was a sort of a black hole, a hole in the universe. I wanted to be part of this blackness, darkness, this mystery of which we knew so little. I would enter the hole and boom, I too would be part of the unknown; I would disappear forever. Space, dark space surrounded me. I too would become part of the darkness. I was darkness. Darkness, there was nothing that could separate us now. I saw myself swirling around in the black hole in the empty space. I was no longer lost. I was part of *something*. Shelter! Total shelter, freedom from people! They can no longer touch me. I can no longer be hurt by words, abusive words launched at me, by the electrical cord. Yes, I was safe from physical and psychological mistreatments. *Oh hole! Infinite hole, protect me! I am protected from everything. I no longer want to be hurt. Infinite black hole, protect me from yesterday. Be my family, for I don't have one. I don't have any friends. I am already part of your family. I feel it. I want to join you, but I am afraid of the unknown.*

I imagined holding tightly onto the imaginary gun. My index finger was caressing the trigger. Then, I had a thought. What would happen once the deed was performed? Done! You cannot go back to fix it. That is how things are. The past cannot be rectified. It's set.

I imagined the bullet residing in my brain. *I need to put it in my brain. That is where it belongs. It wants to be home. It's lonely.* It longed for my blue blood; to swim in it, even for just a second.

I got up to sit on the bed, to have a silent monologue.

I am unworthy to live. I am incapable of living. Oh black hole, render your decision final without recourse I am tired of the confusion, of the hesitation, of the caprice that is compelling me to think one second I wanted to live, and another to perish.

I did not know why I should live anyhow. Life up to this point had brought me nothing but misery and suffering. I was seriously not sure why I should continue living or even to exist. I was tired of existence. I did not even know why I was born, and this was a serious question. I did not know why there seemed to be so many unanswered questions about what or who we human beings really are. *But the mermaid!*

I shifted my position in the bed to render the final act real. *I am going to break the ultimate human law and that of God. Maybe it's immoral, and if it's immoral, then God would never forgive me. What am I saying? God who?* I pronounced this last sentence with determination. There was no God! I was making a decision. I had decided that God did not exist, but then other questions came to mind. What should I base my moral decisions on? Morality as practiced in society was so relative. I did not believe in the theory of moral relativity, but that was precisely what I saw in society for the most part. If you ask people a question about morality, they would give you different answers. Sometimes you get banal and illogical answers that hurt your ears. Given this, I asked myself what I should rely on: the Bible? Universal Law? What the heck is that anyway? Or simply my own intuition? Yes, that was it. But aren't my own intuition relative?

I was convinced that to a great extent, if they came from a place of purity, they could not be relative or wrong.

Farewell my friends, family, world. This is a forever goodbye that I am saying to you. I'll miss you, but that's how life is.

I rationalized death. It is not a bad thing. *If I kill myself, I am only precipitating things. What's the difference?* I thought I had a good point here. If someone else kills me, then it is considered a crime, but when Death takes me naturally, then why would not one consider that a crime? This was also a very serious question for me. I wanted to understand why such an act is forgiven or overlooked simply because it is "natural." *Are we not energy?* I was thinking that perhaps energy was just a source of force, visible or invisible. It should have been at this point that I stopped rambling and question my own last question. If I had considered what energy really was I might have given myself a clue to the nature of immortality. Instead, I continued with that same line of reasoning. I told myself that the problem was that a natural force could be punished because it is invisible. One cannot punish something one could not see. That was one of the worse and futile nights of my life.

Several weeks after moving into the new apartment, my mother made preparations to take my brother's body back to

Togo. She asked me if I wanted to go, but I told her that I did not want to miss a whole month of school. However, the true reason was that I was tired of all the sadness. She struggled to find someone with whom I could stay. Gretchen and Steve, friends of the family were alright with me staying with them on the weekend. During the week, I would stay with my friend Rance and his family. I really did not understand why I could not stay in the apartment alone. I was seventeen years old. My mother departed for Togo with Messa.

They returned about four weeks later. We moved again shortly after they came back. My mother's so-called best friend wanted to share an apartment with her. She was having difficulties with her husband. She agreed because it would have saved her money. However, after moving in, Catherine backed out of the agreement. The new apartment was even smaller than the previous one. My mother searched for work, but was unsuccessful. She needed money right away, so she decided to work at her friends' houses—cleaning. We were no longer thinking about having enough money to pay the rent, but were more concerned about living from day to day. Still, I did not touch the few hundred dollars that I had when I worked at the Italian restaurant. My mother started doing what she resisted for so long—digging into her savings. She realized that there was no way she was going to support a family with the income she was making cleaning her friends' houses only a few times a week.

We were now far away from school. We would stay there for only seven or eight months. This was the place where Messa and I would learn to be parents. Our baby sister was a lot of work. We had to go home early to babysit so that my mother could go to work. She worked in the afternoon as well as overnight. Messa and I practically never went out.

Those were sad days. My mother did not find a decent job. The only type of work she found was cleaning jobs. Sometimes she came home in the middle of the night. At other times, she came after seven o'clock in the morning. That was when she found a job watching over old couples. I recall being very upset at my mother. We were always late to school because she would not get home early enough. And when she came home, she would drag and take her time to get ready to take us to school.

"Hurry up Dada! We're going to be late!" I often said to her angrily.

"Don't rush me!" she would answer back bitingly. "I'll be ready when I am ready."

We were all annoyed. My mother was irritated because she was not sleeping enough. We were irritated for two reasons. First, we were forced to grow up faster than anticipated. Akofa constantly cried at night, and we had to find a way to pacify her. As a result, we often did not sleep much. Second, we were constantly late to school. My first class was French, and my teacher was not so forgiving. She pulled me aside one day and flat out told me that the tardiness was not acceptable. She was quite serious. Her eyes communicated many things to me. They said that what I was going through was part of life, and I had to find a way to resolve my tardiness. Furthermore, they indicated that life is difficult, and I could not have any excuses. I was late a few more times, then the tardiness stopped. I woke up earlier and took the bus to school between the time my mother took to get ready and the time it took to put the baby in the car, I saved a lot of time. As soon as she came home in the morning, I was out of the house. The bus stop was only a few minutes from the apartment. This was good for me. I no longer had to argue with my mother in the morning. The ride to school was peaceful and was relatively inexpensive because I had a student bus pass.

The year passed slowly. I began hanging out with new friends. A few of us were into body building and took it very seriously. We hung out after school at one of their houses, working out as if there were no tomorrow. By then, I had a car, a 1989 Nissan Pulsar to be exact. We worked out so often that I gained a tremendous muscle mass. Some of my school mates started calling me the Black Incredible Hulk. I was a very well-built and rugged-looking teenager going to visit his stepfather in prison. I had not shaved in a month, and could not recall when I last cut my hair. Gretchen and Rance came with me. I signed a sheet with an officer and was told where to stand. We went into the building. Right in front in the back was another door. A few meters to the right was a little office with a Caucasian officer inside. Outside his office were seats for visitors. There were not a lot of visitors that day. I approached the officer.

"Who would you like to see?"

"Avon, Avon Davies."

"Ok, go inside and wait in room 5. He'll come in a few minutes.

"Thank you."

There were six windows, if I recall correctly. Rance and Gretchen were waiting near the door. To the left, way in the back was a young black man who came to see someone. Maybe it was his father. They were talking calmly. Calmness sometimes is nice. The whole room was calm. But the tranquility would not last once I saw Avon's face. He came out in what seemed to be a jail uniform of some sort. I was upset. I was about to surprise myself, not thinking about what I was going to say before uttering my words. Avon approached the telephone behind the glass window. The glass was rectangular and divided the room into two.

Avon definitely seemed miserable. He had his glasses and jail uniform on. There was a jail number sketched on his shirt on his chest. Unfortunately, I do not recall the number. He was silent. What was he waiting for? I expected him to say something—maybe apologize. Fat chance! I found myself launching words into the air like a flame.

"Why did you kill him?" It was a banal question.

"You know why."

He was lying, and it was obvious that he was trying hard to convince himself of what he was saying.

"Answer me when I talk to you!" I instructed him firmly. I was using his line, what he used to say to us.

"Watch your words," he said. Was he serious?

"And if I don't? What are you going to do? Listen you little f--, you know that the only thing that's stopping me from banging your head against the wall, from grabbing you by the throat like an animal that needs a good beating, is this f—n glass."

Images of Avon banging my brother's head against the wall appeared in my mind.

"Now answer me when I talk to you."

I was getting good, too good. I had learned from the best—the man I was talking to, and it showed. He was afraid. His body began to shake from his entire body. I was not expecting this. I was not sure how to feel about this. It was a mixture of emotions. A part of me was pleased and rendered calm, while the negative part of me was upset at his display of emotion. I think part of me wanted him to remain inhumane, for it would have been easier to understand him. He had descended, and a part of me wanted to accept this as the only possibility. Yet, as I put pen to paper many years later in my early thirties, I know without a shadow of a doubt that it was the light within me that was showing a hint of sorrow at the great negativity he had produced. The shuddering was his soul's attempt to get back to the light, the positive, pure Infinity. Yet, his ascent would be slow, for he did not embrace the conscious being talking to him. He sought to deny the purity within his physical vehicle.

"You know why, it's, it was for your good. It was for the good of the family. He was threatening the family."

"How was he threatening the family?" I asked rhetorically.

"He would have killed all of you."

He was desperate.

"How do you dare say something like that? You were the problem. After having abused us for all these years, you began to lose control, control of your power. You could not take it. That's why you killed him, isn't it?"

"No, it was to protect the family."

"It was for the good of the family my ass! Listen you little f—er..." This last pronouncement resounded well in the room. All was rendered to silence; even the young man and his father stopped talking. Their eyes turned to me, to us. Rance and Gretchen could hear me. I was sure of this. Avon continued insisting that he was trying to protect the family. This was an utter lie. His body betrayed him. Perchance he was having amnesia. No! He was clearly lying.

"Shut your f—mouth!" I hurled at him.

"Calm down!"

Was he serious? There was no way he was telling me to calm down. He should have calmed himself down before going into Essevi's room and killing him in cold blood.

"I said to shut up! Shut your f—mouth before I break this f—n glass and smash your head around!" It worked. He was quiet. I slammed the telephone against the receiver. Dumfounded, he held the telephone to his left ear for a long while as if I were going to return to talk to him again.

The preparation for the trial began along with the continual changes in my mother's degrading emotional state. During the summer of my junior year, Dada found a house to rent near the high school. It would be in this house that I would catch her crying in secret *too* many times. She was no longer crying openly. She was trying to be strong, but sometimes I caught her.

One night, I was woken up by a noise. My room was close to hers. I did not really want to wake up, but the noise would not let up. I got up, and turned on the light and followed the wailing. I walked toward Messa's room. I stopped when I noticed that the noise was diminishing. I turned to the other direction. The cry augmented again. I passed the bathroom and arrived at my mother's front door. She was crying and sniffling endlessly. I stayed at the door for about fifteen to twenty seconds debating whether or not to knock on it. Perhaps I should have gone in to comfort her, but instead I returned to my room and went back to bed. That would not be the only time I would catch her crying. She cried in the car when she thought she was alone. She cried in the kitchen. When she spoke about ordinary things, anything that reminded her of Essevi caused her to take deep breaths that seemed to last for eternal seconds.

Even at the murder trial my mother's heavy sighs would continue. She took long painful pauses between each sentence and phrase.

The trial began about a year after Essevi died. I was a senior in high school. Rance was the only friend who came.

I was disappointed at Long, one of my brother's friends, for not coming. He said he had to go to school. This was an excuse, for I too would not be attending. I recalled asking him a few minutes before our French class. His answer was a sharp "no." I was taken aback, a little betrayed. He did not even let me explain. He and my brother were good friends. From that day on our relation would never be the same.

My mother was the first to testify. I remembered her slow, painful walk to the witness stand. I could already tell she was going to be very emotional.

"Please place your hand on the Bible," said the court officer, "Ma'am, do you swear to tell the truth, the whole truth and nothing but the truth?"

"Yes." Her voice was a mixture of sadness and anger. It seemed she was practically yelling as she answered the questions. With quite a few of them she added:

"He's a child killer." Her eyes were budging out. "His killed my son. He didn't do anything to him. Tell me why he did such a thing!"

There was dead silence in the courtroom for a brief second. The defense attorney was now posing her questions.

"Isn't it true that your son was a threat to the family?"

"No, he didn't do anything."

Three weeks later, we were back in court. I was the first to testify. I was questioned by the defense and the prosecutor attorneys. The bailiff said:

"Please place your right hand on the Bible."

This was the first time I had to testify in court.

"Do you promise to tell the truth, the whole truth and nothing but the truth?"

"Yes."

The defense lawyer approached the bench.

"Before I start, I wanted to tell you that I am just doing my job."

I was not sure about this. He did not have to defend him if he felt that strongly. To me, this was an excuse not to do the right thing. People often say this to avoid doing what they should. I was not going to like this lawyer.

"Your name is 'Kossi Agbessi Epou?' "

"That's right."

"Now, I am going to ask you some serious questions. Answer as honestly as possible. Didn't your brother have a knife?"

"No, he didn't."

"You're telling me that your brother didn't have any knives?"

"No."

"I am going to ask you the question a little differently. Didn't your brother have a Swiss-army knife?"

"Yes, he had one."

"Why did you then tell me that he didn't have a knife?"

"Because that's not really a knife. It's used to clean finger nails, to eat little things. It's not a knife."

"Wasn't this knife long?"

"No.'

"How many inches?"

"I don't know."

"Isn't it true that your brother cut you with a knife once?"

"No."

"You don't have a cut in your left hand?"

"Yes, but it disappeared."

"How did it happen. Did it magically appear on your left hand?"

"Logically no. I was cooking when I cut myself."

Did you lie often to your stepfather?"

"No!"

"Never?"

"Never."

I quickly searched my memory to see if I had ever lied to him. One incident came to me. I had changed the temperature in the house because it was cold. I increased it to 76. Avon had noticed and demanded to know who did it. His face was terrifying. I was getting beat all the time. I was tired of it so I told him I did not know. That was the only time I had lied. But, I did not give a crap about what this lawyer had to say. I was not going to help him. Why was he not asking questions about the scar that I had on my back, all the butt whippings that I experienced. I knew exactly what the lawyer was doing. He wanted to show that Essevi was a delinquent and posed a threat to the physical well-being of the family. How absurd!

A few days before the final decision was rendered, a few of Avon's co-workers, including his boss came to support him. The boss spoke from the audience. I watched with calm, registering his every word, labial and facial expressions.

"We don't condone violence, but there are things that happen in life that make people do things…We think he is still useful to society."

I was only partially understanding this guy. He was a little older than Avon, and seemed to be an African American. He seemed to be speaking from the heart, and this gave me pose to consider his words. Still, I could not help but to remark that he was being one sided. I wondered if Avon's job was going to let him go. He himself had mentioned on more than one occasion that there were younger people entering the field with more knowledge and less experience. The result was that they were taking their old computer programmers' positions. If that were the case, was that why they came to support him? Perhaps, it was because they had suggested to him that his time there was limited. As a result of this, the boss felt something culpable. I was not sure about my assumptions, but those were the things that ran through my mind as he finished.

His speech was futile. I had a feeling that the judge and the jury would be on our side. Besides, what did he want to be done with Avon? Did he want to set him free after he had killed? I was considering the possibilities: He would receive life in prison or the death penalty. At the time, I would have said if he had received the latter, then he would have deserved it. I believed in the death penalty, but would say that it was within limits. I did not believe that it is necessarily wrong. It depended on what the crime is and if one knew with absolute certainty that the person did commit the act of killing another with full malicious intent with due cause. Due cause for me was where the perpetrator was the aggressor, and not protecting himself or herself against an immediate face to face physical danger. The key here is that the person was faced with a situation of self-defense within seconds of his or her demise. This did not mean that one could go after someone else for having killed one of his or her loved ones. There was absolutely no exception, for it entailed a planned, preconceived notion of revenge. Revenge or retribution was not sufficient reasons for employing violence. Besides, I had another stronger reason for not wanting Avon to receive the death penalty: Death was so final a judgment. My brother was gone forever, so why should Avon also be gone forever? I wanted him to live, to suffer, to feel the havoc and pain he had caused.

Every experience for each person is different because each person is at a different level of spiritual awareness. Avon had caused much pain, but I doubted he was going to develop any immediate empathy from this experience. He needed to feel the pain to develop his sense of empathy. I wanted this for him. I also wanted his boss to feel a little physical pain to be able to at least acknowledge the victim's family's suffering. He was not. He did not mention a word of sympathy for our family as he defended Avon.

Avon did not want to testify. Even at the very end of the trial, he was given one last chance, and he turned it down. Finally, judgment day was upon us. He was looking at the judge squarely in the face, and I was watching him at the corner of my eyes. One of the jury members rose to speak.

"We find the accused guilty..."

I certainly was not surprised. I looked around. I did not see his sister. I would not have recognized her anyhow. Perhaps, she was among the public audience quietly watching. Perhaps, it was my thoughts running wild.

The judge turned to Avon now.

"Your sentence is twenty-five years to life..."

Avon protested by saying something to the effect of not being properly defended by his lawyer. The guards seized him. The judge silenced him with words that were music to my ears.

"You went into the child's room while he was sleeping, he was defenseless, and you killed him knowingly in cold blood. I have no pity for you."

As the guards took him away, he turned to give us a contorted facial expression.

A few months elapsed since my brother's murder trial decision was rendered. Since then, I have been feeling a deterioration in our familial relationship. We still spent time together, but it was not pleasant. One day I believe during the weekend, my mother asked where we wanted to eat and I told her Burger King. Messa was in agreement. Rance was with us. I preferred eating at Burger King over McDonald because the price was cheaper. At Burger King you could buy a whopper for only ninety-nine cents; with tax the total price was $1.07. This was not bad at all because the whopper was enormous. I would discover years later in France that it was much more expensive there. The whopper was about twenty percent more expensive in French Francs.

My mother drove the car slowly, a Toyota. It was 8:15 p.m. and we had just finished shopping at Sunrise Mall. We were all tired, and above all, very hungry. We had not eaten since 12:30 p.m. My mother parked the car almost at a direct angle to the entrance of the fast food joint. There were a lot of people in the restaurant. Sometimes I like crowds. It's like going to the movies and there being a full house. The full-house makes me think that they are happy to be there to enjoy the show. In this case, to enjoy the food. At that time I truly loved eating whoppers. I could never eat just one. They tasted so good. The feeling was always temporary. How I felt a day or two after eating the whopper was another story.

We were at the counter. My mother was ordering.

"I'll have a whopper with medium fries and a medium size sprite," Messa answered.

"I'll have, uhm, three whoppers and a medium fries, and a small coca-cola," I said. I never ordered a big drink because the refills were free. My mother asked Rance what he wanted. He said that he wanted the same thing as me, with one less whopper.

"Ok, did you get all that?" my mother asked the cashier.

"Yes, I got it," she answered.

"I'll have a chicken sandwich," my mother added.

"With mayonnaise?"

"No."

My mother could never eat mayonnaise because it made her nauseous. The nice young cashier gave her a receipt with the number 55. We sat down and waited for our order number to be called. There were less people in the restaurant now. I guess it was getting late. We sat in the center of the store. There were people on each side of us. To our left was a little girl about eight or nine years old who was eating a salad with her mother. She seemed to be about sixteen years old. The mother was maybe about forty-two or forty-three years old.

I got up and went to the bathroom to wash my hands. During my absence the cashier had called our number. Everybody except my mother rose to get the food. We brought the food and the drinks to her.

"Here Dada, I filled your cup with cherry coke. Is that ok?"

"Thank you."

I knew she would like it, for that was her favorite soda. It was evident that she was distracted by something. She remained quiet as Rance and Messa spoke. She was chewing her food slowly, hypnotically. I wondered what was eating her inside. She shook her head. Her eyes were closed for a brief second.

"Avon! Even after a year I still do not understand you. Killer! How could he have done such a thing?" She stopped as if waiting for an answer. I was looking at her curiously with a mixture of emotions. Part of me felt her great pain, while the other part wanted her to stop torturing me with her outburst of sadness. Rance and Messa were quiet.

"I want to kill him!"

The two families to each side of us were rendered dead silent.

"You'll do no such thing. You're angry. That's all," I said.

"Don't talk to your mother like that," Rance said to me.

"Shut up!" I said with a deep frown. Was he serious? I was upset, and if he wanted a fight, he had chosen the right time. "I'm not talking to you. Frankly, I don't care how you talk to your mother. This is my mother, not yours. Learn to shut up when necessary."

He was quiet now. Messa was observing. He was looking at me. I had my hand on the table. Dada was also looking at me with a mixture of emotion—pity, anger, disappointment, and perhaps the desire to leave the place. I did not finish my whopper, but I was no longer hungry. She ruined my appetite. I took my tray and was about to throw the rest of it in the trash can when Rance asked me if I were going to eat the rest of my food. I returned to the table and handed it to him. My mother's eyes were still upon me. When I sat down, her scrutiny became even more intense. Suddenly, tears rolled down each corner of her eyes. I felt badly. She took a napkin and wiped them. I averted my eyes and pretended not to see. This was too much for me. I went outside to wait for them. It was dark. Cars sped by with their shinning lights. A few minutes later they joined me. My mother stopped at the first red light.

"Why are you like that?" she started again.

"Like what?" I pretended not to understand. She was not going to leave me alone. She started crying again. I purposely avoided her eyes.

"Be quiet and drive."

I knew I was being mean, but I did not know how to stop, besides I was not sure I wanted to. I was conflicted.

"Agbessi—"

"What!" I said, cutting him off, "What do you want? You want to start again?" I roared at Rance. He was rendered to silence, and no one talked for the remaining of the ride back home.

Thinking back, I see now how futile these arguments were. The interesting thing was that I never argued with my mother until after Essevi's death. Well, I was not ever able to anyhow. Avon would have never given me the chance. Another interesting thing was that Avon and I did have an argument—which was one more than with my mother.

With time, I would understand my mother better. I would understand in the South of France that she is just like everybody else. Children have the habit of expecting a lot from their parents, sometimes without being conscious of it. Deep inside, they expect a lot from them because unconsciously we children believe that they are more than they actually are. I have learned that one must take one's parents as they actually are. They are souls just like you and I who are also trying to find their way, to become more spiritually aware.

Sometimes in this consciousness, the opposite is true. Sometimes children are wiser than their parents. People say that you must forgive those who have harmed you. I had often considered such saying, and accepted them as ideals. Such expressions were not concrete enough for me. Besides, how could I forget my past! I could not, but I could certainly make more of an effort, and I did. I realized that what I needed was a new environment, a place to start fresh. France did the job. Having spent a year away from America, I had the time to reflect on my life, I put pen to paper to begin to make amends.

One day I wrote a letter to my mother from Montpellier, France.

Hello,

As I lied on my bed last night with my mind filled with sadness, I thought about the past and you. So, today, I decided to write you a letter to tell you about the past and my present sentiments. The past was not what I would have hoped or liked. A lot of things hurt me physically, emotionally, and mentally. It's the first time I dare write them down. I could have called you, but I preferred to express them in writing. If I had called you to discuss it, we would have gone nowhere. You would have cried endlessly. I do not want to hear you cry or to complain. Despite all that has happened, I have recently become aware that you are a good mother. I do not blame you for anything. I beg you not to deprive yourself of the words "good mother," which you have earned.

During the most difficult moments you were there to take care of us. You worked like crazy and with little sleep at times in order to feed us. You always found a way to pay the rent. All that, as I think about it, impressed me.

It is only now that I am able to be inspired by your courage, of your capacity to persevere. You always took your responsibilities when we needed you. Don't resist the two words I have written. I thank you for all you have done. I don't have anything else to say. I just wanted to say how I felt at this time.

With love

Your son,

Agbessi

P.S.,
Don't forget the two words.

During the beginning of my senior year of high school, a black, middle-aged army recruiter came to visit our high school campus. Bad faith drove Rance and I to his table.

The man made us many promises about "securing" our future. For some reason, this southern black military guy targeted me for months to come, trying to convince me to join the army. I told him from the commencement that I was a conscientious objector and did not believe in war, but he pressed on. He even succeeded in getting me to visit him at the recruiting office. I repeatedly told him that I did not want to kill anyone. It did not make any sense. To kill people who did not do anything to me was a crime of the heart. In war, a lot of innocent people were always dying. I did not want to be a part of that. When he saw that he was being unsuccessful at convincing me, he sought help from one of my classmates in my English class. He was a very erudite white teenage boy who knew way too much about military and world history. He was from a military family, of course. He approached me a minute or two before class commenced. He said that Mr. Joseph was working very hard to help me with my future. Was this kid serious? Get out of here! When my brother died he did not say anything, and now he was talking to me about joining the army to kill people? Insanity!

I listened to his words, but my mind would not be swayed. Before I could join, I would absolutely have to know that under no circumstance was I going to kill anybody. Besides, I did not care much for authority figures. I didn't like anybody telling me what to do morality-wise. Five years with Avon was enough to convince me that violence and abuse was not a good way to live one's life. Besides, I wanted to go to college, and maybe see a bit of the world. College was expensive. I had been going to the library to look for scholarships. I really did not know how I was going to pay for it. My grades were not that high to qualify me for scholarships. I had a B average, and when you took away my weight lifting courses, my grade point average was 2.8. And so, I finally accepted the recruiter's offer to help me find a job in the army that would not entail killing anybody and scholarships to pay for college. I told him that I had heard about the government calling people back to serve even when one is out of the military. He lied by saying that it depended on what my contract is. In college, I would learn that joining the army was like being part of the mafia or the CIA. Once you join them, you can never leave. No matter how long your enlistment contract, they could always call you back if they really need you.

I also explained to Officer Joseph that I had an aversion to blood. He brushed it aside. I didn't appreciate this.

We made an appointment for him to pick me up early one Saturday morning to go to the testing center to take the army exams. He arrived on time. I got up quietly and waited for him. My mother also got up, questioning me about what exactly I was going to do that day. How many other ways was I to explain to her that I was going to do my physical and to take the exam? If she did not understand it before, then she was not going to. I felt she was being dramatic because I had not decided anything yet. Upon hearing the door bell, I went outside. My mother also came, uninvited. She was going to embarrass me. I just knew it!

"I don't want him to go!" She said vehemently.

Mr. Joseph seemed annoyed. My mother would not let up.

"His father was in the military. He died. His brother is also dead. Do you want to take him away from me too?" She was not really asking a question. She uttered the words in such a way that they spoke to his conscious.

"Ma'am, it's for his future," he said irritably. The look on his face betrayed him. "He's not going to die."

"Dada, we need to go. It'll take us about two hours to get there." I got inside the car with the recruiter. As he began to drive off, my mother turned the porch light off. The recruiter had a jeep. It was a cool car, but I did not really know why I was going with him. I needed money to go to college, but if I had another way of accomplishing that goal, I definitely knew that it would not have been through the army. I had one reoccurring thought: I could always change my mind before signing the contract. It was true that I had not signed any papers yet. I was just going to see how much money I could actually get for college. I relaxed in my seat. The recruiter now seemed calm, confident.

"We're going to get you squared away." He was smiling.

He must have thought that it was a done deal and that he had convinced me. He had a lot to learn about my personality. I often turn things over in my head a thousand times before making a final decision.

He dropped me off and waited with me for about fifteen minutes before leaving. A military officer or personnel came to speak to him for a brief moment, then I followed him into a large waiting room. A lot of young men entered the room. The majority of them seemed excited to be there. One in particular caught my attention. He was Caucasian and several inches taller than me. His excitement about joining the army was palpable. Was he ready to kill people, for his country? Apparently he was; because later as he took his physical he was saying "Yes sir!" to the doctor as if he were his commanding officer. He passed the test.

The old man who examined my friend and I was very thorough. My God! He even checked my testicles. Afterward, I found myself following him, naked in front of my peers. I was not comfortable with this. He weighed and measured my height without any shoes on. He made a face.

"Have you ever had a problem with your feet?"

"No, what is it?" I could see from his countenance that he was not satisfied with my answer. At the time, I did not remember, but as I write this story now I recall several instances when I did have problems with both of my feet. As a child, my feet were cut several times by broken glass because I went around barefoot due to the fact that we "could not" afford shoes. I learned later that the clothes that my grandmother was distributing to different people in the house were from my mother in America. There were shoes, but my grandmother never told me about them.

"Walk from there to there for me."

I did and he noted something down on his clipboard.

"Ok son, you can go."

I sat next to my new friend. It was not long before we all followed another military personnel into the written examination room. I thought the exam was difficult. I was therefore surprised when I learned that I received a hundred percent on the mathematics section.

It was now about 3 p.m. and we were being called one by one to review the results and to decide on a job choice. My military counselor appeared to me at the time a nice, tall Caucasian guy, who spoke to me about the choices that were available to me. He wanted me to enlist right there and I was extremely uncomfortable with this.

"The position we have for you…tank maintenance engineer."

"What would that entail?"

"You would be responsible for repairing the tanks after battle."

"Fixing the tanks after battle?"

"So, I would be in the battlefields?" I asked, stressing the "s" at the end of the last word.

"You won't do any fighting." He showed me a picture. Perhaps he should not have because it gave me a visual, and I definitely knew right then and there that I did not want to be fixing anything. I was never into fixing cars or bicycles. In high school, I was put in a welding class. I immediately dropped it. I did not want any sparks flying into my face.

"So, what do you think?"

Was he serious? Couldn't he see the blank stare and discomfort in my face?

"Well, I am not sure, I'd like a few days to think about it."

"It's a good job. All your housing and food are paid for, free," he said with a smile. I was not smiling.

"Yeah, but I am just not sure at this time."

"This position may not be available when you come back. I assure you it's a good deal. You just sign here."

"If I sign, can I change my mind later?"

"No, you wouldn't be able to."

He maintained his calm as he reached for the telephone. He called my recruiter. It was at this exact moment where my apprehension and politeness disappeared. I was upset, for I knew what he was trying to do. These people were refusing to take "no" for an answer.

"I don't know what's going on, but he doesn't want to sign…"

"Let me talk to him," I heard Mr. Joseph say over the phone.

My military counselor passed the telephone to me.

"I thought we were squared away? Go ahead and sign the paper," he said, imploring me."

I was now very upset.

"I am not signing anything. I am a conscientious objector. We talked about this."

Finally, my voice was firm. I did not care what he had to say anymore. I felt the gravity and force within my own voice. He understood.

"Do you want me to come and pick you up?"

"No, I'll find a way home."

"Listen, think about what you're doing. It's your future you're destroying. Sign the paper and you will see that I was right. Sign it and I'll come get you."

I hung up the phone and asked the counselor for permission to call my mother.

"We just finished…."

"I'll come get you."

"That's ok. I'll find my way home."

I wanted to be alone. "I'll see you around six o'clock." The counselor told me about the bus schedule. I left the building and waited at the stop briefly. The trip home was about two hours. I rode the bus to the main intersection near McDonald. I was about forty minutes away from home by foot. I heard a very repetitive honking. I looked and saw my mother's car. What was she doing there? I was sure she had called off from work because of me.

"Get in quickly. There are cars everywhere. It's dangerous!"

I got into the car hesitantly and was quiet. I felt frustrated and upset. The recruiter had wasted my time, and was trying to force me into a decision against my will. In hindsight, this was one of the best decisions that I would ever make in terms of the progress of my soul. The worse thing anybody can do is to fight wars especially for his or her country. By doing so he or she is literally darkening his or her soul which is inside the body. It is an absolute fact beyond culture, religion, time and space, planets, star systems, and dimensional or spiritual realms to kill other people and not have it negatively affect one's soul. We are immortal and cannot die. The negativity is immediately added to the Light Body. When I decided that I would not join the military, I had no idea at the time that I was listening to the purity within me. It is only in the present that I am very proud of myself.

I turned to sneak a look at my mother.

"What happened?"

I hesitated a little.

"They wanted me to sign right away. I asked for a week to think about it and they didn't like that. I didn't sign."

"Good. I don't know why you went along with it anyway."

She was right. There seems to be a calmness about me that sometimes makes people think that they can pull a fast one on me. With people like Officer Joseph, being very firm is the only way to push back their negative energy.

High school quickly came to an end soon after that. I was deeply sad, downcasted, depressed in those days. I do not know how I survived high school. Maybe it was because I worked like an insane person—going to bed late. At that time, I was working at McClellan Air Force Base. I left school early, at about 12:45-1 p.m. to go to work.

During the summer of 1995, my mother moved again. This time she bought a fixer-upper house.

In August of 1995, after having moved again to another house a lot less expensive than the last one we were renting, a forgotten old voice would be heard. Nearly two years had elapsed since the trial. It was a good Californian summer day. It was not too hot. We were all in a good mood and were outside when we heard the telephone rang. My mother went inside the apartment to answer the phone from her bedroom.

"Hello?"

"Hello Ma'am, do you accept a collect call from Avon Davies?"

"What?" my mother's voice shuddered in fear.

I was now in the house, waiting for her. She froze upon the spot as if she had seen a ghost that gave her goose bumps. The phone was loud enough for me to hear Avon's voice. It was thought provoking to think that after two years hearing his voice would render her to physical paralysis.

I went to the closet where I had stored the whip. It was there after nearly a year. I observed it carefully, pondering its power.

Merely two weeks before leaving for college I also witnessed a sadness I thought was absent—a strange sadness from my brother Messa. When Essevi passed away, I had seen him laugh bizarrely and seemed unexpressive. I never saw him cry. He often locked himself in his room. In hindsight, I understand now that he was expressing his feelings differently. He always seemed serious. Often, I would not hear a single sound coming from the room. I wondered what he was doing in there. Perhaps, sleeping. My mother sometimes demanded that he get out of the room to get some fresh air. When he would not, she would insist with "Open the door right now! Open the door right now I am telling you!" His usual answer was "Leave me alone!" Some people after having lost a dear person, have the tendency of expressing their emotions openly. Others prefer solitude. That was Messa's case. I sensed that he preferred to suffer alone in his room. I have learned therefore that it is important not to judge too fast. That is, even if some people do not show their emotions, they still may be suffering.

Some have a tendency of being serious, to plunge into solitude. Sometimes there are also people who laugh more than usual. Their suffering and the incapacity to handle the problem is hidden behind their smile and laughter. Therefore, one must watch and observe their comportment, changes in their behavior. If there is a change in their way of being, then this may imply that they are most likely suffering from the loss of their dear one. Messa was like this. In the beginning he laughed a lot. I recognized it the very next day. He was laughing a little too much. There were a lot of people at the old house who came to offer their condolences. He was in the family room talking. His laughter was the oddest thing I had ever witnessed. For a brief moment, I wondered if he had gone mad. With time, I would understand that he did not know how to deal with the fact that his brother was gone. The excessive laughter was his way of dealing with the loss.

CHAPTER 5

EMÉFA

About halfway through my third year of college, I began planning for a student-exchange program abroad. I wanted to partake in a program that would allow me to take courses in my three degree programs: French, economics and international business management. The director of the program at the University of the Pacific in California suggested francophone West African countries because that was where my roots are. However, I decided to go with France because I had already lived in Africa. I wanted a new experience.

Sometime in late August of 1999, I arrived in the Montpellier, which is located in the South of France. I arrived with a mission—to become completely fluent in French before returning to America in a year's time.

About a year and a half later, my mother and I began planning a trip to Togo. I was still living in France. I felt the time had come for me to return to the so-called motherland. I was at the airport in Montpellier having a hard time boarding because of a problem with my visa.

"You're not Togolese anymore," the well-dressed, short-haired French lady said.

"I'll handle it when I get there," I told her.

She reluctantly let me board the plane. It was still in the afternoon when we landed in Togo. When I arrived at the Lomé International Airport, I met with some difficulties entering the country. My mother was waiting for me. She came to meet me at the checkout exit. A soldier approached me. He asked if I had proof of my yellow fever shots and a visa. I told him that I had neither. A minute later, another airport personnel arrived. This one was not wearing any army uniform. He spoke to us in Ewe, our native language, and apparently his as well, given his accent.

"You don't have a visa?"

"How much is the visa?" I asked him in Ewe.

He quoted a sum, which I recall not. My mother tried to negotiate a cheaper price, but he was resolute. It was clear to me what he wanted—a bribe.

"You have two options: take a shot or pay the visa fees."

I turned to my mother.

"I am not taking any shots at this airport. Who knows what they have in them."

"You have always been afraid of taking shots."

"Let's pay this guy and get out of here."

I paid him off. This was fine. Besides, it gave me the chance to practice my native language, which I had not spoken in almost a decade. We would get through the airport alright. My luggage retrieval was successful, for I did not have to pay any of the guards anymore "tips" to leave.

We did not go straight to Kpalimé, which is located in the south. We took a taxi and went to a relative's house. I had not seen fo Roger, a relative in years. Fo Bernard, his brother, was at the house with Yawavino, my maternal grandmother. I spoke to them in Ewe. They were all apparently impressed that I could still speak the language. I enjoyed the evening with them. Fo Roger, whose house we were in was very hospitable, and his wife seemed like a decent soul, so I thought at the time. To my left, she sat fanning the portable charcoal stove. Sparks flew up, left, and to the right. Later that evening, fo Bernard and I conversed in the living room, where the fan blew above us from the high ceiling. Though it was spring it felt like summer—a bit warm. We slept in the living room, undisturbed by mosquitoes. He told me about his ex-girlfriend, who had deceived him. She was from a neighboring West African country. This would be the last true, good, and heart-felt conversation that I would have with him. Two years later, he would attempt to come to America with my mother's aid. There would be complications, such as the high governmental fraud penalties (i.e., fees) and misleading on his part. I would intervene mostly because the money he was asking for was too much even in U.S. dollars. I strongly suspected that this was the reason for him keeping his distance from me years later.

Morning found us leaving for my former home town. The ride to Kpalimé was physically painful. I was squeezed between buttocks from left to right. Upon arriving, we stayed with Happy and Féfévi. Féfévi was a relative, and Happy worked with her. We stayed with them at a Belgian couple's house. They had a young son, two years old, I believe. He was speaking Ewe, counting with his fingers. The father did not really mind, but the mother objected. The boy was always with Happy, so he was bound to pick up the language.

The room we stayed in was extremely hot and uncomfortable. Fortunately, Féfévi and Happy had a fan, which my mother and I used. I woke up several times during the night, for the fan was too loud. We spent most of the time at my mother's house, where my younger aunt Edi was living with her husband. In fact, there were a lot of people in the house. Navi Edi had three children. Her husband the taxi-driver, who was forever smiling was also living there. She cooked for us most of the time. My mother took charge of the water. She boiled and added some pungent herbs. She said that we should not drink the same water because it was not purified. Perhaps because of the water or the food, I became sick several days later. I clutched my hand upon my stomach. I ran to the bathroom several times at the Belgian couple's house. I vomited a few times. Happy seemed a little concerned. I told her that perhaps the sickness was due to the spaghetti I had eaten for lunch.

A few days later, my mother asked me if I wanted to go with her to visit her home village. Why in the world I agreed to go with her I would never know. I think it was because I did not recall how it looked. I remembered that terrible day when I landed in her native village. Everybody seemed to know her. We walked a little while on the red dirt road. We came across a few Kablé people. My mother spoke the language as if she were one of them. At one point, these members of the Kablé ethnic group had asked where in their part of their country she was from. It was incredible. They thought she was Kablé. I was impressed by her linguistic fluidity, her confidence. Out of this amazement, entered the scene a girl who would forever affect my life for the worse, though, it would take me ten years to understand it.

Eméfa shyly introduced herself. I extended my hand, observing her reserved demeanor. She lowered her head somewhat along with her eyes, as if pondering. Our encounter would last only about two minutes, but a life time of suffering. My mother and I would stroll down Ewomé, saying hello to her old friends and acquaintances. One or two I would vaguely recall. One in particular seemed to remember me. She was making pots out of clay. She was middle-aged, but seemed to be in good shape. She had her legs stretched forward, very fit. Her eyes gazed upon mine.

"No, I don't remember you," I answered her in Ewe.

"He was very young. He can't remember."

A few more words were exchanged, then my mother moved us forward to the next set of people to whom we would greet. I turned back and Eméfa was still staring at me. If I had had any common sense, I would have suspected that this girl was going to be fatally attracted to me, and that my life would never be the same.

Sometime after returning from my mother's native village, I was given a room in one of my relatives' houses. He was my maternal grandmother's first son. As far as I could tell, he was not working. In any case, I slept in that room that night in the mosquito nets. I did hear some buzzing noise a few times during the night, but if I were bitten I did not feel it. Though I did see a bit mark when I awoke, I was too happy to pay attention to it. I had just woken up from a vivid, lucid dream. I was walking in the vicinity of the house. The houses seemed so beautiful, wonderful to the physical touch. Colors and sound were magnified three-fold. It was rejuvenating and peaceful. I went to my mother's house, where Navi[2] Edi and her family among others were residing. At the time, I did not know that my mother had bought the house. Perhaps, I was not paying attention to details. If I had been, then I would have done something about the rest of the land that remained after my grandfather died. I was after all the oldest son. However, my mind was not there during that time. I knew that my grandmother was living in the house in Kusuntu, but I did not feel that it was urgent to go see her either.

When I arrived at my mother's house, cooked food was offered to me. A few seconds later my mother brought up my grandmother's name.

"We should go see her before we leave."

Navi Edi smiled and grunted at my mother's suggestion.

"Amano!" Navi Edi said, laughing.

---

[2] Navi means "aunty" or "the youngest aunt."

"Go see her?" I said without really thinking.

"Yes, she's your grandmother," my mother said.

"She knows we're here," I replied.

"She is not going to come here. You're the guest; you have to go see her."

"Alright, I'll go say hello today."

"I'll go with you. I don't want you going alone."

The afternoon found us at my grandfather's house, a house I had not seen in nearly ten years. We took the passageway where the ram and I used to play. It was pretty much the same. I looked at the field to my left. The tree under which I once slept was still there. We passed the big clay oven, and entered the house.

"Agoooo!" Navi Edi said, excusing herself as she entered the house. No one answered. To the right was Akouvi, near my grandfather's old bedroom.

"Hello," I said to her.

She was looking my way, but did not answer. Her condition had gotten worse. In Togo we called it "adava" which basically translates as being crazy. When she was young, she had difficulty communicating verbally. Her words did not make much sense.

"Amano[3] le afeme?" Navi Edi asked, trying to find out if my grandmother were home. Another silence.

"Maybe she's in the living room."

We walked up to the big living room.

"Ago ooo!" Navi Edi said again, seeking permission to enter the room. We entered the room, and there was my short grandmother. I greeted her in Ewe. She stared at me blankly. It was evident that she did not recognize me. She asked us how we were doing. It seemed that she recognized my aunt and mother, but definitely not me. My mother

---

[3] Recall that "Amano" is my paternal grandmother. "Ama" is her first daughter. Hence, Amano means "the mother of Ama" or "Ama's mother."

132

watched her cautiously. I approached to extend my hand to her. My mother came close to me. The look of dislike in her face for my grandmother was palpable. It could be felt.

"This is Agbessi," said Navi Edi.

"Yes," my grandmother answered, pretending to recognize me the entire time.

"You've grown."

"I did the hair here," I told her, referring to my Jamaican style hairdo.

We went to the open area of the house where Akouvi was. Amano used the word "adava" to describe her. She quickly retorted:

"I am not crazy. You don't know what the matter with me is."

She was fifteen years old. She was very skinny and unkempt. Her hair was disheveled and her clothes torn in several places. I left the house that day feeling sorry for her. A year or two later, she would die of no particular reason—out of madness, I was told. In 2009, I would learn that it was Black Magic—the same way her mother died.

We went outside now to visit some of our old neighbors. This was the neighbor whose house I used to go to purchase aspirin from a white-haired bed-ridden old woman. Two gentlemen were playing a game. We joined them. The older one recognized me immediately and was happy to see us.

"How are you?" he asked me in English.

"Pas mal," I replied in French, then adding, "Alright."

"Did he see his grandmother?"

"She did not recognize him," Navi Edi said slightly laughing.

As soon as she had said this, my grandmother as if she were running, came out of nowhere.

"I have not seen him since he was this big," she said, indicating with her right hand how small I was since she had last seen me.

"How was I supposed to remember?"

She seemed embarrassed. Apparently, she had been hiding and listening to our conversation. The thing that struck me as sad about what she had just done was that she was more concerned about how others perceived her than being happy to see me. Before we left, not once did she hint or ask me to come back to see her again. I watched her as she complained. Nevertheless, no one answered her whining. This rendered her even more uneasy, for she quickly returned to the house, while we continued chatting about days of old. A few years later, this man who was hardly sixty years old would die.

Three and a half weeks later I went to the airport, ready to return to France. I handed my ticket to the lady at the counter. She read my last name, perplexed.

"What is it?" I asked her in Ewe.

"You can't board."

"What is the problem?"

"Someone has already boarded with the same name."

"What?"

"I'll be back."

She went to speak to someone. I was utterly flabbergasted. My last name was unique. My half brother's name flashed into my head. No! That could not have been him. He had written a letter to me asking for money, and that was about a year ago, and I did not think that he had the means to travel abroad. Besides, the lady said that the first and the last name had matched the person who boarded.

She returned a few minutes later and punched a few keys on the computer.

"Everything is alright now," she said handing me my ticket.

I was suspicious of the identity confusion. Deep inside, I thought the lady was being deceived. Sometimes what happens is that there is a list of names that top officials in the government have at airports to keep track of certain individuals. Given my father's brief position in the military, I thought that his name had been kept on this list.

Merely a few days after returning to the South of France, I received a letter from Eméfa. Was it true that my knowledge of my own culture was limited? No, it was my conscience self that was not aware of endless possibilities of existence in this life and beyond. God! I met her only for two minutes, and yet she would cause so much havoc in my life. How! Why? Wasn't I strong enough to resist? No, I didn't know who I was. I had a vague remembrance of my inner Light. As I walked the usual alley-street in the downtown area in Montpellier, I observed the huge street. I basked in the quietness as I read Eméfa's letter.

October 30, 2000

Good morning dear friend in Christ,

I am delighted to know you. I seize the opportunity to wish you a good 2000-2001 year, and why not a good end of year.

I dare believe that you would accept this invitation to wish you good luck at work.

My love, I don't know what to say, whether or not the heart has a door that one opens to discover all that resides inside. I will give you the key to this door.

As I stood in this wide southern downtown street in the South of France, I pondered how quiet and empty the place was. I gazed from left to right. I smiled, unsure. *Who is this girl? Safe?* I continued reading the letter.

Trust that I would accept this direct point that I will keep your promise in terms of our love relationship. I was brought up like you. That's why I had this desire to_____.

I will be the first this year. I hope we will find ourselves one day if you wish. And that would please me very much.

That would not surprise you dear Agbessi, as handsome and charming as you are.

I paused here to digest her words. "Charming?" She must be insane. That's nice of her to say. How could I have been charming when I said very little to her? I read further.

That should not surprise you, my dear Agbessi....Since the first time I saw you, you produced upon me an indelible impression, it is no longer prohibitable.

Have a lot of courage because it is hard work that pays. So, have a better new year.

Be wise in life because there is no purpose to running, it's important to stay focused.

I don't want to bore you my dear Agbessi by an indiscrete insistence. I will stop here and above all don't forget your notebooks.

I adore you with all my heart.

Talk to you later, Eméfa.

My address....

P.S. I am dying of thirst to hear from you.

About a week and a half later, I became very sick. I started feeling nauseous. On Tuesday morning when I was getting ready to go to work, I ran to the bathroom many times only to leave unable to vomit. I suppose I should have gone to the doctor, but I did not have health insurance and did not think I could have afforded it. Instead, I went to the supermarket and bought a big bottle of coca-coca to drink. I took the coca-cola to work with me that morning. I got through the day. The next day, however, proved more problematic. I hardly got through two classes. I excused myself and headed home. I could hardly walk. I was near the mall, to the rear of the Mayor's Office. I leaned my head forward and began to vomit. My eyes took heat. I drank the Coca-Cola. I had to get home to sleep. Yes, sleep was all I needed, and I would wake up myself again. My walk to and from work usually took about fourteen minutes, but this time around it took me forty-five minutes.

When I arrived home, I saw my roommate Lawal in his room chanting along with his music. I brought in a bucket and the small room garbage can, which had a black plastic bag covering the inside. I tried watching television, but my eyes and mind could not focus. I walked meekly to my bed. The garbage can was to the right of me, on the floor near the door. I tried sleeping. I was fading in and out of consciousness. I knew I could not sleep. If I did I knew I might not have woken up. I reached for the garbage can and vomited. I called Lawal as loud as I could, but he could not hear me, though his music was not loud. I called for him for several minutes. My voice was inaudible. I tried to walk, but could not. I felt my blood was thinning. I was without physical strength. I dragged my body on the floor with my hands and the little finger nails that I had. A few minutes later my face was upon Lawal's surprised countenance.

"Hospital! Can't walk!" I said weakly in French.

He asked me what the matter was, and I repeated the same words. He called the hospital, which told him to bring me. He brought a shirt out for me from my room, which I put on. He put my left arm around his neck and I leaned on him for physical support. The debilitating feeling was interesting. My blood was turning into water and I could feel it.

The doctor asked a few questions. I was now able to walk a little better, and my voice could be heard much better. He diagnosed the illness as malaria. He asked me if I had travelled recently and the answer was an obvious yes. He said that malaria is caused by the bit of a mosquito. I went to the bathroom to vomit some more. Soon after, I found myself on a stretcher. I was losing consciousness again. Lawal was gone somewhere. I was in a room where nurses and doctors were passing by in the hallway. I felt a lightness. I heard voices below. Many French voices mingled to create an incomprehensible monologue of conversations. I was dying, yet I felt extremely happy without knowing the reason. I sensed an end of this life and a new beginning, and an uncertain continuation. Before I knew it, I was in an ambulance, being taken to an actual hospital. The lower part of my throat swelled. It was difficult to swallow. I could not eat or talk. I also could not shower. The nurses gave me a warm towel bath, what one of my residences in college used to call a "spit bath." My arms swelled like the cartoon character Popeye. I was fed through feeding tubes. A week would pass before I was able to talk again. My girlfriend Cécile came everyday to see how I was doing. Christine, my older friend, also came to see me once. I expected a few other people to visit, but they never did. I took mental note of this.

In mid-June of 2000, I returned to California. I stayed with my family in Sacramento for about two weeks then headed to New York City with my younger brother Messa to start my master's degree program in economic development. Upon going to the City, there were several dire things I had to take care of. First, I had to find a job. I found a graveyard position (i.e., an overnight shift) about five weeks later at Columbia University where I was also going to do my first master's degree. Messa and I also had to find a permanent place to live. We were renting a mouse-filled, sully room on the second floor from a Nigerian man in the Bronx. The first few months proved difficult. We were surviving on 25 dollars a week for about the first two months. It took several months not to worry about not having enough money for food and transportation. By then, I was single again, and Eméfa was writing to me on a regular basis via e-mail.

By this time, my mother moved to Maryland. It was great because that meant that we could see her more often. I had been wanting to see her face to face to discuss my relationship with Eméfa. Unfortunately, I could not see her until March of 2001, when we had time off from school. I took the Peter Pan bus to Silver Spring, Maryland, where she picked me up.

She was a nurse assistant. I do not know how she had managed all those years. The jobs she had paid very little. At times she hardly made ten dollars an hour. She was extremely frugal. Her home in Maryland at the time was a Victorian-style house. It had two floors. The kitchen and the laundry room were downstairs, while the three bedrooms were up upstairs. There was a full bath upstairs and a half bath downstairs. Upon entering, one saw the stairs immediately to the right, and the sofa to the left. Everything was very clean. As always, I took my shoes off at the entrance. As you might recall Reader, wearing shoes inside the house was not permitted in our household.

After settling in, she gave me a tour of the house and the backyard. The house was extremely clean. In fact, it was so clean that one would have thought that one were in a super hotel. It was cleaner than the house we had back in California.

I related my correspondences and conversations about Eméfa to my mother. She was smiling. She had a framed picture of her. My mother had known her mother and her family when she was young. Supposedly they got along with one or two disappointments.

"It's been a long time since I've spoken to her," she said, referring to Eméfa's mother. "Marry her," she said with a smile. I was listening to her, but there was no way I was going to make such a serious commitment without knowing her.

"How do you know the family?"

"We go way back. She's actually part of your family."

I jolted in the couch.

"Get out of here!" I said with a smile. "No freaken way.

You want me to marry my relative?" I said, my eye brows rising.

"She's a distant cousin. You go back several generations."

"I don't know. I don't think I can marry my cousin. Wouldn't that be like incest or something like that?"

"Don't think like that Agbessi. People do this all the time."

She was right. I did read in a magazine that Albert Einstein actually married his first cousin. I decided to give myself a few days to reflect before making a final decision.

In the meantime, I became interested in politics and development. That was basically what I was studying. I had voted Bill Clinton into office. I was a registered Democrat. However, it was slowly dawning on me that on a structural level, both the Republican and Democratic presidents were producing the same outcomes. They seemed different on the surface, but at the core, they produced the same results and maintained the same status quo.

I wanted something new. I started by changing my political party to independent. I figured that if a new leader appeared, I would listen and judge him or her based on what he or she was saying instead of religiously sticking to one political party. Nevertheless, something else was bothering me. It dawned on me that the political parties were set up in such a way that the people would never really decide who their president or senators would be. This became absolutely clear to me during the 2008 elections. It was a struggle to elect Barrack Obama as the Democratic nominee. It was incredibly ridiculous! I had to change my political party back to the Democratic Party in order to accomplish the task; and to do this, I had to see a judge! It was then that I began thinking about the way the voting system is set up. I seriously thought it would be better to let people cast open votes for the individuals running for presidents and public office. I began to question why the system was set up like this. I was beginning to understand that our so-called leaders wanted to give us the people the illusion of choice. Though I changed my political party, I was still blind, a sheep in the system, following dark souls like Al Gore.

Sometime in 2000, I heard that the Democratic presidential candidate Al Gore was coming to Columbia University to speak. I thought I was lucky to have gotten a seat to see him. At that time, I was not happy with President George Bush's job performance, and was happy to vote him out of office. Al Gore was the candidate in whom I was interested. I wanted to listen to him, but years later I would realize that I had already made up my mind that I was going to vote for him regardless. In any case, I sat in the front row to Al Gore's left. He spoke with assurance and he seemed convincing. He received my and most of the attendees' applause. The attendees were aggressive, but I would not be denied the chance to speak to this guy. Al Gore walked toward us. There was a tall young black man with long braided hair who was now shaking his hand. He told Al Gore not to forget his promise to help the common people. Finally, it was my turn. I stuck my hand out to him and he shook it, briefly waiting for me to say something. I looked at him squarely in the eyes and said:

"I just wanted to shake your hand."

As I shook his hand, something felt weird. I sensed a void, a lack of feeling within the man. Even now, I am still not sure how to describe this feeling. The best words perhaps are "negative vibes." This was more of a sense.

Sometime after meeting Al Gore, I received an e-mail correspondence from Eméfa.

Hello dear friend,

You can't imagine the joy that animates me before taking my pen to write you this letter.

Excuse me for being a little late writing you, but I was not feeling well.

I suffered for three weeks on my bed. As long as God the All Powerful is alive, he healed me so that I glorify his name.

I received the money that you had sent me; for that I thank you very sincerely in the name of our creator.

God almighty will help you to find the double of what you gave me.

To emphasize my thanks, I give you this verse: Colossiens 3: 23-24.

A little later, I received another letter from Eméfa.

Dear beloved,

I would like you to write ASAP about our love relationship.

It is difficult for me to say that I did not pass my BAC, but I know that nothing is impossible for God. And that his moment or time is the best, because I hope that he will help me confront this problem. May his will be done; Amen.

My best wishes, filled with love.

I did not consult the Bible as she had indicated. In those days, I hardly read the Bible or any source of spiritual information. It dawned on me that she quoted the scriptures a lot. *She was a bit religious*, I thought as I walked into the kitchen in our new apartment in the Bronx. I recalled Christine's plea not to marry Eméfa. I walked into the kitchen, and turned on the light. Then, I turned on the faucet. A storm of roaches welcomed me as they scattered away from the sink. There were so many of them. The soap trick I had learned from France (i.e., my French friend) had not worked. Yes, of course, a storm of dead roaches lied in the bowl of soap, but it seemed that they were adapting quickly. I also saw a mouse run away. At this time, my brother Messa had suddenly developed fear of mice.

"They carry the West Nile virus!" he would frequently remind me.

"Why do you keep calling them rats?" I said, "They are mice."

"What?"

"They are mice," I repeated, "Mice look different. Rats are bigger and their teeth are fang-like."

"They are rats!" he insisted, "What's the difference?" There was no point arguing with him. I picked up the bowl of soap with the roaches stuck inside. *When will I ever stop living in such places? Boy, I don't know how much longer I can take this.*

"I just saw a mouse," I told Messa.
He immediately closed his bedroom door. I thought he was being a baby, but most of all, I was going to enjoy his new-found fear of mice.

"Hey Messa, what if in the middle of the night, one crawled up in bed with you, kissing you, right on the lips?"

I was giggling. "What if you enjoy it for a few seconds not knowing that it was a mouse, I mean a rat. Have you ever been kissed by a rat?"

He was not smiling, but I was. He needed to relax. They were just mice. However, a day or two later, he would report that a "rat" had invaded his privacy. He said that it was in his top dresser. I was walking out of the room when he begged me to check it. I hesitantly opened it—nothing! I left the room and returned to thoughts of Christine's advice.

I was thinking about my relationships in general. I wanted someone special, and I so desperately wanted Eméfa to be the one. I wrote a letter telling her that I indeed wanted to try the love-relationship. I think deep inside I wanted more than this superficial world. I wanted deep meaning—deep love. I decided to try out the relationship with Eméfa. I paid more attention to her and tried to know her better. Christine was my close confidant. I told her about the situation with her, and how my mother wanted me to marry her, and how I had initially said no, but was now reconsidering. Christine wrote back. She was utterly against the whole thing. It did not bother her that Eméfa was my fourth generation cousin. I sensed that her major problem with this was that it was prearranged and that I did not really know her; and yet I was going to accept. She wrote to me about this. I specifically recalled her saying: "I knew you were going to do it."

A few days later, I composed a letter during the overnight shift at work and in the afternoon, mailed it to Eméfa via regular physical courier. I do not recall saving it, and if I did, I no longer have the disk. Therefore, I cannot reproduce it here. Basically, the letter stated that I could only be friends with her because we were fourth generation cousins. I assumed that she accepted this friendship because she was still writing to me on a regular basis.

That same year terrible things were going to start happening given that I had told her that we could not be together. However, as blind as I was, I would not learn of the specifics until January of 2009. In the meantime, I was of the opinion that I could be conversing with a girl in her early twenties in another country and the relationship would be purely fraternal. That was the mindset I was in for several years after the Twin Towers collapsed in September of 2001. I had been working on a novel during this time—a historical fiction about the Ewe people, who are currently residing in three West African countries: Benin, Ghana, and Togo. I wanted to know more about some of the spiritual and marital practices, I asked Eméfa to tell me about this via e-mail. On Saturday, May 4, 2003, she wrote:

> Good morning dear beloved brother,
>
> I just read the message that you sent me. That surprises me because I sent you a letter via the post office in January to wish you a good new year. That means that the post office people didn't send my letter or the post card.
> I will take advantage of this occasion to wish you once again a good year, success, health, perseverance in all things. You asked me to help you write a book.
> Yeah, I am able as long as you're not in too much of a hurry, because soon our exams will be in May 26-30.
> But, if you're in a hurry, I found someone who will help to get it done. It suffices to send me the instructions and the places where we can find the documents that you want.
>
> If you want to call me, here's the phone number where I can be reached: 0022844…between 6-7 p.m.
>
> My best wishes.
>
> Say hello to your mother and your brother Messa.
>
> Your sister Eméfa.

When the job was done Eméfa sent me a handwritten report and an e-mail message that read:

Hello beloved brother,

How are you doing? I am doing well. It is good when one knows what one wants to do in the future, but I have no desire to teach.

To be straightforward, I am not strong in English or French. In terms of the research, I had told you that I could not do it. Because of this I asked a friend for help. Without lying to you, it is he who did most of the research that I sent you.

Oh dear Benoît, I would like to tell you that he is very sincere to me. Also, he did not take any of the money you sent. He cannot refuse to render you a service, so you can send me other research topics that you need.

Thank you for your understanding, and give my fraternal greetings to your mother.

Talk to you soon.

Eméfa

Upon reading the letter, several things went through my mind. *What did she mean by: He is very sincere to me? Suspicious!* I knew I was losing her, but I could not dwell on this because I had to deal with a direr problem: the continual deterioration in my physical and inner well-being.

About a month or so after initially sending Eméfa the 400 dollars, the ache all over my body worsened. The major parts of my body that were affected included my chest, my heart, my buttocks, and my knees and feet. Overtime, the physical pain began to take a toll in other forms. Once during the summer of 2002, I was at Columbia University, walking up the stairs to Lerner Hall when I felt an immense, indescribable fatigue. I felt so tired, chronic fatigue. But yet, I could not sleep. I was always tired, and did not know why. I was headed back to the Bronx now. As I sat down in the 1-train, I yawned feverishly pondering why I was constantly tired. I got myself in the habit of working out after work in the morning. When I arrived home, I tried to sleep after watching a bit of television. This was a one-bedroom apartment I was sharing with my younger brother. I set my alarm clock and put my head down on the pillow. I slept for only about an hour, when I woke up suddenly without knowing why. I never sleep all the way through. Why? I thought it was strange to be tired. The worst part was that I did not know what to do to fix the problem. I did not even know what the problem was. I was lost. Was it something I was eating that was causing this bizarre insomnia?

One day I was watching Oprah Winfrey when I would get some ideas. Oprah was talking about soft drinks and how unhealthy they were for you. She said something to the effect of losing about fifteen to twenty pounds a year if one stopped polluting one's body with overfilled sugar drinks. I gave them up that same day. I have always been good at giving up things that were not good for me once I really know their detrimental effect.

After this partial victory, I felt slightly reenergized, but nevertheless, I still had the anxiety attacks. I felt it hard in my chest and my stomach area. I felt it during the day and even when I slept. There were times when these attacks were so strong that I would toss and turn in my bed in agony holding parts of my body. I could not figure out the cause of the suffering. My body and mind were tormenting me without pity. I was in pain physically and mentally.

One evening, in my new apartment near the east side of the Yankee Stadium, the physical component of my suffering augmented. I was in bed when it commenced. I clutched my heart, but the slight did not ease. It felt like my blood was dripping from my heart. I pressed my right hand against my chest. Nothing changed. My heart was still dripping blood inside and I could literally feel it. It would stop a few minutes later. I went to drink some juice. Still not better. I lied in bed waiting for sleep to come, but it would not. After a while, I got up to drink some red wine. After the consumption of a glass and a half, I felt calmer and sleepy. Nevertheless I would only sleep a few hours before waking up in the middle of the night.

In May or June of 2001, we had our graduation celebration in front of Columbia University's Alma Mater. My fellow students and I were sitting to the right, near the Thinker—a statue of a man with his hand in his chin thinking. The major guest speaker was Condoleezza Rice. If my memory is not deceiving me, she went to Columbia University. She spoke beautifully and ended the speech with "God Speed."

There were other speakers, but she was the only one I would clearly remember. In addition to the general school graduation, we also had two other gatherings at the School of International Studies and Public Affairs, which was next to the law school. At the second gathering, we had a distinguished guest speaker—Superman, Christopher Reeve, to be precise. He was in a special wheel chair and had difficulty speaking. His physical pain was palpable. He paused between his words and he spoke about the importance of stem cell research to cure illnesses. At times, I turned away from him because I could not endure his pain. It was too painful.

After completing my master's degree in economics, I turned my attention to two tasks: searching for a job and finding a solution to my suffering. Both tasks proved very difficult. In terms of the job search, I had interviews at Wall Street, at the U.S. Treasury, at the International Monetary Fund, and at the World Bank. I even applied for teaching positions as well as a security guard at different companies. I finally took a job as a stockbroker trainee. It was awful. I quit after two days.

The second task of curing my illness proved to be the most difficult. My knees were hurting deeply every couple of days. Sometimes they became so stiff that I literally could not walk. I was also having major chest pains. I assumed that the solution lied only in the physical realm of existence. I was right to some extent. I experimented with food. I took careful notes of the types of food that I was eating to see if any of it was the cause of my chest pains. It turned out that beef was definitely not helping. The chest pains disappeared once I stopped eating it. My curious mind told me to do some research on how cows are cultivated. I was convinced that the hormones they fed them were responsible for my chest problems. The interesting thing about this is that I would later return to France and consume beef on several occasions but would not experience any chest pains. I learned that cows' food diet were better in France.

During these unfortunate times, I also began feeling depressed sporadically for unexplained reasons. Days would go by and I would not feel comfortable inside my skin or my mind. I felt physically, mentally and psychologically tormented. I used to be a happy person. Even in France, things were not this bad. There were days when I even considered suicide, but I could never bring myself to the act. I always found a reason to continue for one more day. I did not want to be a coward. Besides, I had strong doubts that I would exist after the death of my physical body. In order to pass the time, I kept myself busy with whatever I could. I began learning two new languages—Spanish and German. They took my mind somewhat off my pain. Besides, I also had Eméfa.

In 2003, the problem became so severe that I could no longer ignore it. I had to find help. I decided to seek medical assistance. The first hospital I went to did not find anything in my blood. The doctor said that I was fine, but I knew I was not. I sought a second opinion at Columbia Presbyterian Hospital in Manhattan. It was a big, renowned hospital. The front desk's personnel was hospitable. I waited patiently until I was finally called. The lady wore a white outfit. I do not recall whether or not she was the actual doctor, but she performed all of the medical examinations, including the X-ray. I lied on the bed with the big white paper. I posed a few questions as I looked at the picture of my chest on the monitor.

"What is it?"

"Your heart valves are not closing properly."

"How, why?"

"You have a heart murmur."

"Could you please explain?"

I do not recall her exact words, but I do remember her explanation. She said that most people have it, and do not know it. She also said that I should avoid eating food that contain caffeine. I asked for pills, but she insisted that I would only go on medication if I developed a severe case of the heart murmur. All that was fascinating to listen to, but I still had questions. According to her, children are born with heart murmurs. I was not born with a heart murmur. When I came to the United States at the age of twelve, my mother had to take me to the hospital to run a battery of medical tests. We went several times and the doctor did not report such a health issue. Throughout the years when I have taken physicals and blood tests, none indicated any health problems. *So, how could I suddenly have a heart murmur? How could my heart be leaking blood?* I left the hospital somewhat relieved that I did not have a major illness, but questions would linger in my mind about this for years to come.

Toward the end of 2003, I wrote a letter to Eméfa, accepting her initial invitation to be in a relationship with me. On February 17, 2004 at 6:28 p.m. she wrote:

Hello dear friend,

It is an opportunity for me to give you an answer to the letter that you wrote to me. Please excuse me for my lateness, because I was busy. How are you holding up? In regards to the relation that you spoke to me about, I must say that your desire is too late. As you know, three years ago you gave me an answer concerning this relationship. You told me that we are fourth generation cousins; and for that, it is necessary that the relationship be fraternal. During this time, you have forgotten that everything changes and that we must live in the present. After having received your answer, I told myself that it would be necessary to make a decision. As I write to you now dear brother, excuse me for saying that I have a fiancé whose name is Emmanuel, the teacher whom I spoke to you about. As long as I have made an engagement, I cannot go back to your decision. May this not surprise you because man asks, God gives. It is important that we tell everybody the truth in life.

Thank you for your understanding; God will explain the rest to you in your bed. Thank you, thank you for your understanding.

Eméfa

Given her answer, I naturally assumed that we would remain just friends, and that our long distance communication would dramatically decrease. That was the decision I made.

I had not written or talked to Eméfa for about a year. I had basically stopped thinking about her. Then on Wednesday, February 16, 2005, I received an e-mail from her. She wrote:

Good morning dear brother,

How's it going? It has been a long time since we have communicated. How's your job? I would like to hear from you at the number 00228-912…on February 25th from 4 p.m. and on.

My best wishes to your mother and your brother.

Take care of yourself and goodbye.

I called her, but not right away. First, I sent her an e-mail message on February 20th at 9:54 p.m. from work. I wrote the message in French. The English translation reads:

> Always on the search for something better. I just moved again. The apartment is very clean and I love the kitchen. I love being home. It has only been four days since I moved, so my new telephone number has not yet been activated. My phone number will be 917-507...I am currently residing in Manhattan, New York. It's very close to my job. I am doing an internship—I am teaching. I will start working really hard in September.

A few days later, I called her after 4 p.m.
"Hello Eméfa. It's Agbessi. Comment ça va?"
"Good, thanks to God. How's your family?"
"Ok."
"Your mother and your sista?"
"She's ok."
"Here's Emanuel. Say hello."
She passed the telephone to him so fast that I did not have time to say no, to tell her that I did not want to talk to her fiancé. I did not understand why she did such a thing.

Emmanuel took the phone with an irritated voice. He asked me how I was, but it was clear from his voice that this guy really did not like me. Well, why would he? I was a threat to him after all. Here was a guy calling his fiancé across the world. *I do not even know why I called*, I thought to myself.

"Let me say goodbye to Eméfa."
Upon taking the phone I said to her:

"Have a good evening. Goodbye." And that would be the last time that I would ever speak to her on the telephone.

I received an e-mail from her a little over a month later. On the 31st of March 2005, she wrote:

Hello dear brother Benoît.

How are you doing? I have the impression that you celebrated the Easter break well because this celebration is exceptional for all Christians. Are you already in the house that you promised to buy? Say hello to your mother and your brother. How's work going?

Your little sister Eméfa.

I would receive several other messages from Eméfa, but I found no reason to answer them.

By late 2005, much had changed. I received my second master's degree in education, was living in a none-roach-infested studio apartment in Manhattan, found a teaching job in ESL and French, bought a house, and started travelling again.

The person I visited most was Christine, in the South of France. I have always enjoyed spending time with her. She too was a writer. She even helped me with my first book which I wrote in French. She was more open-minded spiritually than I was at that time. She was certainly unafraid of what lies beyond physical death. She always seemed happy and laughed a lot. I was particularly impressed by the way she dealt with her husband Jacques's death. She said that he died while driving his car. He had a heart attack.

"He had a smile on his face," she told me when I went to see her in December of 2005. I was not sure what to make of this statement. Was Jacques going to be alright? Was he departing this world and ceasing to exist? I could not be sure. For the most part, the French were existentialists—which to me pretty much was quite ambiguous about what actually happens after the death of the physical body. I recalled Jacques—quiet, thoughtful, and had a peculiar throaty laughter. Now he was gone. The next time I would visit their household he would be absent. I used to go to their house all the time. They lived by the sea, near Montpellier. Those were very interesting days. I enjoyed the bus rides home to Montpellier. There was everything there in this downtown place. There was Gaumont, a popular French movie theater, where I saw the spectacular film The Matrix. I was so impressed with this film that I saw it twice—in French. In hindsight, the real fiction was my physical existence. The Matrix was an underrepresentation of the real nature of existence. This, I would learn several years later after the awakening of my soul from its deep amnestic sleep.

By late 2005, I did not think Eméfa would write again. I was wrong. On Saturday, November 18, 2006, I received an interesting and curious e-mail from her.

Hello my dear Benoît,

How are you? Everything is alright with me. I take advantage of this occasion to say hello to you and to ask news of how you've been.

I wish you a good new year with good health, and success in all your affairs.

Your wife Eméfa.

"No freaking way!" I said aloud in the computer room at the public library. Then, I turned away from the computer users and offered them complete silence. A sketch of a smile emanated on my face. It widened and I laughed hard inside. *My wife?* As I walked out of the library I gave a boisterous laugh. Even as I entered my 1995 crappy Toyota car, the smile upon my face remained.

"Ha" I said several times. As I drove home the entire time, I was unable to stop smiling. *Dada is going to love this story.* I arrived home within a few minutes of driving. I knocked on the first floor door of the house. My mother answered it. She was cooking.

"Guess what?" I said taking off my book bag and shoes.

"What is it Agbessi?"

"Guess who wrote to me today!"

"Who wrote to you?"

"You're supposed to guess. You're not guessing. Ha, ha!"

I waited for her guess.

"Eméfa!" she correctly guessed miraculously.

"Yeah, guess what she wrote to me?"

"Just tell me Agbessi."

I maintained my smile.

"She ended the letter with the words 'your wife Eméfa.' What do you think is going through her mind. Ha! This is the silliest thing I have ever heard."

"She still likes you."

"Yeah, but she's married. Why would she like me? She's nuts! Ha! Ha! Dada, you're supposed to be laughing. Isn't this the funniest thing you've ever heard?"

My mother smiled.

"She still likes you," she repeated.

"But why?" I asked with a smile.

CHAPTER 6

A VISIT FROM MY FATHER

In December of 2006, I was still living in Harlem, waiting for my lease to expire before permanently moving to the house that I had bought two months prior. On the economic level, I was doing alright, but my body and mind were still causing me unease. I seemed to think that somehow all these maladies would disappear with the passing of time. I reinforced this idea with positive thinking. I was in one of these states of mind when I went to bed. About two hours later, this changed completely with one phone call from my brother Messa. He told me that Dada was in a major car accident, but was alive. My bewilderment expressed itself with silence. "She's alive?" I finally managed to ask as if I had not heard him the first time.

My mother was coming back from a job interview from another state. As she reached the intersection near the main road to our house, a car made a sudden left turn very rapidly, striking my mother's car, and flipping it over completely. The windows shattered, and she was thrown out of the car and fainted right on the spot. She injured her feet, knees, broke her neck and several disks in her back. To add insult to injury, the ambulance personnel took one look at the color of her skin and decided that she would not have enough money to pay for the hospital near our house, which was merely two or three minutes from the scene of the accident. Instead, they took her to another hospital, across the Bronx, which was over an hour away.

For the ensuing six months, my mother was bed-ridden, unable to sleep, moaning in pain every night. I slept on the couch and thus heard her pain throughout the night. She was in the wheel chair for the first month and used a walking equipment to move about short distances.

Things were not getting better in my life. In fact, 2007 would be the beginning of a long series of disasters, which would finally lead to the end of my amnestic state of existence that most of humanity is currently in.

On the morning of March 22, 2007, at about 6:27 a.m., I walked out to the street. There was snow everywhere. My 1995 Toyota Camry was completely covered. I cleared it and tried turning the vehicle on, but it would not budge. It was stuck. I put the engine in reverse and pressed upon the gas. The engine gave out completely. The car would not go anywhere. *More expenses to pay for, and I don't have the money.*

I left the car and the sad trip back home, to the first floor of the three story house. I opened the door. My mother's eye met mine across her bedroom.

"You're still here?"

"Yes," I responded as I took off my shoes. I passed the living room. There she was standing at the threshold of the bedroom. I approached with a look of seriousness.

"It's almost 7 a.m. It doesn't look like I'll be going to work today. The car is not starting. It's not moving. It seems to be out of gear. I might have to tow it."

My mother said nothing, but in those few seconds of silence and the curious tinge of sadness that appeared on her face, I knew she cared. I was on her left side.

"I have to call out. I won't be able to make it on time. I don't know how I'm going to get to work tomorrow either. The gaze upon her face onto mine grew with increasing sadness. My mother asked me if there were something that she could do. I answered no. Then, she solemnly said:

"We'll need to go shopping today."

There are moments in one's existence when one is absolutely sure of love. This was one of those times. She would have bought me a thousand cars, but I would have refused them all in exchange for that look of love beyond words. People say that a picture is worth a thousand words. In this case, my mother's look transmitted a love that I would carry with me for years to come.

At that moment, I knew she loved me beyond measure. It was not because she wanted to purchase me a car with her retirement money. It was the fact that in her gaze upon me, I would forever understand the extent of her care. It was a gaze of love, one that I had never seen in her. In that moment, I also understood that if I should ever doubt her love, I would always refer to this image, and I would feel self-assured.

The intensity of her energy was saddening, too loving, so I pulled away from her stare, and reluctantly accepted her offer. She turned again toward her bedroom near the bathroom. There she was. She could hardly walk yet she wanted to go shopping for a new car for me. I called out sick from work, and we went out to find a vehicle.

The months passed slowly and stressfully. My mother began to walk again, but slowly like a turtle. By June, she insisted on getting behind the wheel. I disapproved, but once my mother had made up her mind, it would take a mountain to dissuade her. She accuses me of being the same way. My answer to that was always a smile accompanied with the words "Like mother like son." She ignored my pleas and bought a new car with the reimbursed insurance money. She complained that her neck was hurting every time she turned to look out the window. My opposition against her driving became stronger. As a result, she stopped telling me how she felt. In June of 2007, she bought a plane ticket to go to Togo. By this time my tenant on the second floor stopped paying her rent. I asked them to leave. Both the second and the third floors were a complete mess. The third floor was completely inhabitable. I spent about ten thousand dollars renovating it. I thought about renting either the first or the third floor, and worry about fixing the other floor later. I had to find another job and fast. I went back to my old part-time job—teaching writing workshops at Hostos Community College. I taught mostly on the third floor of Building C. It was there where I would meet Jennifer. She came for tutoring for writing a couple of times and took one of my writing workshops. Our first real conversation took place after my last writing workshop that summer. She launched a question at me.

"You said that you have difficulties in your life…Do you have Jesus in your life?"

I did not answer, for I did not know what she really meant. To me, it was a vague question.

"Do you go to church?" she asked.

"Usually not?"

"Jesus is the way."

I looked at her calmly with slightly confused eyes, trying to understand. She was smiling as she wrote her phone number and e-mail on a piece of paper for me.

"Come to church with me."

"What denomination do you belong to?"

"Seventh Day Adventist."

We walked out of the building and crossed the 149 and…intersection. When we came to the post office, I stopped, turned slightly left to face her.

"Where are you headed?"

"Home."

"Yeah, me too. Wanna a lift?"

She got into the car. She liked it. Well, as you know Reader the car was new, and was very clean, and still had a new car smell. I drove her home. Jennifer was tall, and a bit skinny. She was very polite and very religious. She went to church three times a week, I would learn later.

A few days later, I sent her an e-mail. Once she responded, I called her the next day. I recalled the phone call very well. I was in my room on the first floor, sitting at my desk. Jennifer had given me two phone numbers. The first was her cell phone, which she had warned me might not work. I was therefore not surprised when it did not. Upon dialing the second number her mother answered right away. I expected this. I introduced myself to her, but it seemed that she already knew who I was. I left a message for Jennifer. She called me back the next day. I invited her to go see a movie with my younger sister. We did not go right away. We ended up eating akple and some stew dish. We went later, but I cannot recall the movie we watched. However, I do remember sitting at the left side of the aisle, because it was a very small theater. I always sit in the center aisle. I did not recall enjoying myself that much.

After the movies, we went back to my house. We were all in the kitchen, trying to think of something to eat. Jennifer had not slept much, but she seemed alright with this. I had a sense of how she was feeling; I used to work the graveyard shift. Jennifer and my sister Akofa were in the kitchen. She was trying to get to know Akofa. The door to the backyard was open. I looked at the yard and the immense rock to the right. The yard needed weeding. I went to the kitchen to see what was transpiring. Jennifer was alone now. Akofa had gone somewhere, probably her room or bathroom. I had caught a few words of their conversation, which was about working hard in school.

"My sister can be a bit lazy," I said to Jennifer. Akofa was not there.

"You should not judge her like that," she said with a wise smile.

"Judge? Get out of here! Really? What word would you have me used?"

She smiled again.

"You could say that she doesn't work very hard."

"Sounds like you have a point, but she's still lazy."

"Agbe," she said softly, "Do you think that maybe you're trying to do it alone?"

I sensed the emanation of Jesus's name.

"Jesus can help."

I was right.

"You want her to go to church with you?"

"Yes."

"Alright, if you think it'll help," I said, slightly smiling.

We went to church with Jennifer the ensuing Sunday. We dressed up a little. Dressing up a little was a big deal for me because I did not use to care much about my physical appearance when I went out. Jennifer seemed well dressed when we picked her up. I recall her wearing a dress with black and light colors. The church was in the Bronx. It was not very big. The building seemed old and stony looking. Akofa and I exited the car and we followed Jennifer, who was greeting her fellow churchgoers with a warm smile. We sat in the center toward the right. Underneath each seat was a Bible. I followed along with the singing. I helped Akofa to turn to the right page. We sang along with them softly.

Then the priest spoke about God. I cannot recall his exact words, but I listened attentively, trying to discern what was true and what was not. Then, there was an announcement that Jennifer would play the piano. I was impressed. She sang nicely as she played. She had not told me about this beforehand.

After the signing came the hardest part of the church ceremony. The priest asked us to pray aloud, to admit our sins. Everyone stood up, praying feverishly with their eyes closed. I had my eyes open enough to be able to see what Akofa was doing. She had her eyes open and was blankly staring into the void. Moving my lips as if I were really talking, I turned toward Jennifer to see if she were doing it. She was. In fact, she was so serious that I thought perhaps I too should have tried harder. I could pray for what I felt comfortable with. I closed my eyes and began speaking.

"God, the Most High, please heal my knees, my feet. In the name of purity, I beseech Thee. You are the Most Powerful, the Most High. Hear my prayers, amen!"

I opened my eyes and waited for everyone else to stop.

After the service, I met the priest, who officially welcomed us into their church. I explained to him that I had come because of Jennifer and was not sure I would be coming on a regular basis. He assured me that "God will make it happen." I did not buy this, of course. But, if "God" were to make anything happen, He or She was not helping me vis-à-vis women.

During the last week of July 2007, while on the third floor of Building C at Hostos Community College, I received news from my mother from Togo via e-mail. She reported that things were going alright and that walking was still difficult. She also took some pictures of a few relatives and three girls whom she thought I might like. The girl in the center was very attractive. I decided to get to know her. I did not see the harm in this, for Jennifer and I were just friends. Up to that point, I had not even kissed her nor did I make her believe that we were together. So, I wrote to my mother: "The girl in the center, what do you know about her family? Are they good people?"

My mother wrote back, saying that she would discuss my questions when she returned to the States.

Another Sunday was fast approaching and Jennifer again asked us to accompany her. I reiterated to her that I was not a church-going person, and would not be going. She kept pleading until I told her that I would go. That same day, I began to notice a difference in my body. There were palpitations or "ticks" all over my body. There were underneath my skin. Most of them were in my arms, my buttocks, and my thighs. I was confused. I did not know what was going on. I was not sexually active with anyone; I did not do drugs or drink hard liquor. So, what in the world was going on with my body? I would pray for this on Sunday when I went to church. And I did. I even kneeled to ask for healing, and to understand what was transpiring. I went to church twice more with Jennifer and prayed for the ticking to cease, but my condition did not improve. The negative things that were going to happen were going to occur with an increased speed and intensity. Sleep would not come. Thus it was one day when Jennifer came over after work. She made me some toast, and some coffee. I had begun drinking coffee on a daily basis now. I had tried it in France, but did not like it. It was too strong. However, this particular coffee that Jennifer made had much flavor and was not as strong. It had a sweet vanilla taste. Jennifer sat to my left as I ate. She did not make anything for herself. She said that she was not hungry.

"I am tired. My body is sore," she said.

"Maybe you need a massage."

She smiled and said no. I understood this, though I was not thinking what she was. Massages lead to other things, and this she was pretending not to want. I sensed it from her, but I was going to have a bit of fun, for humor's sake.

"Yeah? I give really good massages."

She remained quiet. I suggested that she sleep a little.

"You can use my bed. I'll run some errands while you're sleeping."

She preferred to go home. So, I drove her to the Bronx. When we arrived, we parked on the right side of the street, which was just across from her apartment complex. The building was a low-rise. She and her twin sister were sharing an apartment with one or two other people. We had to wait in the car because it was not yet time to park at the location. We waited for about fifteen minutes. As we waited we spoke about many things. But, the central conversation was about being "saved."

"Do you really believe that all those people who are not Christians are really going to hell?"

"Yes, the Bible says…"

She was basically saying that in order to be saved, one had to be a Christian and go to church. I looked at the clock, we still had about ten minutes left before the parking sign would permit us to park there.

"And all those Muslims are going to hell?"

"You need to be a Christian."

I stopped to consider her words. The implication was crystal clear. I too was going to hell.

"Jenny, there's about two minutes left. We can start walking to your apartment now."

When we arrived, she turned on the television as she cooked. After she ate, I was supposed to take her to the church in the Bronx. She was preparing to move again. As I sat there watching the film (i.e., <u>Medina</u>), my arm and heart area began to tick again. I placed my hand over the palpitation and pressed against my biceps. It stopped, but as soon as I took my hand off it restarted. Jennifer did not tarry in her preparation. I dropped her off at the church.

In the evening of the same day when Jennifer had made breakfast for me, my stomach began to hurt severely. I could not sleep when I went to bed. My stomach was torturing me. I twisted in bed in agony, holding it tightly, as if to squeeze out the pain. It hurt so much that I felt like taking a gun and shooting out my intestines to stop the pain. I tried drinking some tea and took Tylenol, but such medications were useless. The pain was formidable to battle. I thought that perchance it was the food that Jennifer had made for me, but this did not make sense, for I had drunk the tea before, but did not experience any stomach pain. The following evening was the same. The next day was also the same. I minimized the amount of coffee that I drank. I also stopped drinking red wine. This helped somewhat, but the pain returned sporadically, every few days.

The days I had a reprieve from the stomach pains were joyous. I spent much of them reading Dr. Weiss's book <u>Many Lives, Many Masters</u> as well as books about African history. Maybe I wanted to become African, who knows. I preferred rereading Dr. Weiss's book. Reading it was more fun, a reprieve from the mundane world. I had actually been given a copy by a friend at Columbia University when I completed my master's degree program in Economics Development. My friend told me about it because I told her about my brother's death. At least six years must have elapsed since I read it. There was one thing that held me back from believing the whole story. In the book, Catherine, the main character, held back some personal information about being a prostitute when Dr. Weiss regressed her in one of her lives in Europe. Basically, Catherine, or rather her soul had chosen not to reveal this because she was ashamed. At the time, I had difficulty accepting this. I thought that because she was being regressed, she would not hold back information in her memory bank. Years later, I realized that I had been wrong. I was incorrect for one main reason—souls have free will and no one or thing can ever force them to do or reveal anything that they did not want to share. I would learn the importance of this two years later with my own spiritual experiences. There is no force, absolutely no force that can make you do anything.

I had returned to this book because of Jennifer.

One day in the afternoon, she called me while I was on the terrace of my first floor. The conversation centered on faith and God. She was trying so hard to understand me.

"You're not an atheist, so what is it?" She wanted to know why I was constantly refusing to go to church with her.

"Yes, there is something, though I am not sure what."

"Jesus loves you. Come with me."

"I don't do church Jenny," I told her.

"I am having these weird dreams. I don't understand them. I can't tell if they are real or not."

She was listening, but it was clear to me that we were of two different mindsets. She did not have to try so hard to convince me that Jesus or God was the way. So much confusion! I walked toward the white door. Yes, I would go to church again with her; to learn more about her; but intuitively I already knew. Even more importantly, I knew that the answers to the general questions of existence that I was seeking would not lie with her or her church or any church for that matter. I needed to find a solution that was not of the rhetoric type. I did not simply want to believe. I never really liked the word "belief." I have always felt that we human beings are supposed to know, by peeling away layers from the onion until we get to the center, the essence that cannot be seen by the exterior façade. I felt the same was true for worldwide religious belief systems as well as scientific theories. We are to arrive at what we know, not what we believe. I strongly felt there was a difference between the two. So, as I explored Dr. Weiss' works, I sought to learn what I had long forgotten. I was not simply interested in intellectual knowledge. I wanted experiential knowledge. From one of his books, I was able to find his self-hypnotic cassettes, which I purchased later. The cassettes would help me to unlock my memory bank in order to uncover my soul's memory from time immemorial.

Toward the end of the summer—late August, Jennifer moved to my area. She was a mere four-minute walk from me. She and her twin sister moved to the apartment complex across the street. She became a big sister to Akofa and this pleased me, for I thought maybe Akofa needed a female influence. I was happy that she had a female role model.

Sometime at the end of September of 2007, I took half a day off to pick up my mother at the airport in New York City. Before my mother went Togo, she could hardly move or walk because of the accident. Now, she was showing a tremendous improvement.

We went straight home. Upon returning home, she and I discussed her trip to Togo on the third floor. She took a lot of pictures, which were of family members and relatives. Among them were the pictures that she had e-mailed me. I was looking at Hawa's picture. She was skinny, tall, and was holding her crossed hands behind her back. Her stature was extremely erect. My mother had taken the picture at her house in front of the crimson-like living room door. Her attention was on the last girl.

"What's up with the hair?" I said, smiling a little.

"She's nice. Her father is also a good person."

"So you know the family?"

"It's been a while since I've seen him. He's looking for a good guy for his daughter. He'll give you a few hectares of land."

"Sounds like he trusts you," I said.

She was more excited about this last girl then I was.

"Marry her Agbessi." She was smiling, but was dead serious.

"Naw!"

"You're not attracted to her?"

"She's ok. I can get to know her."

"But you prefer to get to know the other girl," she said, lifting up the picture of Hawa.

"Yes," I answered, "Do you have her phone number?"

"I have her mother's number, their house number."

"I'll call her mother and ask to talk to her."

"Write a letter first."

"A letter?"

"Keep it simple, and see what she says.

The ensuing Saturday, I drove her and Akofa to Manhattan to see my brother Messa. She wanted him to transfer the pictures and videos she had taken on her trip onto a disk. He had difficulty accomplishing the task. I began writing the letter to Hawa with my mother's help. I wrote two drafts before being satisfied. The letter basically said that I was impressed with her picture and would like to get to know her. I included my phone number, mailing address, as well as my e-mail address. It took about three weeks before

Hawa responded with an e-mail. In the meantime, my so-called relationship with Jennifer would soon come to an end.

On her birthday late one evening, I gave her a lift to the gas station where she worked. We had arrived early and we were chatting in the car. When an opportune moment of silence arrived, I seized upon it and leaned forward to her in the passenger seat. My mouth moved toward hers. She pulled back suavely and gingerly with a slight smile.

"My lips are for my husband," she said.

I was dead silent, stupefied. I stared at her, my mouth half ajar. *Alright*, I told myself in my head.

"Is it ok?" She asked.

"What? Yeah, understood."

I understood the refusal of the kiss in my own way alright. It meant that before I could kiss her, I had to marry her, to be her husband. But, did a kiss have to wait until marriage as well? I thought she was overdoing it. This was worse than "p-control" I pressed the button for my seat to lean back. I closed my eyes and waited for her shift to begin. She waited with me in the car. I decided to let myself fall asleep.

So much was happening that Fall that at times it was a little overwhelming. In September, I began having a reoccurring dream about having children. In all of these dreams there was a baby being born, but I could not identify the child's mother. That is, I saw bits and pieces of the mother, but never her face. In one particular dream, we were in the open part of a house, and I was holding the baby. Her mother was a few feet away. I saw her silhouette, her arms and lower body. She was tall, and was black.

In the dreams, I was certain I was in Togo. I know now that these were not dreams. They were possible glimpses of my future.

One particular glimpse was so awesome that I did not want to wake up. Thank God not all of these dreams were negative. It was one of the most beautiful visions that I have ever had. It was either a Friday or a Saturday evening. I fell asleep. I found myself in the streets of a city I had never been. I turned left. Every step was sensuous. It was wonderful. I was walking around and could feel it physically. I walked down a hill. It was an enclosed area, a neighborhood within a neighborhood. I was aware of the feeling—the way the ground felt as I walked upon it, the way I descended the hill, and exactly what I was wearing: a white jacket. Upon reaching the bottom of the hill, I woke up.

Other "supernatural" things were happening. Night after night, and sometimes during the day, I would be in bed reading or relaxing and could feel an energy. Some of it did not feel good, but some was positive. The positive presences actually brought me calm. I was aware that I was not alone in the room, though I could not see anything physical. I ignored these happenings, for I could not understand what was transpiring.

On December 8, 2007, I got more than I had bargained for. It was about 8 a.m. on a Saturday morning when it commenced. I was in bed, but I was awake when all this happened.

It started with the twinkling of the feet. I opened my eyes, trying to understand what was happening. Then, slowly the presence, an aura moved its way up the upper portion of my bed, toward my chest area and it began to speak. I heard the voice say, "You will die beaucoup." What I sensed, but could not see was the care and the worry within the aura on top of my upper body, near my face. I could feel it physically, but could not see it with my physical eyes; I lied in bed pondering this over, for I had never had such an experience. Finally, I decided to go back to sleep. As I fell

173

into a strange sleep, I had a dream warning me of my death. It was a very physical and vivid dream. In it there was a plane explosion. The steward was only a few feet away from me. I seemed to have exploded into her. In a matter of a second, we were reduced to nothingness. It was an awful way to go, and I was afraid.

I was downstairs in my three-story house which I could barely afford. I had a lot to digest. I chose to focus on the inter-dimensional visit. I rose from my bed pronouncing the word "wow!" I recognized the voice as someone I definitely knew. This was an absolute. There was no confusion about this. I knew it deep within my bones or soul or whatever one wishes to call it.

My mind identified the voice as Essevi, but was not sure of this. I was, however, absolutely sure that it was someone I knew in a past incarnation. For a few moments my soul was in control once again of my physical body and mind. All questions in my mind were suspended, seized, and I knew what I really was beyond the visible, solid world. However, this would not last, for I would try to find a "logical" reason to explain away this incredible experience. I spoke to two of my work colleagues. The one with expertise in science said, "The brain plays tricks." Given that I am left-brain, I would take this statement seriously.

My other colleague was in one of the science classrooms. He was sitting behind the counter. I was standing up as I spoke.

"I can feel them," I said, referring to my brother Essevi and my father.

He froze. His eyes did not blank for a good second and a half. He stopped talking. I did not expect this. I understood that I could not share anymore with him. He could not handle it. This information conflicted with his old paradigm.

Despite my colleagues' disbelief and my own skepticism, what would ensue the next two years would eradicate any doubt in me that these experiences were not only real, and that I would come to the understanding that I as well as the vast majority of humanity had forgotten who we really were beyond the physical.

One particular evening when I was in bed, I could feel a strong negative energy above my body. It was so negative that I had to move to the right, next to the window. Every couple of days I would feel this negative energy with the same intensity. Once as I leaned over to lie down with my stomach facing forward, and again I literally felt none-physical energy upon my chest. I was uncomfortable with this. I turned over, my back on the bed. I did not know what was going on. I was trying to understand it with my limited five senses instead of my intuition.

The negative energy I was experiencing was not the only source of energy that would visit me that fall. At other times, I felt an energy that was neither negative nor positive. It was an energy that I could not see, but could feel physically. Little did I realize that it was the same energy that came to warn me about my imminent death. In either October or November of that year, the physicality of this energy became stronger and stronger. During one particular night, it was so strong that I felt a movement from my lower body to my upper body. Intuitively, my soul recognized the aura moving about me in the bed. Thus, I was not afraid and did not experience any negative emotions.

Night after night I would feel this particular presence. The interesting thing about all of these experiences thus far is that I was fully awake when they occurred. I did not know who to talk to. I wanted to talk to someone who would not overtly or inwardly make fun of me or judge me.

I turned to one of my co-workers at Hostos Community college. Christina and I worked at the Writing Center on the third floor: Building C. After about 3 p.m., I asked her if I could talk to her. We went into one of the rooms near the exit. She had her laptop and was going to work a little as we talked. I told her about the book that I was rereading, and asked if she believed in reincarnation. I was trying to verify what Dr. Brian Weiss had written.

"Do you think reincarnation is real?"

"Yes," she answered.

I was a little surprised at her answer. I suppose I was expecting her to say no or maybe, but her answer was a definite yes.

"Have you ever seen or experienced anything of this sort?"

"In Costa Rica..." she began, her eyes leaving her computer and focusing them on mine.

"I once went to this place..."

I do not recall her exact words, but she basically said that she went to a celebration where a man could look at a person and see that person's past lives. I was impressed.

"Well, this is a good book, it's called Many Lives, Many Masters. It talks about reincarnation. It's about this young woman who has phobias—you know, difficulty sleeping, hiding in closets, and things like that. She has been reincarnated eighty-seven times on this planet. It's a good read. You should check it out."

"Why are you so interested in it?"

"Because I am having these strange dreams. I am wondering if they are mere dreams. I don't know. They just come out of nowhere, which makes me think that they might not be fantasy."

I did not tell her about the dreams. Instead, I helped her a little with her lesson plan and headed home.

Instead of going straight home, I went to the library. I needed to know whether or not reincarnation is real. I signed up for a computer to use the internet. I wanted to check out Dr. Weiss's self-hypnotic disks. I ordered them online on the same day.

It took about a week for the CDs to arrive. I was not sure I would be successful with it, but I had to try. I listened to the CD titled "Regression Through Mirrors of Time" every night, but had no luck. It put me to sleep every time. I would often wake up in the middle of the night finding the little light on the cassette player. I had begun making another plan—to save money to see Dr. Weiss. But, that idea would take years, for I figured his sessions would be too costly. I had to get to the bottom of these dreams especially "the last one."

In my last reincarnation dream, I found myself going into some sort of public bathroom. Upon entering, I went into a stall to sit to do my business. The stall's door was closed. Then, I heard two voices. I opened the door slightly to see the people whose voices I was hearing. They were two Caucasian men, perhaps in their thirties or early forties. They saw that the stall near them was occupied, so they advanced toward me with a frown in their faces. Then I woke up. It was a bizarre dream. I was black, and I intuitively knew that the dream had occurred in the United States of America and I was about to experience the physical consequence of slavery and racism. The interesting thing about this dream was that it reoccurred with fewer scenes and elements.

A few days later, I had another. I was in an old train, and the section I was in was vacant. The train operator was white. The inside of the train itself seemed old and was not very clean. I was a young man, sitting on the right side somewhere close to the entrance. Words were not spoken, but the young black man sitting there was absolutely me. I was absolutely aware of the reason why I was on that train: to escape from slavery.

One night, I finally succeeded at hypnotizing myself. I was in bed on the first floor, where my mother used to sleep. The particular night was different because I was more relaxed. It was a Friday. On Friday nights, I usually did not worry or think as much about my jobs or my other problems such as the mortgage and bills. I was in bed and had the CD player on my right dresser next to the mirror. I listened to the CD, trying to visualize different invisible colored lights such as purple, white, and blue surrounding my physical body. I visualized everything as instructed by Dr. Weiss on the CD. I even focused on the movement of my eyelids. Then suddenly, there was a loud ring in my head, as if there were a bell. It felt as if a door had opened that was leading to a massive space of knowledge. The restriction to my Infinite Memory Bank was gone. As I rolled my eyes, a scene of a past incarnation came to me. I was on top of a skyscraper, and all around me were very tall buildings. I was on top of one of them. I was a Caucasian young man, probably in my 20s. I was wearing eye glasses, and talking to someone I could not see. The person I was conversing with was definitely there, but was out of my field of vision. The Caucasian young man was carrying a suitcase in his right hand and stood completely erect. It was obvious that the young man was upset, for he had a frown on his face as he spoke to the person who could not be seen. I had the sense that the man was posing bitter questions because something unjust was done to him. I observed from above in my light body form in the sky to the right. I was a lucid, intangible, fluid source of energy. I was absolutely sure of the fact that I was simultaneously the Caucasian male and the spirit form above. I got a little closer to my soul, but could no longer maintain my focus. The hypnotic trance was wearing off. I lied in bed in wonder. After so much effort, I had finally succeeded at cracking upon My Infinite Memory Bank. The hypnosis was awesome! I was fully aware of the experience. I was not asleep. I was in control. It was amazing! I knew that was absolute. I could not doubt it. Nevertheless, I still wondered how it was possible. I did not get close enough to explore or to better understand my spirit form. Like my childhood mermaid memory, I would again tuck away this experience, and not really use it to better understand the world until years later.

Six months after my father came to warn me about my emanate death, the visions and dreams were still occurring on a regular basis. In the early months of 2008, I had a vision of one of my poorly misbehaved student. I was still living on the first floor of my house. At first, I thought it was a dream. I was in my regular classroom, 92, which was near the Dean's office. The class had not quite begun. I was walking toward my desk when something had suddenly hit me behind the head. I turned to the boy to the front of the classroom. He was sitting near the right side of the window. In the dream, I had clearly seen him thrown the piece of object at me. In hindsight, I should have paid a closer attention to the dream, but this was the beginning of my awakening, and the distinction between dreams and visions were still not quite clear to me. Unlike the vision, I did not see who had thrown the object at me. I knew that it came from the right side of the classroom. The student, whom I had seen in the dream, had his eyes wide open with guilt.

"Did you throw the bottle?"

"No!"

"Really?" I said in disbelief.

The bell rang for the class to commence. I sent him out immediately to the Dean's Office and then wrote a discipline referral on him after the class was over. The student was there the entire period.

"I don't know why you behave the way you do, but this is absolutely ridiculous."

"I didn't do it."

He chose to continue lying. I looked at him straight in the eye.

"Right, we'll talk later."

Toward the middle of the day as I was walking toward the main office, I saw the student's dean who told me that he admitted to having thrown the bottle, but that it was an accident. Somehow, I had believed him. The news had reached the principle. She too took it as an accident. The report was never inputted into the school's computer system.

A few weeks later, I had an out of body experience. I was sleeping on the first floor. My mother and little sister were on the third floor. It was during the snow season. I felt myself, my light body drifting in the air. My light formless self was out in the street right in front of the house, in the air. I made a right turn, passing several cars on my left. I passed a car repair shop on my right. I reached a three-way intersection. I flew diagonally to the street. I was by my car, a few feet away. There was a white man there writing something on a piece of paper. I floated away back into my room. I woke up. It was past two o'clock in the morning. Before going back to sleep, a thought occurred to me: *I just got a parking ticket*. The next morning, at about 6:45 a.m. I left my house with this thought. Surely, upon arriving, there was a piece of paper on my windshield, indicating that I did indeed get a parking ticket.

At work, one of my male colleagues would enter a religious discussion with a female colleague. It was in one of the staff rooms. The 2008 presidential elections were inciting a lot of intense and passionate conversation. The two of them were having a discussion about abortion. This was not a topic that I was passionate about. My male white colleague sat directly to the left of me, while the other tall, white female teacher sat across from him. They were talking about the horrors of abortion. He tried to involve me, but I squirted the topic. They insisted, and I finally said:

"We're all eventually going to the same place."

He stopped to think about it.

A few days later I was in the room again when he came to call his wife. I had difficulties with the computers, so I sat down to do some of the grading by hand. He sat down in the same place as before. Before I knew it, he was talking about Christianity. I recall a few of his exact words.

"Christianity is different than other religions."

I listened without judgment. I have had a lot of religious and spiritual discussions in my life, and I did not think having this particular discussion was going to heighten my spiritual awareness.

"Unlike other religions, Jesus Christ has done it for you. He has suffered so that you don't have to suffer."

I did not say anything, but this was absolutely not making sense to me. I was experiencing negative vibes in my bed, and have suffered a lot in my life. For me, his statements were completely incongruent with my experiences and to basic logic. Nevertheless, I did not criticize. He went on to tell me about a guy from India who had converted to Christianity. This guy had a website that my colleague wanted me to check out. I actually meant to check it out, but pernicious spiritual things were going to start happening to me that would force me to focus on my physical survival.

In the summer of 2008 while I was at Hostos Community College, I received an e-mail from Elomvi, informing me that our grandmother Amano had died, and that he was now alone in the world. I did not feel sad or happy about her death. I related the news to my mother, who said that I should send some money for the burial. Though I was struggling with a myriad bills, and a ridiculously high mortgage, I felt an obligation to do something. So, I sent the money to my aunt's father's older half sister. Several weeks later, I learned from Koku that Amano had awoken from death a week later, and that she wasn't really dead. I made a joke to my mother.

"Maybe God sent her back for being so bad."

After waking up, she became a completely new person. This was according to the village people in Kusuntu and Kpalimé. She started going to church and became a Christian. Her daughters took care of her. She could hardly move and had an unexplained skin condition.

"Her skin peeled off all over her body. She was in agony!" Amélino[4] would tell me in 2009 with a look of unease.

Despite the suffering, she remained true to the course. In 2009, I would learn that she was capable of change; we must change if we wish to reach the purest part of Infinity. This was a comforting thing to know. Personally, I thought that my grandmother was sent back to this consciousness to suffer in order to learn that hurting people spiritually is categorically unacceptable.

---

[4] Amélino literally means "the mother of Améli" because Améli is her first child. So, we have **Améli** + *no*. This can be done with any name to refer to a mother. Another example is Hawano, which means "the mother of Hawa." Again, this is because Hawa is her first child.

CHAPTER 7

FOUR MONTH COMBAT WITH INTERDIMENSIONAL ENTITIES

Fear is a debilitating negative energy that holds us as prisoners. It keeps us from doing what we truly want. It prevents us from seeing a greater beauty beyond its small, limited perspective. It was this negative energy that prevented me from returning to Togo since 2005. However, I was determined to go sooner or later, but for now the fear would be in control, at least through the summer of 2008. For one reason or another, I thought I would probably be safe if I went anywhere accept Togo. Given this assumption, I went to the Dominican Republic to work on my spoken Spanish. The plane ride was literally rocky. While I was airborne, I thought about my brother Essevi and my father, wondering if they were with me then. When I woke up at the capital the ensuing morning, I had my answer. My brother visited me in a dream in his old form; that is, the way he was in his late teenage years.

I did not enjoy the Dominican Republic as much as I should have. I did not really plan it properly. I stayed at a friend's house in Navarette, Cibao. The family was too protective and was against me going anywhere alone, not even to the store. I spent most of my time reading in Spanish. My stomach problem temporarily disappeared. For the most part, my melancholic state was greatly reduced.

There were a few times, however, when my depressive state seized me strongly.

Overall, the five weeks in this country offered me the opportunity to reflect about my life in general. I revised my six-year plan. I eliminated my plan to do a PhD, and replaced it with establishing a family. I thought about my relationship with Hawa, or the lack of it. I had accepted Hawa's wish to be friends, but thought that one day we would be more than that. Nevertheless, I decided that it would be best if I kept my options open until she was able to commit. That is, if I met another girl, I would date her.

Upon returning from the Dominican Republic, things went back to their usual, depressive state. I felt a bit lonely, completely uncomfortable inside the skin in which I was residing. I wondered why I was not able to control this on and off depression. I also wondered why I was having such a hard time meeting a girl who would truly care about me. The majority of the girls whom I had met thus far were incompatible and some were flat out dangerous. The extent of this, I would learn in the ensuing eight months. The last girl was from Trinidad.

I was using the computer at the library in the basement at Lehman College to find out about my fall semester educational administrational courses when my new friend asked for help. I helped her for a few minutes. When I turned to leave, an older woman also asked me for help. I found my new friend by the elevator. We ascended up together and began talking. While outside in front of the library, she mentioned something about her boyfriend, and soon after that I bid her good evening.

From then on whenever I returned to the library to use the computer to do my assignments, I found Terry-Anne there nearly every time. By October, she asked for a car ride home. She lived close to the school. Thus began our weird relationship. She called me a lot each day. I was working on my master's degree in educational administration and was swamped with a lot of work. I felt she was overbearing and I could not breathe. I explained this to her and directly told her to stop calling me so many times each day. She took offence to it. I did not know what I did wrong given that I was calm about it. I tried to soothe things out with her by explaining to her generally that I was going through a lot spiritually and needed some space. She was upset for a while, then she was back to her normal self. I thought by telling her that I was not looking for a serious relationship, she would have lost interest. She did not.

Two months elapsed. My bizarre relationship with Terry-Anne continued as my spiritual battles were about to unfold near Bedford Park Blvd, where I used to live in 2001. Presently, I was walking back from the 4-train station. I had my black, heavy jacket on with a thin hood. The sun was waning. It was not strong to begin with. Fall had already arrived. There was a bit of wind, and the air was a bit chilly. I do not recall the exact date, but I believe the month was November. I was almost at my car now. My Toyota was stationed near the C-Town supermarket.

I walked to the front of the car, the passenger side, and opened the door and put my book bag down on the floor of the seat. I closed the door, then walked to the driver's side. I opened the door with the same motion as I have a thousand times. I was feeling alright, calm of mind. Given that it was a bit chilly I wanted to put the heat on as quickly as possible. Upon turning the key in the engine slightly, I was completely stupefied. I stared at the dashboard. Silence enveloped my being for a long, eternal few seconds, as I stared at the clock in amazement. The clock had been set back exactly twelve minutes. It was always ahead. This is the way I liked it. Immediately, a thought occurred to me—

my father and my brother. I felt that one of them did this. In hindsight, I would understand that they were trying to tell me that they were there for me, though I could not see them physically. I drove off, trying to understand how they were able to do this.

It was during this time when I sat down, a pencil in hand and started thinking about how to resolve my main spiritual problem, which the vision that I had about dying if I should fly on a plane to Togo. I eliminated science as a possible source of answer as an option because I had already gone to the hospital and the doctors basically did not find anything. Furthermore, I eliminated church as a solution because none of my prayers at church worked to ease my physical and mental suffering. I thought my solution lied in finding someone who could see beyond the physical. Thoughts of psychics kept coming to me. I searched online for someone to help me. I called several. None of them answered. Those who answered wanted my credit card number and charged a lot of money. I kept trying, but did not find anyone. I stopped trying for a month. Then, on January 3, 2009, I went to shop in the outdoor shopping mall near my house. I saw the sign which read "$5 hand reading. Tarot..." I knocked on the front door from the street. A tall, very overweight woman who identified herself a moment later as Linda answered the door.

"Hello, how are you? Are you giving readings?" I asked with a hint of weariness.

"Sure, come up, and give me a few seconds," she said.

I mounted the stairs to the second and only floor. Before I reached the top, Linda began to speak.

"Your father and grandmother are with you now. I can sense your brother's presence, though he is not here."

I was a bit incredulous, for I didn't think these things were really possible. I, nevertheless, didn't say anything. We sat at the foot of the stairs. Linda had gotten a chair from the apartment at the end of the corridor on the left. She took my hands and began asking questions such as my name and birthday, questions which I ignored to see if she were authentic.

"You used to have really vivid, colorful dreams, but now you can't remember them."

I gazed up at her. We were on top of the stairs.

"You're supposed to live a long life…"

She was looking at the creased lines by my pinky finger.

"You're behind. You're supposed to have three children: two boys and a girl."

"I had a dream, more like a vision, that I would die in a plane explosion on my way to West Africa. I just want to know if it's safe to fly there."

"The spirit with you now died in his twenties. I see a uniform."

"There was a curse put on your family fifty or sixty years ago that has been killing all the males in your family. There was another placed on you seven to eight years ago."

I sat there in the chair pondering everything, not really believing a word, but trying to obtain the information for which I came.

"So, is it safe to travel?" I asked aimlessly.

"Come back in about 45 minutes. I'll do some research.

I was not sure about this lady, but I was going to let this thing run its course to find out whether or not she was credible. I gave Linda my name and date of birth. She said that she needed this information to do the research. I returned later with the items she indicated: some money and a closed bottle of water. Linda instructed me to sit down, and she began her work. I watched her carefully. I was not going to do anything that was against my will. She asked me to take a sip the of water from the bottle that I brought. I drank a bit of it and put the cap back on it.

"Repeat after me! I, your name, in the name of Jesus Christ want to rid my body of negative entities and influences."

"I, Agbessi Epou, in the name of the Most High and the Most Pure, want to rid my body of negative entities and influences."

I did not know why I had modified the words. It came instinctively. Linda did a simulated prayer with the water bottle: in front of my head, followed by my chest, then to my left shoulder, then the right shoulder. Then, right in front of me, the water turned to a dark red-dish color. She had not opened the bottle after I drank it.

"We have to ship it to Israel overnight to bury."

"How did you do that?" I asked, still stupefied.

"God has helped you."

"God?" I asked with doubt and hesitancy."

At this time, she was walking toward the door, then she turned to pose a rhetorical question with a knowing smile.

"You still don't believe?" she asked with a smile, "It is very urgent that we bury it as soon as possible. It will come back tonight at midnight." Linda then cited a price, which I do not recall. It was over a thousand dollars; I was becoming a little suspicious because of the high cost.

"I don't have that kind of money. I have a lot of financial problems. My house is falling apart, broken pipes."

Linda became a bit impatient and agitated.

"It'll be back tonight at midnight," she said emphatically as if to startle me or to compel me to action out of fear.

I walked downstairs, and was on my way back to my house. My body felt slightly different, though I could not put my finger on it. As I approached my house, I turned to look back at my preceding steps. There were marks of reddish stain on the snowy ground, the same color that was in the bottle from which I took the sip of the water. They

188

were imprints of my footsteps I considered the correlation, and then tried to find a logical reason. When none came, I left the whole thing alone. Several hours later, I was ready for bed. I closed my eyes to sleep, I felt a presence forcing itself upon my left arm. It was not comfortable. If this were a dream, it was not at all a cool one. It felt negative. After awakening, I could not sleep for a while, a good hour and a half. Linda's words came back to me loud and clear: "There is an army of demons after you. You have to do something!"

I would fall asleep only to awaken an hour or so later again. I began to consider what Linda had said about the army of demons, and if this was really the reason why I wasn't sleeping. I took Linda only slightly serious because ever since college, I could never sleep all the way through the night. Back then, I did not have a hard time falling asleep. It was staying asleep that was the problem. I usually wake up at least three times before my planned morning rise. As a result, Linda's demon warning had not yet registered. However, something was definitely different that night. My feet, especially my toes took fire. They felt like they were burning. They were hot and uncomfortable. Throughout the week I had a burning sensation in my feet and I still could not sleep all the way through the night. My insomnia was worsening.

I remained in contact with Linda via telephone. She had an associate who went by the name of Lisa. I would later learn that her husband's so-called last name is "Ristick." Sometimes when I called the apartment phone number, Lisa would pick it up then pass it to Linda. About a week and half later, I returned to pay the money that Linda had asked. By then she had done a lot of "spiritual research." I went to see her and the following is what I learned:

"A curse was put on your family about 60-70 years ago, before you were born. It has killed every male in your family since then. Now, they're after you."

I gazed at her for a good second or so, unsure about whether or not to accept part of the story or any of it. All I knew was that I was suffering. She asked me to pick a tarot card and I did. Though I do not recall the details of what the card looks like, I do remember Linda's statements.

"You trust no one. But you trust me. Pick another card."

I picked a card with a being of light.

"You will find salvation."

She paused, as if attempting to comprehend, she gazed into the open air, and I watched her attentively, trying to understand beyond the silence of her words.

"We have to go to the root of the problem, to remove the original curse," she said with all seriousness. "We must now protect the people dearest to you."

Before salvation would come, however, there would be a lot of deceptions, lies, and a lot of money loss. And Linda and Lisa would be a part of the manipulation.

Merely a few days later, I came to the understanding that Linda was right. It was about 9 p.m. I was at the computer lab at Lehman College working on a research paper when it began. The world of the unseen and the physical were converging. Thitherto, I was on my computer doing lesson plans. I looked around at the students at the lab, most of them were working feverishly. It was late. My sense of "invisible touch," if you will, was expanding. The top of my head was full of activity. There were beings above my head, but I could not see them. However, I could feel them very strongly. I thought about my work colleague's statement: The mind plays tricks. *Tricks?*" I shouted in my head. *Bull-shit!* I was being attacked as I drove. I was still trying to understand how all this could be possible. There was no time for logic, only time for intuition. I rubbed my head with my hand, but could not seize anything tangible. The physical activity above my head augmented in strength.

"*I have to get out of here!*" I heard myself say in my head. I headed toward the printer. A couple of what looked like Dominican girls were conversing a few feet away in front of me. I raised my right hand to the top of my head, then brought it down. I retrieved the things that I printed from the printer. This printer was nearer the entrance than the others. I looked at the girls in front of me, and then I turned my head to the right to have a look at the general ambiance of the room. I made a-360 degree turn to observe the room. I had a thought: These people were not aware of the world they cannot see. The feeling or need to exit the room increased as the activity above my head augmented.

"*To the car, home!*"

I took my right hand to the top of my head again and rubbed it profusely. This did not help. I instinctively knew that two of the mass-less beings above my head were my father and my brother. I was now passing the Lehman College Library. The wind was cold. The noise of the air and the trees were relaxing. As much as I was enjoying this brief reprieve, I wanted very badly to be in my car, to be warm.

As I drove home that evening, I felt like I was in two worlds, the world of the unseen and the physical. I had to pay attention to two things simultaneously: the ever-increasing activity above my head and my driving. At one point, the fighting above my head was so great that I could not but help pronounce the ensuing words:

"Essevi, Fo Yema, if this isn't necessary, then ease up on the fight." As you may recall fo Yema is my father, which is his first name. I made it home in one piece that night.

A few weeks later, I lost access to Linda. One afternoon, while in the living room on the third floor, I called her to inquire about the original curse. Lisa answered the phone with:

"I am taking over the case. It's one of the biggest we've seen in a long time.

"Tell me more about the original curse."

"It was placed while your great grandfather was alive, about fifty or sixty years ago.

"Why? Please explain!"

"Your grandfather had an affair with a woman. She was fatally attracted to him. To get back at him, she casted a really strong spell against him and your family. All the males would die young."

"After all this time, the spell is still working?"

"Every couple of years, she added to it."

"So, how do we rectify this?"

"We have to go to the root of the problem. It'll cost some money."

The words she uttered should have been a strong clue that this woman was interested in only money. Something told me that there was something off here, but yet I pursued the course in the hope that this money grabbing, unenlightened soul would get rid of the negative souls that besieged me.

"I don't have any more money. Your church, can't they help? How much money are you talking about?"

"I don't know. I have to do a little bit of digging first. I'll let you know."

That night, very late, at or around 11:30 p.m. Lisa called to inform me of the cost. She told me that it was $10,000. I was outraged and very upset and would refuse to pay anything.

"I don't even have that much money in my bank account."

The phone suddenly cuts off. For a minute, I would wonder if that were a sign of some sort. Then the phone rang again with the voice of a very agitated and irate Lisa.

"This is your last chance."

Her tone depicted a strong sense of anger.

"I'll take my chances. This is insanity. Asking for money I don't have." My voice was firm, angry, and expressive.

She hung up. I went to bed a few minutes later. I stayed awake most of the night in the dark. When I awoke, my sides, right above my hips were hollowed, curved in, as if I had lost a lot of weight.

At about 10 a.m. at work I received a voice mail, and it was Lisa saying that how my brother didn't let her sleep the entire night; and that he kept annoying her to help me. I did not call her back. However, she did not give up. I was not sure about the validity of her claims. She left several messages asking me to tell my brother to leave her alone.

After work, I was near my house. I was still very much confused about going through with this whole thing with Lisa. So, I called my mother.

"So did you talk to Yawavino?" I asked, referring to my maternal grandmother.

"She said she's a Christian now."

I was even more stressed and anxious.

"So, she's not going to do it? Wow, this is a great time for her to be a Christian."

I looked up at the post office, then toward the bank, trying to decide whether or not I would take the money to Lisa. I really did not want to, but I felt I was running out of time. Whatever was transpiring was happening to me physically. I put my hand to my left waist, and then to the right. Both sides had creased in tremendously. In addition, my thighs also took immense heat. This was totally supernatural. I had to act.

"I'll ask her again."

"When will you talk to her?"

"Tomorrow."

"Tomorrow?"

That would have been too late. I went to the bank and took out the money and headed to Shoprite to first purchase some food for dinner. I was on foot now. Descending the little hill toward the entrance of the store, I felt so confused about what I was doing. Questions after questions popped into my head. *Should such a decision be so difficult to make? Shouldn't it be easy?* My heart was literally uncomfortably beating strangely as I walked into and out of the store. *Am I blindly following her? I didn't really like her the first time I met her.* The cold air caressed my cheeks to the right on the small sidewalk.

I went home, cooked, and finished my lesson plans, and then late in the night at or about 9 p.m. I headed to Lisa's place with the money. She came down to the first floor. She smiled and swore to me that everything was going to be alright. I believed in her words, for I needed so badly to believe. I remember calling my mother that evening and telling her that my brother and my father were with me and that I could sense their physical presence, though I could not see them. She said to tell them "welcome."

"I am sure they already heard you," I said as I approached the intersection. I gave Lisa the money and walked back home. I was optimistic because I wanted to believe that she would help me.

Nearly two weeks passed and Lisa's words were merely hot air. I began to doubt in her ability to get the job done. I went to the library to do my own research on psychics and demonic possessions on the internet. I found a couple of listings and phone numbers. I wrote a few down, and made some phone calls upon exiting the library. I was only able to speak to a young psychic in New Jersey.

"I need some help. How do I say this…I have been cursed. Spells have been casted on me in three continents, and I can't sleep. I have been told that an army of demons is after me. Can you help?"

"I don't believe in demons, but I do sense a lot of negativity around your aura."

I thanked her and hung up. I did not feel she could help me. I did not believe in demons either, but I knew for certain that something or things beyond the physical were after me. If she could not see this, then there was no way she could help.

For the ensuing four months, I would wait, battle negative souls in the middle of the night. Until 2009 I was not aware that these things existed. I had forgotten much before this incarnation. Sleepless nights would ensue, and I would wake up being attacked in the middle of the night. I questioned everything, but the logical mind did not find any logical or scientific answers to explain away these occurrences. What was happening was not only real and multi-dimensional, it was dangerous.

The morning after I had let myself be deceived by Lisa and her cronies, things had taken a turn for the worse. I was now able to sense other entities' presences. In the middle of the night as I lied down, I needed not even close my eyes before sensing negative auras. My father and my brother did come everyday and every night to check up on me, to fight for me. I usually felt their presence around my head area, as I do now as I write. They were there, and they have always been there to protect me. However, they could not be there 24 hours a day. The negative entities were always waiting for their absence to attack, to enter my body again.

About a month after I had gone to see Lisa and Linda, the ticking or rather the palpitations all over my body augmented. I was convinced I had more negative energy inside my body. In February of 2009, the assistant principal and the chair person of the foreign language department and I were going over my post observation. The chair person sat to the left of me. I was closer to the door. Calmly flipping through her notes, the assistant principal said:

"I have a few recommendations…"

The palpitations augmented with force as she spoke. The major area was my chest, just above my heart. The palpitation was so visible and fast that I thought that the assistant principal noticed. She did not say anything. I was relieved. I pulled up my shirt, in an effort to cover it. I heaved my chest in, trying to leave room between my chest and my shirt. That is, I was trying to make sure that my chest was not touching my actual shirt, as to hide the visible palpitation. This was an intriguing experience. They were both so caught up in what they were saying that they did not see what was transpiring right before their very eyes.

About two and a half months passed and things had gone worse. One Saturday before leaving my brother's apartment in New York City, I called Lisa to inquire about how the job was going. I was in the driver's seat of my car. With a low-spirit and feeling really down, and could not shake it off. I wondered when all this would come to an end. I dialed Lisa's phone number.

"Hi," I said.

"You don't sound well. Linda called me from abroad. She had a really difficult time today."

"Difficulties with what?" I inquired with a defeated voice.

"She had to fight off a lot of negativity. There were a lot of them."

"How long is all this going to take Lisa? I am really tired."

"We should be done in about two weeks."

I would wait impatiently for the two weeks to past. I breathed slightly looking out through the dashboard into the void. I turned the engine on and started driving. An image of Linda working with her church in Togo entered my mind. I felt uneasy, drained. When I reached the bridge, the feeling of deep void, depression, and really low energy augmented. I heard voices laughing boisterously and mockingly. I felt a deep negativity around me. The energy was very negative. These voices were to the left, right, and in front of me. I was nearly surrounded. I felt the negativity, but could not see their souls. Despite the deepness of this low energy, my soul pushed me on. I had to get home safely, to survive if only to endure one more day, and whatever happens in this life or the next I would be able to say that I did not surrender, capitulate to the army of negative lower dimensional and inter-dimensional entities.

The feeling that I had on the bridge would be repeated a month or so later in a different place. It was early in the morning, about 7 a.m. I was going about 68 miles per hour, and was on the highway. I recall vividly changing from the left to the middle lane. I literally heard and felt the negative souls again. This time, the feeling was different. I frowned and uttered the word "no!" Again, I could feel their negative vibes, but could not see them. I decided to slow down a little. I tried to stay focused on my driving in order to avoid an accident, but the negative souls' vibes increased. It felt strange. This feeling ran deep, and it was a general feeling about the progress of their souls. My chest area waned in hopelessness. The words "cannot do it" sketched in my mind's eye with a loud inaudible force of itself. I remained calm. As I drove off the bridge, the meaning of the vibes that I was feeling became more concrete. What I was feeling was not my own. It was that of the negative souls' feeling of hopelessness; an infinite fear of not being able to reach the purest part of their inner beauty. In other words, to reach the Most Pure, the Most Positive, God. As I think about this experience in hindsight, I understand now how much these entities were suffering. Their souls were literally covered and imbued in darkness. They have sunken so, so low that their ability to ascend to the ultimate purity seemed impossible. Instead of being brave, they have chosen cowardice—to exist while causing havoc, to suck other souls' positive energy.

The peak of the dark entities' attacks would result in a rediscovery of the nature of who I truly am beyond the physical, solid body. As usual, the evening commenced with me lying in bed, waiting to fall asleep. My back was against the pillow looking straight up, I closed my eyes, but still sleep would not come.

Finally, I turned my stomach touching the bed. My brother and father came come to visit, travelling above my head. Somehow, I always knew it was them. That night, after "visit of surveillance," they left. This was the dark entities' chance to attack me. What transpired next was absolutely amazing, life changing, beautiful, incredible, lovely, cool, and would help me in my awakening process.

After my angels left, I still could not sleep, though my eyes were closed. Sleep would not come because I was being vigilant. After a while, my mind began to calm down, for I could no longer sense the negative entities around me. I began to relax and to fall asleep again, not really thinking about the fact that these negative beings were just waiting at a distance, waiting for their chance to enter my body again.

I was in a state of sleep now. I would say that this state of rest would last for about fifteen or so minutes when suddenly I would be jerked awake by one of the entities trying to get inside my body. My head was facing the left wall, resting on the pillow. It pressed hard against the back of my head, kissing it. It was very solid. In its desperation to gain access to me, it had taken a physical form. My mind struggled to make meaning of what was happening, for I had never experienced anything like this before in this consciousness. I felt this negative soul all over my physical body. The entity was very clever. It actually took the form of my so-called girlfriend Hawa. I raised my head a little and said out loud "Has it begun?" Upon the pronouncement of these words, there was an understanding beyond the mind. That is, my light body or soul understood what was happening. It immediately suspended all mental activities to take charge. I quickly became aware of many things. One such thing was that my mind was a denser, solid form of consciousness and even it cannot die. As the thoughts came, they left rapidly. Quickly now, It shut down my mind and existed my physical body with resolute authority and absolutely no hesitation whatsoever. There was a complete separation of my soul from my physical body. The mind was no longer in control, my soul was. A life time of deception, manipulation, and forgetfulness was going to be undone in one night with only a few minutes of "a near battle" with this negative soul.

199

Upon exiting the physical vehicle, my Light Being stood near the foot of the bed, observing its human form. My body just lied there on the bed, half naked, with the sheet partially covering my buttocks. I was also taking notice of my own soul, the being that was observing its physical body. I understood that the mind itself is a "separate" energy with which the soul interfaces. I was aware of the fact that It is aware of very little of the nature of the universe when it is in the physical vehicle. I sensed that my soul was much more aware of what It really is. I knew things without knowing how. I had no questions. I was a being of light that shone in the room. I saw everything around me, but not everything could see me. Now, I was focused on my physical body, as if nothing else mattered. As if that very dark entity on the left side of my bed posed no danger to me whatsoever. I felt no fear, only calm. I paid It no attention. My Light eyes were focused on my physical body. Yes, even my soul had eyes, but not in the physical sense of the word. It was luminescent, extremely fluid, and possessed no physical form. These mass-less eyes would be turned to face the entity only after it had observed its physical form on the bed.

Turning now to my left, I saw the negative entity on the foot of the bed, scratching its head in bewilderment, trying to comprehend why it was not being successful at entering my body. It was not yet aware of my presence to its right. Still scratching its head, I observed It without judgment. The essence of this entity was much like my own soul, except that it was literally very dark. In terms of intelligence, it was completely brilliant. It was smart beyond imagination, beyond an intelligence any human being on Earth might possess. At that point, I also understood that I too am brilliant beyond imagination. The major difference between our two souls is that my soul was much, much brighter. My essence or soul is a being of light, literally. I could see very clearly in the dark room.

It was now time to battle. With infinite calm, I reached deep within the bosom of my soul to select a weapon that was not physical. Now, the dark soul sensed my presence. As I turned to face it, it fled toward the left at what appeared to be the speed of light or even faster. I sensed its fear—it was afraid of me. A bully, it was. Bullies are always deep inside weaker than the soul they are picking on. Such abuse which comes from a place of great negativity and weakness, is to some extent a lack of awareness and bravery, and sometimes food.

Upon the dark soul's flight, I went back into my physical body, and decided to sleep. I woke up that morning knowing who I truly was, though I would have more questions. Next to my "father's visit," this was the single most wonderful experience I had ever had. Physical sex does not remotely compare to it. There was no trace of fear in me. I knew the entity was there on my bed, yet I took my time to observe my own physical body. "No fear, no worries?" I asked myself that morning. I was doing things I didn't know I could do that night. I was aware of the fact that in this form of consciousness or existence, I had a feeling of endlessness, infinite possibilities. I was not a man or a woman. I had no sex or gender. I simply existed. It dawned on me that the West African or American or whatever one may wish to call or identify me is not who I truly am. I am not even my experience. I am not my body. I am not my culture, race, religion, or science. And neither are you Reader. These things are merely tools to learn in this consciousness. This latter point is paramount to understanding who we really are. For one reason or another, we have forgotten our essence or soul, which is literally inside our physical bodies. The connection between the physical body and the soul is so intimate that if one is not careful, one will mistake the physical vehicle for its true self. The body is very physical and solid. The soul is not. It is mass-less, intangible, fluid.

Ever since this experience, I have been careful identifying myself with mundane ideas and belief systems. As the months passed, I tried to remember more and more that the mind thinks because it is not all-powerful like the soul. Furthermore, I would also remind myself that this life is only an experience. There is no death, only a departing or a moving on of the soul to another level. As a result, since May of 2009, a new intuition was solidifying in my day to day way of thinking—one should never fear death. The soul is ageless and cannot die, no matter what. The worse thing in life is suffering.

Though I was successful that night combating the dark entity, I wanted to get rid of the rest of the ones waiting in the shadows to attack me. After the official workday ended, I was in the middle of working on my lessons for the ensuing day for my classes when I felt the urge to stop. I was sitting at the computer to the right of the big printer. I logged onto the internet and typed in the words "psychics in New York." A score of them with their phone numbers immediately appeared. I searched through them all. A lot of them looked satisfactory, though I did not know what I was looking for exactly. With a stroke of the key, I returned to the general Google search. This time, I simply typed in "psychics." An infinite number of them appeared on the screen. I was in a new territory and was not quite sure how to proceed. I decided that the best way to do this was to carefully read what ability they were professing to possess, and to see if there were entrapments. There was a guy in New York, but his biography was a little dubious and I had to leave a message for him to get back to me. I did not want to leave anymore messages for any more psychics, so I left it alone.

Finally, I came upon a website with a lady in Texas. I quickly skimmed through for any ill-will. One gave me a slight pause. She was offering to help people in various ways, including love. I was desperate. I had to try something else. I had to try anything, without telling Lisa. She was taking forever to help me. Doubts filled my mind about her ability to help. She had taken so much money and produced no results. I was still being attacked at night, and she claimed to be working on things.

I dialed the lady's cell phone in Texas. She picked up right away.

"Hi!" I said.

"Hello my son," said the voice of an older woman, "My name is Savanna."

"My name is Agbe."

"What's your date of birth?"

"No, if you are any good, you can access the information without my date of birth," I said, thinking back to what Lisa had said about not giving my date of birth to people. I was not going to fall for the same trap twice.

"I am calling to—"

"She's not strong enough! This is urgent! All those equipments! She's not meant to finish the job. Think about it."

I knew Savanna was referring to Lisa. The equipment was the physical things I had given to her. I remained silent.

"It should have only taken a few weeks—two or three at the most."

"Tell me more. Why can't she help me?" I said without emotion.

"She's not strong enough. It's probably an ego thing. She'll never, ever stop!"

I knew that this Savanna lady was telling the truth. She had never seen or spoken to me before, and yet she was describing Lisa's personality as I too saw it. Lisa was not a quitter. There was a stubbornness about her. I had asked her once if it would not be logical to seek additional help, and she refused. Furthermore, Savanna was right about the equipment. That was my car.

"Why won't you let me help you?"

I listened to Savanna, still not completely trusting her.

"How much do you charge?"

"$78," I heard her say.

"You can help me, and you will charge less than a hundred dollars?"

"Only $78 my son," she said with calm.

"Ok, I'll think about it and will call you back."

"Have a good afternoon my son."

As I drove home, I considered the possibilities. This lady was offering to help, and the money was not much, and I was not asking her to do anything bad, only to free me from the dark entities.

There was no wrong in this. I was at the Tappan Zee Bridge now. I paid the tow, which was way too expensive. It was either $4.50 or $5.

That evening upon getting home, I did my chores—cleaning the bathroom a bit, cooking dinner and putting some finishing touches on my lesson plans. After showering, I prayed while sitting at the desk as usual—reading the Bible, modifying the text to fit my prayers. Then I went to bed. That night, like a hundred nights during the four months that I fought these entities, sleep would be difficult. I would awake several times during the night. In the morning, I would be extremely exhausted. Given this, I decided to give Savanna a try.

I sent her $78 via Western Union the next day. She called me a few hours later. I was lying in bed.

"Good evening my son. How are you?"

"I am ok. Just need some sleep. I haven't really slept in a long time. I sent the money order."

"I received it. To get started, I'm going to need some information from you."

"Go ahead."

"Your name."

"Epou, you already know my first name."

"And your date of birth?"

"We have already been through this. You can do this without my date of birth."

"What's the lady's name?" she asked sternly and sharply.

"Her name is Lisa."

"What else do you know about her?"

"Start with that. She's been helping me. I can't betray her."

The next day, I called her from work, and she explained to me what I needed to do in order for her to help me.

"You need to get five dollars in quarters, and a white handkerchief."

"And what do I do with them?"

"Get them and then call me back. I imagine it will be very difficult for you to do this?"

Was she serious? Hadn't she ever heard of a bank? I just had to go to the bank right after work.

"The candles, I was told I should order special sets. The ones in the stores have been tampered with, prayed on. Isn't this a problem?"

"I have been doing this for fifty years. It's perfectly alright."

"Alright, I'll talk to you later."

I walked into Citibank and asked for change for $5. They gave me a roll of quarters for $10. I took it and left. Now, it was time to go to the supermarket to purchase the white handkerchief. Neither of these tasks was difficult at all. That evening Savanna told me to write down my wishes on a piece of paper. I took the piece of paper and wrapped the handkerchief around it and put it under my pillow. It stayed there for two days.

Now we were ready to tackle the big task of permanently getting rid of these entities. Like Lisa, she explained to me that the problem lied in money. She told me what to do and I followed her instructions. I put half of the money in my left shoe and the other half in my right shoe.

"Now put your shoes on and walk on the money. The money is nothing. Think this."

After a few minutes I asked, "How long do I have to do this?"

"Take the shoes to your room."

I did this and waited for her next instructions.

"Now we're going to pray my son."

I was sitting at my desk with a huge smile. Somehow, I must have known intuitively that these dark inter-dimensional entities' days were numbered. Savanna instructed me to repeat after her. Since I do not recall her exact words, I will explain them. She told me to say my full name, to ask for protection in the name of Jesus Christ, to send the bad souls back into the darkness, from where they came. I did all of these things. However, every time she said "Jesus or God," I changed it to "The Most Pure."

I went to bed that night with a smile on my face. I recalled my eyes being opened for a few minutes in the darkness, in dead silence of the night, contemplating what the night would bring. As the minutes passed and nothing negative happened to me, I began to relax, thinking that perchance they were gone forever. However, I was terribly wrong. They were waiting at a distance, waiting for my soul to forget about them. I closed my eyes and tried to sleep once again and I did. However, it would not be long before they would return.

My neck!

They held me at a choking position. A strong arm, but it was not really an arm around my neck, and it was not my real physical neck. They had joined forces, attaching their souls to one another to form one massive, gigantic arm. They tightened their grip around my neck. My light spirit body remained cool as a cucumber. It even smiled. It knew what to do. I sunk my spirit teeth into this giant arm, and they released me immediately, for the pain must have been great for them. Then they were gone only to return sometime later that night.

It was like a downpour of dark souls upon me. I was below, and they came from above, behind me. They quickly centered above my head, the headquarter of my soul. The descent upon me was so fast that there was no time to think or strategize. Quickly now, I changed from one consciousness to another, smiling, for I knew they could not win. I was enjoying the battle. I opened my eyes and uttered the word "wow!" I was flabbergasted at the quantity of them. To say that there were a hundred would be an extreme understatement. It is only now, November of 2010 that my physical brain is able to understand the scope, the magnitude of what the none-physical beings I was fighting were. The shifting from one consciousness to another was not a dream. All of these things happened, but in a different dimension, right in my room. The opening of my eyes put me in another sphere of consciousness—the physical. In this physical state, they could not enter my body, not because my eyes were open, but because I knew they were around, and I was expecting them.

Whatever else transpired that night, I do not remember. I only recall the height of the battle. In the morning, I would stand, gazing at the physical room. It was a small room.

Not much space for anything. My desk was right by the door, so tight against the bed. I looked around, and smiled.

The next day, I sent Savanna the money that I prayed on that night. It was about ten thousand dollars. She said that she needed it to complete the job before sending it back to me. She called me in the evening at about six o'clock, sounding joyous.

"I wasn't sure it would work."

"Yeah, we'll see."

Several days later, I received a telephone call from Lisa after work. At first she said that she and her church were making great progress to remove the original curse. I do not know why, but somehow I ended up telling her that Savanna had helped me get rid of the dark entities. She became very worried and nervous, almost panic-like. She began asking me all sorts of questions about her. I told her that I could not reveal her identity because she helped me. She was worried that Savanna might do something to her. I tried to soothe her by saying that she really helped me and there was nothing to worry about. She asked me to "at least" give her Savanna's phone number. I refused. However, I did give her the 800 number listed on the website. She told me the next day that she called the number and asked for a reading; and that Savanna called her evil, and asked me if I thought she was evil. She told me to stay away from her. I was quiet.

In the evening, Savanna called me and said the most bizarre thing.

"I don't know what happened," she said with concern in her voice. She was talking to herself.

"It's probably Karma."

Now, the sound of her voice was directed outward toward me.

"It doesn't make any sense."

"She called me and I answered. She said that her six-year old son was screaming, crying hysterically all night," I said to Savanna, referring to Lisa

"Listen my son, she'll be fine. She's exaggerating."

At about three o'clock the next day, I was working on my lesson plans at school when I received a phone call from a woman. It was the voice of an older woman.

"Hello."

"Good afternoon," the woman said, "Is this Agbe?"

"Yes, it is."

"I am Savanna's boss."

"You're calling from Texas."

"Yes. We need to know more about Lisa."

"It's not good to betray someone who has helped you."

"There is something wrong with her. She's not well."

"She's not well? What do you mean?"

"She knows everything about us and we don't know anything about her."

"I sensed that she was a bit scared."

"Please, we don't know what she might do."

"She only has the 800 number that's listed on your website."

"Savanna, is Savanna there?"

"Yes, my son," she answered quietly.

"She doesn't know your name. Alright, I'll tell you what I know. She lives on….Her partner in crime is Linda, and she's tall and very overweight. Lisa has taken over the case, but nothing seems to be improving. I knocked on their door on the third day of January 2009. I don't know them. Her husband is…Her phone number is…Her English grammar is not that good. And she still has my car. That's it. You promised not to do anything bad…"

"No, we just need to prevent her from doing anything bad to us."

By the use of the word "bad," I would understand "spell." This whole thing was very peculiar. Here was Savanna's boss on the phone pleading for information. They know something. They were psychics, and I guess they saw something dangerous about Lisa that I did not. Something rubbed me off about her. In any case, I was talking to the two women. *Savanna had a boss? Why did she have a boss?* Lisa's words flashed in my head immediately.

"He's just a baby…There is someone above her, and above her someone else. That's how it works."

So, Lisa was right. Savanna was part of an organized group of witches? What does that mean really? They used Jesus Christ's name a lot. Later when our relationship would come to an end, a thought dawned on me: *Lisa too is part of a twisted religion.* The use of "God" was a cover. All their biblical citations were a cover for their real purpose. They do some good deeds, but they are also involved in the dark arts. A year later, it dawned on me with utter clarity that they were part of secret religious societies and that secret societies existed throughout the world. These were the conclusions that I would reach later, but for now I still needed help.

That night, Savanna called to see how I was doing. I told her that I wanted to get this whole thing done and over with and that I had doubts about Lisa being able to help me. This was where she said the most shocking thing.

"She had you scared out of your mind, asking you if you wanted to be in the spirit world or in this world. I mean, think about it. She did help you, but it doesn't make any sense."

I was utterly dumfounded by what she said. How did she know that Lisa had said those exact words to me? The palpitations began again all over my chest, biceps, and triceps. Savanna hung up the phone.

I was tired. I had a long day, working late into the evening, until about 8 p.m. I poured myself a glass of red wine. I had earned it. After eating and watching some television, it was time to go to bed again. I sat at my desk, opened the Bible to Psalms 91 as usual and began reading, but altering the words to fit what I really wanted to say. I uttered:

"We who dwell in the shelter of the Most High, the Most Positive, the Most Pure, who abide in the shadow of the Almighty, will say to the Lord, 'Our refuge and our fortress; our God, in whom we trust…A thousand may fall at our side, ten thousand at our right hand; but they will not come near us…"

Sleep was overtaking me, and so I surrendered to its command. I slept that night without interruptions, though I would wake up at least once, it would not be because of any negative entities. I was being vigilant. They were gone. Savanna had done a good job, though she stole nearly nine thousand dollars from me.

Several days later, I was at school. My first administrative educational course would begin in a few minutes. I was in front of Carman Hall, near the bookstore at Lehman College when I received her call.

"Hello my son."

"Hello Savanna, how is it going?"

"I have great news my son."

"What is it?"

"They are gone. All of them."

"And the money? When do I get it back?"

"No, my son. There was no time. I had to use it to buy gold. We did not even have enough. We had to be sure that they would not return."

I offered her dead silence.

211

"You must be really happy my son. Aren't you happy my son?"

"Savanna, you lied to me and you're asking me if I am happy?" My voice strained, hoarse, full of despair and anger.

"What am I supposed to live on? That was my mortgage money. I need the money back."

"It's gone my son."

"I don't have anything to live on. I need some of the money back."

"I'll see what I can do."

After hanging up the phone, I took a deep breath and walked inside the building and entered the first floor of Carmen Hall. The professor was already there. My group and I had to give a big presentation that would be a big part of our grade. I was so angry and despairing that I did not really know what I was going to do. As I sat there in that room to the left wall, I stared straight ahead hearing my fellow classmates' incomprehensible words. A thought occurred to me—*leave!* I looked at my presentation papers, trying to figure out what to say. I was not in the right frame of mind, and wanted so much to leave. However, I thought if I left, then I would probably fail the course. *So! It's just a useless course. An educational administrative leader? Forget it! I would be a leader in some other way. But, you're halfway through the program. Stay!*

It was clear what I had to do. I had to stay to do the presentation for my group's sake. I did not want them to receive a bad grade. I just had to get through it. My two group members did fine. I thought that I did the worse. Words came out of my mouth, but I did not really know what I was saying. Finally, it was over. I took a seat on the left side of the long rectangular table, feeling mentally beaten and drained. It would take about another two hours before I would calm down. For now I would go to my next class.

The second class, which was the last class of the evening, was two hours and forty minutes long. Luckily, we would get out a bit early that evening. The good thing about that course was that the professor was amiable. I sat in the back of the class, more toward the right side if one were entering the classroom. This room had movable desks. Given that I had already done my presentation on a sample lesson, I just sat there in my seat and listened to the last few presentations. This opportunity for quiet reflection was good for me. Besides, when I am really upset, I do not talk. I prefer silence. After the course ended, we students said our goodbyes.

A few of us lingered outside to chat. I had the opportunity to say goodbye to my professor, who asked me how I was doing. He must have read my countenance. I felt I could trust him. I told him a little about my battles with the negative entities. This guy was different. He saw that I was going through something serious, and tried to help.

"They can't touch you," he said solemnly with excitement.

"But they did."

"No, they can't touch you."

We were standing by the bus stop. The bus came, but he did not get on it.

"You're going to miss your bus."

"It's ok, there is a reason why we are talking. Come to church with me."

"What church are you a part of?"

"Seventh Day Adventist."

"I don't really go to church. I did a little while ago with a friend, the same, but these things were still happening."

Though he did not succeed in convincing me to go to church with him that day, I will always remember his attempt to help me, his kindness. He missed two buses that evening. He even gave me his home and cell phone numbers. I still have them. It has been nearly a year and half since I last saw or spoke to him. I have been meaning to call and thank him for this display of kindness, reaching out to help another soul.

A few days later, Lisa and I were talking about resolving the original curse. I changed the conversation to learn more about my father. I felt she was being evasive, and would not tell me what I wanted to know. A part of me felt that she was being that way because she did not know. I believe that it was about 5 o'clock in the evening. I was walking toward my bedroom with the cell phone to my left ear. I stopped at the door's threshold.

"I would like to know exactly who killed my father."

"I can't go into that."

"Why not?" I said. "I am going back. They will know who I am, and I won't know who they are."

"Your father doesn't want me to say. He said what will happen to those who killed him will be clear in time."

I turned off the phone and went back to my dinner. I do not recall what I ate that evening, but I do remember doing my lessons and praying with Psalm 91 before going to bed.

After conversing with Lisa that night, something amazing happened. Other than being out of my body, what was about to happen that night would shake me to my inner core and alter many of my life long beliefs and practices. In a span of merely three months, the old me was dying and had to die in order to experience the beauty within that had always been there, dormant, watching, and suffering, but trying to become unconsciously aware all along. I went to bed thinking that it was going to be an ordinary night. The demons had gone, my sleep had returned to somewhat of a normal state. However, little did I know that evening that everything was about to change. I went to bed hoping to have lucid, vivid dreams. I lived for these.

The lucid dream did come, but with much more intensity than I would have ever imagined. I cannot even say that it was a dream, because it was not. It was not even a vision. It was a message.

It commenced with an argument. My mother and my stepfather Avon were to the left toward the corner of the room. There was someone else present, but I do not recall who it was nor do I remember exactly what my mother and Avon were discussing. I simply recall that my mother was the cause of me being upset. However, I took my anger out on my stepfather. They all appeared relatively calm except me, who was getting angrier and angrier by the second. Before I knew it, I had some sort of a bat and was beating my stepfather. Every strike was real, so physical. Even the stick in my hand felt physical as in this so-called physical world we live in. I hit him over and over again all over the body. He received them with moans and cries of pain. The last strike landed somewhere across his chest. His body receded against the wall. The pain and suffering on his face was immense. He landed on his buttocks. That was the end of him. The blood about the floor and his face was dark red. Colors within the room shone so, so brightly. This was so real that there was literally no difference between what I was experiencing and this so-called "real physical world." As the life receded from his body, I literally screamed out with Infinity, and Infinity was absolutely God. I felt the pain of killing my stepfather deep within my inner body, my Light Self. The intensity of the "No" that I shouted out was omnipresent. The colors became even more vivid. The "feelings" were more intense. I felt the "no!" deep within my Self, my mind, chest, the ensemble of my entire being. I felt what God felt. God and I were in absolute accord.

That is, what I had done was totally uncool and would hold back the Universal Plan, and that whatever that plan is, is also my plan. It was a great and devastating feeling.

The other overwhelming feeling that seized me was that I knew without a shadow of a doubt that I was literally a part of the Universe. Everything was me, and I was everything. There was absolutely no hierarchy between God and me. We simply were. No being was higher or lower than others. At the same time, I was also aware of centers of energy (i.e., beings) that one might call "superior" within the Whole, but were not. It was completely clear to me that this was because of their total acceptance of the Universal Plan to help all beings reach their ultimate purity. I understood that "God" was not really a separate entity. There was a breaking off into pieces some time in the "past."

Presently, the conscience killing of my stepfather overwhelmed me. I was absolutely not judged. The Whole did not judge me. There was only the bitter feeling that I had pushed back the Universal Plan, and that I could not live with. I felt as if I had killed myself and that was what hurt the most. I screamed as if I were being physically and spiritually harmed. God does not judge. At least not in the way most people have been manipulated since birth to believe. My being was penetrated again with: There is no hierarchy between God and us so-called human beings. In the grand scheme of things, every soul, dark or bright is absolutely indispensible to the well-being of God. I felt an interconnectedness that was beyond words. Instantly, I understood that we are all connected to each other within the planet and beyond. The Universe needed not give me a reason. Furthermore, I was aware that my stepfather would have another chance to learn from killing my brother. He would not be tossed aside. He could not. God cannot get rid of Itself. This experience reinforced my gut feeling about death. There is none. Suffering is the worst thing in existence, not death.

From the moment I opened my eyelids in the morning, my concept of physical death had begun to change. Death was no longer anything to fear, but something to look forward to at the end of life. This feeling would take several months to solidify within my mind. As a result, I began to question everything. I mean literally everything. Images of my childhood best friend invaded my mind. I recalled the day I was curled up, my head down, against the brick wall. I recalled the ram coming to comfort me. I was leaving the contradictory state of existence that most of us live in and becoming more spiritually aware.

As a result, I had difficulty eating meat the ensuing days after the message. I had a hard time bringing it to my lips and when I did, I was no longer enjoying it. Goat meat used to be a favorite of mine. Even this was difficult. When I traveled to Togo two months later, this feeling grew even stronger.

In late May of 2009, I had a vision of something bad that would happen to one of my colleagues. I was absolutely convinced that this was a vision of the future and not a dream. In the vision, I was at my desk in the foreign language office in room 124. There were several of my colleagues there. Near the door was my boss's desk. One of my colleagues entered the room. It was February during the midterm examinations. Upon entering the room, the chair person asked her in a suspicious manner where she had been. Her facial depiction and tone was clear that she was micromanaging her. This was enough to set my colleague off. She lost her temper, and said in Spanish:

"What does this woman want?" she demanded, looking at one of the other colleagues to the right. Her face depicted frustration and anger. My boss's face was one of surprise. She held this look for what appeared to be a few eternal seconds. My colleague had not only pronounced those words, but with so much emotion and gestures as to render my supervisor silent and stupefied. My boss said something to her. I tried to intervene, but my colleague's frustration was too strong. I gazed upon the two of them in neutrality, trying to understand their feelings. That was how the vision ended.

Two days later, I called my colleague from the Duane Read drug store to relate the message. The interesting thing about all this was that at the time it appeared that she took the message seriously. However, after she became tenured, it seemed to me that she avoided any conversation about this topic. I also supposed that I was changing too fast for my colleagues and most people in general. I also suppose it is easier for them to offer me silence and then to speak about spiritual development. I know that my spiritual experiences will seem really fantastic for a lot of people, but what is bewildering to me is why some people absolutely refuse to even listen for even a brief second when they are the ones posing the questions themselves.

CHAPTER 8

AN ETERNAL PROMISE

After the last major battle with the inter-dimensional entities, I made a promise that I would take better care of myself no matter the circumstances or who is in my life. Hawa, who was a very important part of my life, would test the strength of this promise. By May of 2009, our relationship had become more serious. We were officially together. We communicated almost everyday via telephone, text, or e-mail. I kept her mostly informed about what was going in my life spiritually. At times, we seemed so far apart while at other times so close. Monday, May 11 was one those days that I was glad she was in my life. She sent me an e-mail that read:

Hello,

The more I read your letters, the more I want to be with you. These last days I felt as if you needed me as I needed you. I have never seen you, but I have the impression sometimes that we have known each other for years. I would like the time to be with you in these difficult moments in my life and yours as well. Every door to believe that certain people don't want us to be together, but let me reassure you that you find peace of heart, you live life as you understand it.

I saw mother (I will tell her to call you) and Kokovi. They went to the Bokono as planned. He recounted the story of your life. Your story with Eméfa and he also said that you continued, maintained contact with this girl and her mother despite the fact that she is married to a man who is living in Germany. These two want your downfall. Kokuvi's mother (she wants you to call her) has declared the facts and I thought that as the Bokono knows all and since he is in the process of working on this, I have give all power to my mother to stop all that they are preparing and all that is. Because Kokovi said that the Bokono said *that there are still things that connect Eméfa to you.* If this guy can help us, don't be against it, please!

As for me, I want to see you as planned in July, as long as none of these things hinder you. My mother will handle it and everything will be alright. Trust me as I have trusted you.

I am not sure if you are really coming, and that's why I have not said anything to anybody about your arrival to Togo: as long as I don't see you in Togo with my own eyes. I'll end up telling myself that you will never come and that it will be me to come if ever I want to be with you.

You are so afraid to come to Togo that I am also afraid.

Well I don't know what I am writing to you and I am not going to read it because I am very angry with the world and I believe I wrote what I think about your story, our story…

Why don't they want us to be together? I don't understand people. Really…We'll call each other?

Take care of yourself.

You're the only person left for me.

I embrace you.

Understand the signs of each situation.

This was the only letter that I felt Hawa's sincere attempt to express her love. I would never experience such brightness of her heart again. As I read her letter I pondered the message she wished to have me understand. She was not appreciative of much—especially me in her life. She did not share much with me. In fact, she was very secretive because she did not want the information "to be used against" her. It was very difficult to know her, and this aspect of her personality would give me pause and when I would go see her a few months later, I would have the answer.

Looking at this letter like the others, it was clear to me that she had difficulty expressing how she felt. This letter did not specifically say that she loved me. I remember telling her once on the phone that I loved her and that I was happy that she came into my life. I also told her that I was looking forward to getting to know her better. Dead silence! She did not say anything in response.

On May 13, 2009, I received an e-mail from Eméfa. It read:

Good evening dear brother,

How are you? As for me, nothing bad. I am actually with my husband in Germany. And you? I think you're mother is doing well. Please give her my hello. And Bella, is she doing well? I just started learning German. I will stop here.

Thank you

Your sister Eméfa.

I was in the library in the computer lab when I received the e-mail. I was sitting to the right corner of the room. I was totally dumbfounded. I shifted back in my seat with unease and surprise. Given that only a few minutes remained, I quickly began writing to Hawa about the e-mail that I had just received. I thought we were both on the same page when I wrote to her about Eméfa's e-mail. But, I was to discover that I was terribly wrong.

On Thursday, May 14, 2009, I wrote:

Hello,

Thank you for all that you're doing. I spoke to Koku yesterday at about 10:45 in the morning your time. He told me that I needed to do something in terms of my brother. That's ok. It is not really bad news. It's only one thing to resolve, which I did not know about. I thought that everything was taken care of, but I am very happy to have done the verification. It is about

19h45 (1h40 in Togo). It's really unbelievable what's happening, but now, the solutions seem clear to me. Do what you must do. There is no hurry. However, I don't have any money. I will have some next Friday. You know, there is something that told me to check my e-mail inbox before the library closed. Below is an e-mail that Eméfa just sent me today. I didn't answer. It has been two years since we haven't

That was how the e-mail ended. I did not have time to finish it, for I literally had only twenty something seconds before the time on the computer expired and would have lost all that I had written. Thus, I pressed the send button hoping that it would work.

In the evening of the ensuing day after work, I went to check my e-mail, hoping that Hawa had written to me. She did indeed receive the e-mail I sent her. However, her response was not what I was expecting. From the very first line, I felt her anger. This was surprising to me because I had explained to her how this girl had hurt me. I moved my chair closer to the computer monitor, riveted, and read her message in disbelief.

I am doing better,

It has been two years since you haven't done what? (with Eméfa). The message is incomplete. You still have some clarifications to do if you really want me to understand. Koku tells me that the guy wants to buy certain things to do the job correctly for you.

He said that the ceremony that you did in Kusuntu was not complete and that he can do it. As for me, I trust what he said because he revealed very old things about your story.

Was Koku able to tell you that your life was in danger? And that it is not coming from your girlfriend Eméfa, but from your grandmother, whom I do not know. I even forgot her name. She cursed you all, and swore that you will all die. And that she has something to do with your brother's death. Your stepfather was also under her control. This is all according to what he told us.

I am going to ask mom and Koku that they get the information from the guy about the total amount of money for all the things that we don't know or we don't know where to buy them.

I don't know if Koku has enough money, so I will let you know.

There is a saying here, you can't kill a snake without cutting off its head. So, I think that the situation with Savanna York and the others will have to wait and we have to first save your life. That's what I think.

Take care of yourself.
Later

Hawa

My eyes remained firmly glued upon the computer monitor, silent. After a moment, I began writing:

Good evening,

I came to the library yesterday very late at the last moment before it closed, because I don't have access to the internet at home. Therefore, I didn't have enough time to complete the message that I was writing you yesterday. First, I'm very tired. It has been thirty-two years since I have been fighting without knowing why. You have only learned a little bit of the story. It doesn't matter what my grandmother did. It's only the beginning. When you mentioned my grandmother, I assume you mean my father's mother, who didn't want my father to be with my mother. She tried several times to kill my mother when she was in the country and apparently when she left. In terms of what you just told me, I understand a lot more than you think. My girlfriend? I saw that girl only once in my life, a few minutes. Maybe you should do a bit more research yourself. It seems that you think that I'm hiding with the words you've written "your girlfriend." I'm tired and I would have preferred death, I was not permitted this. I could not kill myself because it's against the rules. And afterward, where would they have sent me (They--God). The last four months were worse, because sleep did not come. They attacked me in the middle of the night and I did not do anything, and now you're telling me that I must clarify certain things? That is why you wanted to help me? That's why you wanted Koku to go all alone? I sent you the last message because I was taken by surprise. I only had a few seconds before losing everything. The text messages that I've sent you say 2005. The last e-mail between her and I was in 2005. For the moment, maybe I don't see clearly, but there is only one thing that I want— I want to finish the job that God (i.e., I think) wanted and afterwards, I will be free...

The computer lab was about to close, so I gathered my belongings: my book bag and my USB flash drive and walked out of there. I was thinking about Hawa's e-mail. *Cutting off the head of a snake. Amano! Cursing everyone in the family. Killing the snake. So many deaths in the family.* As I passed the circulation desk on my right, an image of my little grandmother appeared vividly in my mind. None of what Hawa had said made any sense to me. How could my grandmother have influenced my stepfather to kill my brother while he was asleep? How in the world was this psychic or witch or whatever one wishes to call him in Kpalimé able to learn all this? Lisa and Linda didn't say anything about this to me. Did they know? I suspected that they knew. *How do I ascertain this without telling them?*

I reached my car. It was a little chilly outside, but it was not too bad. I drove off.

"This is incredible! Incroyable!" I said aloud in a combination of English and French.

"How could this be possible?"

I was alone in my car, so I felt alright about talking aloud to myself.

"That bitch! But why?" I was laughing now.

When I arrived home, my mind was still in a shudder. I climbed up the stairs in the backyard to reach the third floor. *Killing a snake? I don't want to kill any animal to save my life. Why does any animal have to die for me to live?*

"No!" I said loudly.

I was at the third floor door now. I entered the kitchen. *Ah! Warmth! Why would Eméfa and her husband be planning things against me?* I poured myself a glass of red wine, and sat down to reflect some more about my newly acquired information. I killed a snake once. It was pointless. Why does another conscious being have to take my place? Deep inside of the essence of me, I knew this was not the path to take. *No! Hawa cannot help me this way. It is not my path.* My mind was made up. That evening I was also slowly coming to the conclusion that I would later never kill or eat an animal or fish again. The reasons would be clear to me with the passing of time as my awakening became more and more complete. But, that was a triumphant night, for I was brave. I made a brave decision: to accept the possibility of death and not harm other sentient beings. I felt a bit light. Perchance that was my soul rejoicing inside.

I lifted up the glass of wine slowly. My immobile eyes were poised at the air, the void. *He said that the ceremony that...What ceremony?* When my mother buried my brother Essevi, she did not do any ceremony, unless this guy thinks that the actual burial is a ceremony. Who was this guy that Hawa, her mother and my aunt went to see? He was beginning to sound suspicious to me. According to Hawa's e-mail, he was surely going to ask for us to purchase some sort of livestock to sacrifice for the ritual to protect me spiritually. *This won't happen! Hawa was upset at me for writing about Eméfa. I understand that she was suspicious, but I did not know why. To me, the matter was pretty simple. I thought that she understood that there was nothing between Eméfa and I. I sent her the e-mail because I trusted her, and because I was shocked that Eméfa was still writing to me after I decided to permanently ignore her.*

On May 16, 2009, I wrote the following message to Hawa.

> After this message, I will stop bothering you. As this message concerns you both, I will write only one.

> First, I asked you to go do the verification for me in relation to the issue because I trusted you, apparently too much. You said that my grandmother was the person who was responsible for all the curses in the family. You didn't explain. Maybe, you will say that you didn't have the opportunity to do it…

I thought perhaps my last message was a bit harsh. So, I decided to write to her again, to soften things a up little.

> Hello,

> I am writing to find out how you are doing and to tell you how things are going here. I know that you've told me that you're angry with me, but I am not angry with you. I know that it is difficult to learn all that you just learned about me. None of us deserved what they tried to do to us. They failed because we do not have anything to do with this whole affair. All this was done before our birth. So, if even if you're angry with me, I will write you as much as I can to find out how you are and to tell you how things are here in my side of the world. I am also working hard. Given that money is difficult in this moment, I don't have the means to call or write you via text message right now. I wasn't even able to pay the

bills this month. Fortunately, e-mail is free. In any case, I will be able to work in a restaurant soon—as a second job. I think everything will be resolved in July.

Agbe

Hawa's response to my second to the last e-mail letter was very strong. She wrote:

After this letter, I will also stop annoying you. **You must understand that I don't understand anything anymore about your story,** and I am not going to ask someone else in your family or a psychic or a clairvoyant.
You must understand that I don't speak your language (Ewe) very well, and it is possible that I say silly things. I have never seen you and I thought for an instance that I could trust you and we could understand each other. But, I understand that you didn't see things like that you preferred keeping things to yourself. I didn't say that Eméfa is still your girlfriend; (the clairvoyant) assured us that she will continue to cause you harm and I don't know why you're insulting me about the opinion that I have about things. I am really sorry that we don't understand each other and it's not by chance that you have a lot of things in mind. I have no desire to annoy you. You deserve to be free and I deserve to understand things that are not clear to me. As you believe that I don't have the right to know, I'll leave you alone. I was wrong therefore to worry about you.

As I have told you, I have not told anyone about your arrival to Togo that you yourself don't trust anyone, and I too do not trust enough. You will do as you wish.

I only wanted to support you a little and to be with you during the times of tribulations, but you disappoint me with your assumptions. If you need to talk to someone, I am here. I await your email.

On June 16, 2009, I wrote to inform Hawa that I was planning to purchase a plane ticket. I had sent her two messages but did not hear back from her. The first read:

I am working fast or rather I have been helped (i.e., my brother and God). Things are moving a little now. At the end of this month, I will have the necessary amount to purchase a ticket. On Friday I will be paid. However, I can't call you yet. At the beginning, the trip seemed impossible, but now it is a reality, and I want to make sure that that stays the same. There is only about two weeks left at work. With the rest of the money that they will pay me, if I am calculating correctly, I only have about one hundred dollars left, an insufficient amount to eat and to travel. It is therefore essential that I be frugal before coming. I am leaving on Friday, July….in the morning at John F. Kennedy Airport. I will have a 12-hour stopover in Morocco. I will arrive at the capital at about midnight…I will do my best to have a little more money, but it seems impossible. However, the impossible has already happened with this flight. I want to tell you something important. After this summer there will be no more blockages, especially financially.

Now only the details of my arrival remains to be handled. I would like very much to stop at your place, but it will be too late. So, what would you like me to do? Would you like me to wait at someone's house for you? Oh, isn't it the weekend? In any case, you will tell me.

Agbessi.

On the 17th of July, 2009, I boarded the plane at John F. Kennedy Airport to begin my journey to Togo. I landed in Morocco in the afternoon for a stopover. I recalled my mother specifically telling me about asking the airline personnel for accommodation. I learned from her that if you have a stopover longer than a few hours, the airline is supposed to find you temporary accommodation. So, upon exiting the plane, I asked a young Moroccan guy about this in French. He told me where to go, in a mixture of English and French. Outside the airport doors, I mounted the bus. I sat near the front and thought: *I love flying.*

The bus rid was about forty-five minutes. It was great. I was able to see hotels, medium buildings, and undeveloped terrains. The buildings were definitely distinct. There were much red colors. The signs were in Arabic and French. Upon arriving at the hotel, I went to the reception ladies to inquire about my room. The lady toward the left side of the entrance gave me a key, informing me in French that I had a roommate. I took the elevator up either the second or the third floor. The room was nice and simple. It had an alarm clock. I selected the bed next to the window. I took off my shoes and prepared to take a shower. There was a knock on the door. I opened it. It was my roommate. He was black, but with fair skin. He was also skinny and tall. He seemed friendly and spoke English well. I asked him how he learned it, and he told me that he acquired it at school. His accent was good and it was easy to understand him. We conversed a bit. I recalled him telling me that he was from a country in West Africa, but I do not remember where. I went to the bathroom to take a shower. Afterwards, I set the alarm clock and went to bed. He also took a shower. I vaguely remembered the noise of his feet and the bathroom door, for I was somewhere between the state of sleep and awake.

The alarm clock rang, and I opened my eyes. I packed everything, and my roommate and I headed down in the elevator. The dining area was on the second floor. The place was bustling with tourists, mostly American and French. Brunch was being served. We sat at a table with a few American girls. One of them spoke about Togo. She said that she was there on a mission with her church. She posed me questions about the currency. As I was answering, a middle-aged Moroccan man arrived to take our orders. I ordered some chicken, some rice and a bottle of water.

Soon after the meal, we boarded the bus and went to the airport, the transition was smooth. I boarded the plane to Togo. I felt that the tone of the stewards was different. They spoke only French to us passengers. I found this very disappointing, for ten years thither, they had also addressed us in Ewe. Nevertheless, it was good to see some of the passengers conversing in Ewe.

I arrived late in the dusk of the night, at about two o'clock in the morning. The plane had been delayed for a good hour and a half. When we arrived, everybody was palpably tired. The soldiers appeared extremely fatigued as well. I walked toward the baggage claim area. I placed my luggage in the security check machine. It came out at the other end. I walked to retrieve it. A soldier or rather the security personal stopped me. He opened my suitcase. My bag had already gone through the scanning machine. Everything checked out, but he opened it anyway. It overflowed with bed sheets on top. He told me that I could not get through.

"Do you have something for me?" he said with calm and his eyes upon me.

"I don't have anything to give you. It was hard for me to come here. I literally only have a few dollars left in my bank account. I would give you something if I had the money, but I don't."

"Just a little."

"Next time, I'll give you something. My name is Agbe."

Still, he stood there refusing to let me pass.

"I don't have any money. It's a miracle I am on this continent."

"You can't pass until you give me something."

"You're kidding, right?" I said to him in my native language.

"Next time I'll give you something. This year was very difficult for me. My name is Epou, remember it."

Still, he was not satisfied. He observed me closely with his steady brown eyes. Suddenly, I was tired of his game.

"Do what you must, and may the Most High and Positive help you."

Upon pronouncing these words, he promptly stepped aside, apologizing to me profusely in Ewe. At first, I wondered why he moved out of my way so quickly, but later I figured it out. He had assumed that I would use Black Magic against him. My pronouncement was a verbal curse; one with such stern pronouncement that I believed it would produce an effect in his life so that he would not do it again.

In hindsight, I understand that the security personnel had misunderstood my intentions. This after all was a continent that was more open about the possibilities of existence than other continents. This guy, perhaps, feeling my resolve and sternness thought that I would do something against him. I don't know. Maybe he understood something else: spells. A curse or a spell can also be casted simply with the strength of the spoken word, without magic if the will is strong enough. Later, my older aunt would confirm this. It is possible to verbally curse someone without the use of Black Magic and have it come true. At that time, I had doubts about this, but now I consider it a possibility. Hence, the expression "Be careful what you say, it might come true."

The few people who were at the waiting area all seemed very tired. Koku was lying on a bench sleeping a few yards away to my right. A tall girl was sitting to the left side of the room. She smiled a little and her really white teeth showed. I recognized her immediately from the pictures. Her body sagged from fatigue. I walked toward her. She recognized me. Koku approached, and hugged me.

"Welcome," Hawa said in Ewe.

I was going to give her a hug, but she took my suitcase before I could. We went outside. I remembered the exact configuration of the parking lot. Fo Roger had brought me here about nine years ago. It looked the same. We walked to a taxi. We put the suitcases in the trunk. Koku had reserved the taxi for us. The driver came from Kpalimé. He paid more for it so that we would be alone in the car. Otherwise, the driver would have stuffed as many people in the car as possible. I was happy that I had a lot of room in the back of the cab. Hawa sat to my left. I asked Koku for his phone to call my mother.

"Nyaga, me va ro," I told my mother.

"Great! You got there safe."

"Yes, I am really tired."

That was pretty much it. Hawa and Koku laughed at my use of the word "old woman" to refer to my mother.

"Why do you call her that?" Hawa inquired.

"Because ever since the car accident, she seems ten years older."

I leaned my head back to sleep. I slept until I was woken up by voices. They were "police officers" in soldier uniforms who were carrying big riffles. They spoke to the driver for about a minute, and then they let us go. I went back to sleep, leaning my shoulder on Hawa.

"Do you mind?" I mumbled out.

"No."

Since she did not mind, I put my head on her lap in order to feel more comfortable. About twenty-five to half an hour later, I was awoken again. The car had hit a huge pot hole, and we came to a stop. The front left tire was damaged. The engine went out. The driver tried and tried to reignite it without success. He asked us to help. We came out to push the car while he was inside. It worked. The car started. Just as we were about to get back into the vehicle, it stopped again. We pushed it again. It started without a problem. This time it worked all the way to Kpalimé. However, we were stopped again by a final check point. The driver had to exit to plead his case to a soldier, who said that he could have given him a ticket for not having good tires. He explained his case, describing what transpired on the way there. We were lucky, for he let us go only after a few minutes of pleading.

When we arrived in Kpalimé, the driver dropped us off at my mother's house. Hawa went home by herself. I was impressed at the house. The last time I saw it, it was like a complete dump. There were wild weeds, stones and rocks all over. Now, it was basically finished. It had several rooms, toilets, and electricity. It was impressive. It took my mother ten years to build it. The front porch was elevated and was spacious. To the left corner when exiting were wooden seats and an arm chair. I was on the front door on the veranda. Massavi, Koku's girlfriend, came to greet us. Koku had explained that he asked her to delay returning to the capital a few weeks because I was coming. This was the first time meeting her. She was full of smiles and seemed amiable. Koku escorted me to my room, which was my mother's. It was the biggest room in the house, and it had a full bath. Straight ahead and to the far right was the huge bed. My mother had sent a king-size bed from the United States. The bed was directly in the wooden frame.

Morning found me more or less rested. Massavi asked me what I wanted for breakfast and lunch. I told her that I would only have lunch. Then accompanied by Koku, I headed toward my older aunt's house. I saw Améli, who definitely did not recognize me right away. She is my oldest aunt's first child. She had a silver oversized bowl on her head, which was full of water.

"Agbessi yé!" I said in Ewe, trying to refresh her memory of who I was. Suddenly, a smile sketched upon her face, illustrating that she had finally recognized me.

"Ah, Agbessi! Is that you?" she said in astonishment.

"We're headed to the house," Koku told her.

"We'll see you there," I said.

Koku and I entered the house. Navi Edi and her children were no longer residing there. Recall that they were living there in 2000 when I last visited. Améli and her children and her mother had taken over as was related by my mother. I walked in slowly, putting my right index finger to my lips, and indicating to Koku that I needed his cooperation and absolute silence. A few short steps ahead was a woman by an open fire, fanning a stationary clay stove. Sparks of fire flew in many directions. Her back was turned to us. Gingerly now, I tiptoed toward her.

"How are you?" I shouted in Ewe.

"Ohhh!" she said, frightened. She seemed a bit confused. Her eyes searched my face for clues of remembrance. A few seconds later came the scream.

"Ah! Agbessi. Is it really you?"

"When we came in 2000, I was told you were in the Côte d'Ivoire."

I smiled. An image of her walking with me in Kusuntu by Yawavino's house dawned upon my mind. I had not seen her since I left Togo when I was twelve years old.

"It's been a long time," I said.

"Twenty years," she said, being more precise.

Yes, it had been that long. Nevertheless, I recognized her right away. She hugged and kissed me on the cheek profusely. Koku smiled. Chairs were brought out for us. A little girl of about eight or nine years old was helping with the fire. She did not have a shirt on. I said hello and asked her name.

"Jacqueline," she said in a high-pitched whisper. She had been listening and was observing us at the corner of her eyes as we adults talked.

A man in his forties knocked on the gate. He entered the house after Amélino shouted that it was open.

"Fo Kossi!" my aunt said excitedly. He was a doctor who was helping her with her blood pressure and general health problems. She introduced me to him as her younger sister's oldest son from abroad. He seemed like a decent person. He started talking about how Africans in the U.S. were always talking about how difficult life is in America, and how if he had the chance he would go anyway. He posed a question.

"If life there is so bad then why do they keep going?"

I told him that he had a point there.

"You have to understand how the system works. The sooner you understand this, the better you are able to plan for the future. If I had really understood the system in 2005, I would not have bought the house in America. I am working two and a half jobs just to survive."

I stopped talking. I was wearing a short sleeve shirt. My heart area, biceps, and triceps began to palpitate, to tick heavily and visibly.

"Do you see it? It's moving about."

"What is it?" Amélino asked.

"I don't know. They put something in my body," I answered, not knowing who the "they" were.

A few days after I arrived, Hawa told me that she was going to the capital to take care of a few personal things. I asked to go with her because I wanted to meet her siblings. Hawa had told me that there was a chance they may not come before I leave the country. Koku, Hawa and I arrived at the capital about ten o'clock in the morning. Agusta only had three girls. One of them was studying at the university to become a lawyer. We were in the living room. It was very small. Koku and I sat on the couch. The sisters came out to introduce themselves. The two of them had a blackboard which was leaning against the right wall. They had words written in Ewe. I began reading them. Ninda seemed very warm, and was impressed with my regional Ewe accent.

"After all this time you still have the Kusuntu accent. It sounds better than yours Koku," she said.

"He retained the little he knew before he left," Koku responded with offense in his voice.

"What do you do?" the lawyer-sister asked.

"I teach foreign language. I'm doing French now."

They were both studying me carefully. This was understandable, for I was going to be their future brother in-law. Koku and I left together, leaving Hawa behind to handle her errands.

Hawa returned the next morning and I was happy to see her. We were sitting in the entry way, the veranda. I wanted to spend as much time with her as possible. I was making every effort to know her. I thought the best way was to share relative stories. So, I started with the accident she had in the capital a year ago.

"What happened with the motorcycle? You did not really tell me much about it."

"We were hit by a car," she said. And that was it.

"You know we don't have to talk about that. We can talk about something else, anything you want. I am just trying to know you better."

Still, she did not share much about herself. Instead, she asked me questions, and I did most of the talking.

I left feeling very frustrated. Even with my friends around the world I did not have to struggle to know them. Even those people I was not really close to shared a lot more about their personal life than Hawa did. I went to Amélino's house to vent my frustrations, but she was not home. Améli was.

"Da Améli, she doesn't talk."

"She does," she said with a frown.

"She told her mother about the fight you had."

My eyes opened vividly.

"She is telling her mother what's going on between you."

I was silent. I left to go out for a walk. I ended up at Koku's barbershop. Koku cut my hair and I went back to Amélino's house. Hawa was sitting near the left side of the tree, nearly at a straight angle from the main entrance to the house. She was talking to Amélino. The conversation ended with my entry. I went to kiss her as a way of greeting her. She accepted it expressionlessly. The conversation resumed, but was general. She spoke about the things she had to do for the day. Then she excused herself to leave. I was close to her and was walking away and was watching her with sad eyes.

"He wants a kiss," Amélino said softly to Hawa.

She stopped, hesitantly, walking toward me. She had a slight frown on her face and her body dragged. She kissed me slightly on the lips. After she left, Amélino told me the same thing Améli said: Hawa told her mother about your fight the night before. Amélino had told her that it was not a good idea to be telling her mother everything. I became more conscious about what I said to her at that point. I was also convinced that she was not sharing her personal stories with me not because she was a reticent person, but because she simply did not want to let me into her life.

One day I left Amélino's place and headed toward my mother's main house. I was approaching the water pump when I saw Hawano walking home. She asked how I was doing and motioned for me to walk with her as she took my left hand with her right hand. She inquired about how things were. I told her that I was making a major effort to know Hawa, but sometimes it was extremely difficult. She asked me what I meant, and I was very direct. Unlike her, I was never schooled in the art of making things seem sweeter than they actually are.

"She doesn't talk. She doesn't share. Well, that's not entirely true. She did tell me about her ex-boyfriend abroad."

"Boyfriend abroad?" she asked, pretending to be confused.

"She doesn't have a boyfriend abroad."

"Ex-boyfriend," I corrected.

Several thoughts entered my mind. One, Hawa had lied; and two her mother was merely feigning to be surprised that I knew, and would have preferred that I did not know. I accompanied her up to the gate of her house and left.

The following day I went to see Hawa, but she was not home. So, I found myself alone with Agusta. She was saying the most bizarre things.

"Hawa said she didn't have a boyfriend abroad," Agusta explained.

Hawa told her mother that she did not know what I was talking about and that the three of us could sit down and talk about it. She even told her that she could print out her e-mails. I was astonished.

"Really? I have the e-mail that she sent me. I didn't delete it. I wonder why she's lying?" I said, more talking to myself than Agusta.

In the evening I saw Hawa.

"You lied to your mother. Why?"

"I didn't want her to know."

That was her answer. I was not sure I believed her. There was one thing I was sure about—she had lied to her mother about never telling me that she had a boyfriend. I pressed her to explain further, but she became upset and gestured with her finger for me to stop talking about the issue. I stopped. I left shortly after that.

I went back to Hawa's house in the evening at about 6 p.m. We sat in the veranda, the porch, near the entrance to the living room. She was near the door, and I was sitting directly opposite her. She leaned forward a little.

"I have something to tell you." She spoke about her cousin who was a judge.

"We have a history together."

So vague were her words that I was not sure what to make of them. For a moment, I considered the nature of their relations. Were they intimate? I was sure they had been. But, why was she telling that now?

"*History together*, what does that mean?" I found myself asking.

"He is a friend of the family."

In hindsight, as I have said a thousand times, everything is clear. As I sat in that porch, I thought that Hawa was finally opening up, but not as fast as I would have liked. As I write now, images of us walking back from Kusuntu entered my mind. I do not recall how the conversation came about, but I do remember her telling me about a guy making a proposition to her. He had another woman already. He wanted her to be his second wife, to be in charge of the hotel business he was establishing. At times, Hawa was so vague that I had not made the connection.

A few minutes later, her ex-boyfriend judge knocked at the gate-door. He came into the house and greeted everybody. He sat directly across from me. I stared at him intensely. He mumbled when he spoke Ewe. He talked and talked, for what seemed an eternity. He just would not shut up. He was looking at me now.

"How many languages do you speak?"

"One," I answered trying to stop his nosy inquiry about my background.

"Wait! Where are you from?"

"Are you asking an Ewe kid where he is from?" I asked him in my native language with distaste.

I got up brusquely.

"I have to go. Amélino, let's go."

Amélino's face was full of questions. She seemed to be surprised that I wanted to leave so soon. She was conversing with Agusta.

"Leaving so soon?" Agusta inquired.

I nodded my head in confirmation.

"Hawa, go accompany him," her mother said.

I was already at the gate when Hawa pursued me. She was calling me. I ignored her. By the time she caught up, Amélino and I were already out of the gate.

"Wait Agbessi, don't be like that," she said tenderly.

"Be like what? You have not spoken to him yet about us, have you?"

"I have mentioned—"

"You need to stop beating around the bush and have a real conversation with him."

"I will," she said, trying to reassure me.

The next person whom I would catch in a lie was Hawa's own mother. Recall that Hawa had told me that she and her judge friend had "une histoire." This was how I caught Agusta in a lie. One afternoon, Agusta and I were talking in one of her empty rooms, the section of the house that was being constructed. I was a little concerned about the relationship between Hawa and the judge, so I asked her mother about it. She explained to me that he was "just" a friend, a friend of the family who had helped them with some court matters after her husband died.

"I didn't know that he is her cousin."

Apparently, he was not a direct cousin.

"There's nothing between him and Hawa."

"I don't know."

Later, I would put a few clues together and would understand that Agusta was definitely lying. Reader, recall that Hawa had said that her ex-boyfriend wanted to marry her and to put her in charge of a hotel business. As it turned out, Amélino knew this guy and he did have a hotel. Furthermore, I would learn that he had sworn to kill me using Black Magic if I should marry her.

A few days later, I learned about Hawa's bokono. Recall that bokonos can be considered either as healers, psychics, clairvoyants, bad sorcerers or witches. Neither of these descriptions were appropriate for this guy. He was a sorcerer and Hawa knew he was going to come to my house. She was calculating. I was in her porch, under the shade of the roof. We were alone. A hen and its chicks passed by the construction area by my right side, next to which there was a tall palm tree. Hawa was sitting directly across from me.

"His antenna told him that you were in the area."

It took a second or two to digest the words. This was apparently the same man to whom Hawa, her mother, and my aunt had gone to do the verification. *Why would this man's "antenna" be keeping a radar check on me?* It did not make any sense. I turned my eyes upon her.

"How's that? Please explain."

"He came by earlier today."

"Here?" I was surprised. I had never met the guy. *Why did he come by to see them? I sent them to do a verification, and now he was coming by? Strange! Very strange!* Hawa did not explain further.

The next day, the sorcerer whom Hawa called Papa came by Amélino's house. Hawa was there in her very bright white dress shirt; her white teeth shinning with a reserved-knowing smile. I did not know who he was, and Hawa kept quiet about him. He walked directly toward me, shaking my hand in what seemed to be between reverence and jealousy as he uttered something in Kablé. I did not speak the language. It was fast and unusual. This was not a greeting. I had never seen him before and had no idea who he was. His hand shake was firm, his facial expression devious. Amélino greeted him in Kablé. I had a confused look on my face, for I could not figure out what this guy was saying let alone the language. And why the firm, devious handshake from this punk?

After he had gone, I posed Amélino a few questions about what he was saying. She informed me that it was indeed "papa." I related the antenna story to Amélino, whose eyes opened vividly, suspecting that something was awry.

Despite these recent thought provoking experiences and doubts that I was having, I continued visiting Hawa. The next day, I found myself in their veranda. Hawa was sitting in the wooden chair directly facing me. She seemed focused, quiet. Her eyes were looking at my direction, but were not looking at me.

"Are you comfortable in that chair?"

The chair was wooden. The base was inserted into the upper erected part. It did not seem comfortable, yet she sat there completely composed. She put on my sunglasses.

It had rained just a while ago and she seemed cold. She was wearing a sweat shirt. The weather was perfect for me. I was living in the East Coast of the United States of America and was used to the bitter cold snow. She wanted to sit in the sun, on the green grass. She grabbed a chair from the living room and I took one as well.

"Do you like me?"

"Yes," she answered.

"And physically?"

"You're handsome," she said shyly.

"Really?" I asked, confused. I was not understanding her at all.

"Do you like me?" she asked in turn.

"Yes, that's why I wrote to you initially."

"But it's just a picture," she said with a slight smile.

Her words reached my inner light self. I could not talk.

"Is there something you came to do on this trip?"

I looked at her—awestruck, silent and pensive. The question and her facial expression said it all—she wanted to get married, but was not going to be direct about it. So, she posed the question indirectly, to suggest it to me. What came next was a confirmation of this for me.

"I will try to be more open, to talk," she said.

I was pleasantly surprised. My heart was at peace. She was warm and her body language depicted it. I left her that morning feeling reassured that the relationship would get better. I promised to return later in the evening. I was happy. I could not stop thinking about what she said earlier. *It is definitely true what people say about what's inside.* The fluid or intangible part of us, which is literally inside the physical body is what really matters. As I approached Amélino's house, I was absolutely sure that Hawa was right. I was now paying attention to the "what's inside." Physically, Hawa had met my expectations, but I was not pleased with the "inside" part. I knocked on the gate and went inside. I reported the good news to Amélino.

In the evening, I returned to Hawa's house. We ate dinner together on the veranda. After dinner, she brought out her laptop computer and put on some music. She was sitting to my right, and was doing something on the computer as I was captivated by one of the best music I had ever heard. The beat, the sound, and the words were literally music to my ears. My heart surrendered to the melody as I savoured it. A woman started with:

"Hier, c'est déjà passé. Je ne sais pas ce qui m'a pris cheri, mais j'ai compris que l'amour pardone. »

The next verse was in Ewe.

"Nye ma te nzro gbe wo o. Nye ma te nzro gbe wo o. Ma lo wo tso ma vo yi mavo me. »

Then a man with a deep voice took over in Ewe. The song ended, and I just had to ask.

"Hawa, could you please play it again?"

The second time I listened to the song, I considered its lyrics and thought about my own life. The woman was saying, baby, yesterday has already passed. She did not know what came over her, but she knew that love forgives. My favorite verse was the repetitive Ewe line:

"I can never forget, never forget what we once had; I will love you for an eternity, infinity."

The music ended and Hawa packed her things and we went to my mother's main house. On the way, without me posing any questions, Hawa begin talking.

"Sometimes you go through things and no one can ever understand."

That was a precursor to her motorcycle accident. We arrived and sat on the couch in the veranda and she continued relating the story. She told me about how her knees hurt terribly as she lied in the hospital bed. She complained about a few males making crude sexual comments about her. I did not say very much. There she was sharing a bit about her life story with me. Up to this point I did not know anything significant about the girl I was going to marry. I felt close to her. That was the type of love for which I longed. Unfortunately, that would be the first and last time I would ever feel so close to her.

The ensuing day found me at Navi Edi's house. She was in the kitchen cooking akple. I told her about some of the things that had happened to me such as being out of my body to defend myself. I sat there more or less observing the dirt floor as the sound of her cooking seeped through my mind. She was beating, pushing the akple against the side of the pan with a grey wooden cooking utensil.

"I don't know why I still have these palpitations in my body. It's not normal. It's really annoying. It keeps me up at night."

I was quiet now, still meditating the ground.

"There is someone, a priest. He sees things," she said.

"You mean he sees beyond the physical?"

"Yes. Maybe he can help."

"Yeah?"

"You'll have to go to church with me."

"He doesn't do anything bad? No killing of animals?"

"No, he is a priest."

"So, that doesn't mean anything. You never know what goes on behind closed doors."

"Just come with me. You'll see for yourself."

"Fine, when?"

"Tomorrow morning."

"What if Koku asks?"

"He doesn't need to know everything you're doing. Just tell him you're going to the farm with me. We're passing by it anyway."

I woke up very early in the morning at about half past four. Koku heard me and came out to the veranda.

"Where are you going?"

"To the farm with Navi Edi."

"Why?"

"What do you mean why?"

"Why didn't you tell me?"

"Do you have to know everything I do? The next time I go to the bathroom, I'll let you know."

I was laughing, but he was not.

"I'll see you later Koku."

Navi Edi and I took two taxi-motorcycle rides to get to the church. It was a make-shift church, a tent, which was to the left of an actual church. Perhaps they were making reparations to it. My aunt and I went inside. Though it was made out of bamboos, it had electricity inside. The ceiling light was on. We sat in the back in the right aisle and listened. A short man in front of the podium was reading a line out of the scriptures. He left the podium, walking slowly from one side of the stage to the next.

"Everything you need is right here in the Bible. Why go to a bokono?"

It was obvious to me that he was trying to convince the people to stop going to healers for their spiritual problems, but why was he so interested in doing this? *Who above him told him to do this?* I recalled the new Pope taking a trip to Africa a few years ago, and making the comment that Black Magic is one of the reasons why the people in Africa are suffering so much.

I turned to my aunt.

"Is that him?"

"Yes. We'll see him after church. He'll be calling people down for healing."

I turned my attention back to the priest.

"Some people are so proud that they don't want to go on their knees to pray."

Some of the women in the left side of the aisle shifted uneasily in their seats.

"Are you too good for God?"

I was definitely not seeing his point. When I was a child, I did what I was told. I went on my knees to pray. Many times after that during my life when I went to church, which was rare, I also kneeled before praying. In hindsight, I recalled how and what I was feeling each time: I did it because that was what was expected of me. I did not do it because I thought God really wanted me to do so. I did it because people like him demanded and sanctioned it. They were the authority on my spirituality. However, as I sat there for the first time in my life, I began to question such authority. The silent voice inside objected to the priest's words. God is great. This sexless Whole is so great that "Ello" does not need us to bow down. Here, I am using the Spanish subject pronoun which is a sexless because it is what fits best for me in describing God.

The priest's words went in one ear and exited the other without affecting me. His preaching went on for nearly another hour before he began calling us. He would see those people who came first, on the stage with his four assistants. One of them was a woman. She went into a room to the left, where candle flames were emanating. The priest was sitting on the left of the stage while his two other male assistants were sitting at the far right side. Next to the priest was a bench against the door. A woman sat there waiting for the priest to receive him. He called her a few minutes later. The healing session had begun. I could not understand what the older woman was saying to the priest, though I knew she was relating her problems to him.

I looked around, pondering all these people. I was convinced the majority, if not all of them believed in God, but yet they go to see bokonos and priests like these who pretend they cannot see or feel beyond the basic five-sense reality when in reality they can. These people like most part of the world understand that most of their questions are not being answered at church or by science, known as the formal educational system so they try different things. They even have this guy here who is pretending to be a mere priest,figure d it out already. Word of mouth spreads quickly, and that was why I myself was there.

"He sees things," my aunt had said. The priest was hiding and in a few minutes I would learn this. The woman left him and went to the two priest helpers. They spoke with her briefly and then they both began praying for her. One of them put his hands on her head. When they were done, she thanked him with a huge smile on her face and went back to her seat. The process went on and on, until finally it was clear that I might get a chance to see him. He too realized that there were too many people there, so he made an announcement. He said that he would see those who had come from far away first before the rest, and that he would be around the ensuing days for those who remained. I was thus moved to the front of the line. I sat on the bench. There was one person in front of me. I could see clearly now what the healers were doing. They were using the Bible to pray for people. To my right was a room I had mentioned earlier. It was full of burning candles. The other assistant, the woman, was in there. I spoke to the priest as I would speak to anyone else—direct and straightforward.

"I have been attacked in the middle of the night. I sought help with a few psychics. Most of the problems is almost gone, but I still have palpitations in my body. I've heard you are able to see things, is that true?"

He ignored my question. I looked at him, trying to figure out why. He had his head down, preparing questions.

"Are you in any sect?"

"Sect? What? For a long time, I thought that this life was all there was, with a few exceptions at times. No, I could not be in any sects, unless you consider science a sect," I smiled, making a joke.

"Do you drink or use drugs?"

"No, so what do you sense?"

"Go to the two men over there, and briefly explain to them what you've told me."

I explained to them about the curses and Lisa and Linda. One of the men raised his hand.

"Before you begin, I always have to ask: You don't do anything bad, do you?" I inquired.

"Our prayer will break off any bad connections between you and Lisa and anyone else. If the connection is good, then it will reinforce it."

I was satisfied with his answer. I had to ask because I had to protect my soul, even in church. The prayer did not last long. A few minutes later, I joined my aunt and we were on our way back home. We stopped in the open market. The market sold everything from fresh and, preserved food, clothes, you name it, and they had it. I bought my aunt some fish for having brought me to church. I was home by 11 a.m. Neither Hawa nor my oldest aunt ever knew that we had gone to church that day. Koku, however, felt betrayed and would not stop talking or asking questions. He even used the exact word "betrayed" to describe how he felt. This was too much I thought. Ever since I arrived, I had been treated like an infant. Everywhere I went, I had to be escorted or I had to report to them about where I was going and why. I was tired of it. Thus, I decided to make myself understood. I turned to him.

"I've travelled more than you have, and have experienced more danger than you know. Stop bothering me about my whereabouts."

A few days later, Hawa and I found ourselves temporarily alone in the right side of her house, the section in construction. It was completely empty except for the seats. The walls and floors were still being built. The entire left side of the house was being worked on. I had asked my aunt how Agusta was able to afford all these things given that she was not working, and she told me that she was living on what her husband left. This was also confirmed by Hawa. Her husband had died suddenly.

Hawa was attending to her cooking outside. Her two younger sisters were able to visit after all. They were in the kitchen preparing fufu. We were sitting in the open area by the second part of the house in construction. Hawa was fanning the metallic portable stove; the charcoals were beginning to take light. She fanned it below from where the ashes were falling. She was boiling yams. Agusta came to sit by us. We heard a child's cry coming from outside. Less than a minute later, a couple of children walked into the house. One of them was crying. She must have been about nine or ten years old. She held her hands to her forehead. Blood could be seen between her fingers. She was in pain. Apparently she was playing with the other children when she fell. Agusta took her into her arms to comfort her.

"Let's have a look?" she said softly, removing her hand away from the wound. It was huge, reddish, and covered a good portion of her forehead. The skin had pealed. I felt a shudder within my body. Agusta applied some alcohol to the edges of the wound, and the child cried some more. She was wearing a black hood sweater. After a while, the little girl stopped crying and took off to another section of the house. Less than a minute later, a young Ewe woman entered with a baby on her back. Hawa came out to greet them. All eyes were on the baby, who if I recalled correctly was about a year old. The mother took the sheet off and handed the baby to Agusta. While this was happening, Hawa told me that the girl was one of my cousins' wives. My eyes went up, and I looked at the woman closely. Hawa explained that she was part of her family. The woman was married to Mawuto. I knew Mawuto very well. We grew up together. He was very smart and worked hard in school. The woman stayed only for a few minutes. I went into one of the empty rooms in construction. Agusta came in and started asking questions about my life. Before I knew it, I was telling her too much. I spoke about leaving my body to defend myself. I was now complaining about how long it was going to take me to fix my credit score and build my life again. She was full of smiles and reassuring words.

"It will come."

"Ten years to get things back from scratch? That's too long," I said frowning.

"It'll pass by fast. Let's talk a little about you and Hawa. How do you see your lives together?"

"What do you mean?"

"What do you want? Do you want her to be here? To come with you?"

"Well, since she's going to be my wife, it's only natural that she's with me. Otherwise, what's the point?"

She smiled. I understood exactly what she was doing. She wanted to make it seem like it was utterly my decision. I was looking at her now, trying to anticipate her words while reflecting on what she had said.

"If you want, the kids could stay here. You could send money, and I will be happy to help."

She was serious.

"While I'm in America?" I said, my eyes brows rising in disagreement.

"No! Souls travel in groups. Children don't come into our lives by chance. Their souls choose to be with us, to be with their parents. My children will be with me."

"Isn't there anything we can do here to help you?" Agusta asked.

She was talking about using magic to help me fix things.

"I have it taken care of."

She smiled. Before I knew it, we were talking about what I had experienced the last few months. I was sad and I dared to share my sentiments with her.

"There were days that still leave me bewildered. This whole thing was very serious."

Agusta's confident smile still remained.

"I was even arguing with my father out of body."

Her countenance depicted surprise.

"You were fighting with your father outside of your body?" she asked.

"I don't understand why all this had to fall on me. I lost so much money…"

I was staring at the void.

"It will all come back," she said, smiling with the same confident and demeanor.

I frowned.

"It'll take anywhere from seven to ten years."

"It'll pass quickly. It's not a long time."

I was considering her last words, still upset. Why was she so confident, so happy?

She returned to talking about how we could raise our children. I was beginning to think that she was micromanaging our relationship, and I was not comfortable with this. Soon before I knew it, she was talking about "knocking on the first door." This was the first step in the engagement process. This was what I wanted—to be married, to have someone special, to have someone to really love, to be graced by her presence, embraced by her radiance, the invisible glow of her love, her aura. Someone to love—a very dear person had once said to me. *Wait!* The wizened voice inside of me cried out. I felt like I was being manipulated, but I kept quiet, trying to comprehend. I was not happy. Should not I have been in euphoria being engaged? The ticks in my body augmented and I felt melancholic.

Soon after leaving their house, I put pen to paper to set the limits of our social contract—a prenuptial agreement. The words came easily: they were straightforward and specific. I shared the letter with Hawa the next day. She was in my room, sitting across the table. A bland look sketched upon her face, and I wondered about what she was thinking.

"How do you feel about it?"

At first she was silent, but my eyes remained upon hers, obliging her to respond.

"Ça va," she said.

"Is there anything you want to change or add?"

"I'll think about it."

"Ok, let me know, so that I can draft the final copy."

The next time I was to my aunt's house, I received a message.

"Agusta came by twice," Amélino said.

"Twice?"

"She mentioned something about the letter, how it's not necessary. She was upset."

"Alright," I said thinking, "She's upset about preventing them from doing whatever they wanted with any future possible resources I might have."

"I'm glad you did it."

"I needed to know where their heart lies."

When I went to their house, Hawa was there. Her mother commenced the conversation smoothly, asking me how I was and other irrelevant or off topic things which allowed her to ease into the real conversation that she wanted to have with me.

"You wrote a letter?"

"A contract," I specified.

She explained to me how her middle daughter was studying law and much more.

"It's not necessary. All you need is a will. You can put all that in a will," she said with a tender, loving voice. Despite her attempts, I could not be dissuaded.

"I feel that it's important that we both express what we feel. For me, it's important that my wife and family respect the land we have. I absolutely do not want anyone selling any land that I might acquire in the future. Hawa and I have discussed it."

Agusta asked to see the letter, but something told me that her daughter had already shown it to her. She pretended to read the letter again.

"Yeah, all these concerns can go in a will. That's what my husband did."

Her husband died two years thither. It was clear to me that Agusta was frustrated. At that point, there was absolutely nothing she could have said that would have altered my mind. The atmosphere was a bit much for me. I needed to take my leave. I excused myself, citing an appointment with Amélino. I went home to sleep.

The next time Hawa and I would be together something simple, but wonderful would happen. I was sitting in the veranda of my mother's house while Hawa was in the kitchen cooking. I went inside to offer her help, but she refused. I returned to my seat. I took out the medicine that I bought the night before for my cold. I was about to take it when Koku came in. A guy, a stranger sneaked in with him. Koku had not closed the gate all the way upon entering. The guy was carrying bottles of herbal medicine. He approached me, then ceased walking all of a sudden. His mouth was agape and he was staring at me in astonishment. I waited in silence for him to close his mouth and to begin selling me the product. I figured that was the reason why he had sneaked into our house. After a few seconds, he was still staring at me. I knew he was not gay, for the manner in which he was staring was one of reverence and awe. No one had ever stared at me like that before. I wasted no time going straight to the point.

"What do you see?"

"I am clairvoyant," he said.

"What do you see in my soul?"

"Propre[5], très propre!" he answered in French. This translates into English as "clean, very clear" and "pure."

"How much for the medicine and what does it do?"

"It cures all types of sicknesses: foot ache, earaches, stomachaches, and headaches."

"How much?" I repeated.

"10,000 CFA!"

I sensed an exaggeration in his voice.

"No! Get out of here!" I said, smiling, "This was only 3,000 CFA."

I showed him the medication on the table.

"Agbessi!" Hawa called out from the kitchen.

I got up, hesitating, because I wanted to talk to the guy about what he was seeing beyond the physical. Hawa called me again. I left him, wondering if what he said were possible. I did not feel pure. I was still angry about what was done to me. How could my soul be pure? If it were so pure, then why did I suffer so much. Those were the thoughts that entered my mind as I went to Hawa. She did not really have anything important to say. I wish I had stayed to talk to the guy, to learn more about what he was seeing.

About twenty minutes later my older aunt, my grandmother, Améli, and Jacqueline showed up to our house unexpectedly. The food was ready. Hawa brought all of us a plate. I handled the water. Everyone was sitting at the veranda eating accept Hawa. She said that she was not hungry, but I sensed that she did not feel comfortable being among us. She stayed inside the house.

A few days passed. During this time, I thought about how things were progressing between Hawa and I. I was beginning to put aside the doubts that I was having about her being the one for me. I went to her house in mid-morning.

---

[5] Propre is French for *pure* or clean.

She was not home. Her mother was. She greeted me warmly and offered me a seat. Then began her inquiry about Hawa and I again.

"You've gotten to know her a little. Do you like her?"

"Yes, but it's difficult to know her. She doesn't talk. This bothers me a little."

A little? Was I insane? It bothered me tremendously, but for the most part I rationalized it away with *"We just need to get used to each other a little more."*

"That's how she is. Hawa has always been quiet. Ninda is more talkative. Some people talk more than others."

I thought Agusta's answer was an excuse. Nevertheless, I began making preparations "to knock on the first door." In the traditional Ewe culture and to some extent as it still is in most of Africa and other parts of the world, marrying a woman required many steps. The knock on the first door is the beginning of the engagement process. I spoke to Amélino about this. Amélino went to Agusta to inquire about the items that she as Hawa's parent was seeking for permission for her daughter's hand. The list was long, and rather expensive. I was thinking that even back in the days when the boy asked the girl's parents for permission to marry their daughter they could not have spent that much money. Agusta's figures were surpassing a thousand dollars and that was just the beginning. She went to speak to my aunt at one point. After she had gone and I went to visit, my aunt told me about the possible increase in price.

"What's the purpose of all these items? Weren't they basically to provide for the girl?"

My aunt answered affirmatively.

"Something feels wrong about this. They know that I don't have a lot of money at this time. I can't borrow anymore."

"Are you buying this girl?" fo Koffi asked with a joking smile.

I raised my head and eyes as if I just had an epiphany.

Fo Koffi was right. I needed reassurance that we would really work out our differences. I asked to talk to her at my mother's main house. We were in my bedroom, sitting to the left of the bed. I looked at her with calm eyes and she waited for me to speak.

"I feel like I've been trying to know you now for two years, but I can't get through. Is there a reason why you're not communicating with me?"

"You never let go of an issue. Didn't I tell you to drop it!" she commanded with her right index finger, and jolting eyes and eyebrows. She was sitting at the head of the bed to the left corner. I was sitting a few feet away from her.

"Are you going to do it again?" she inquired with a roaring, commanding tone.

I felt a wave of confused invisible negative energy. So close physically, yet so far apart we were.

"Is it clear?" she roared.

"Yes, I understand," I answered meekly. I was completely stunned. I wanted to tell her that *that* was not the way to talk to someone you're supposed to love, but no words exited my mouth. I had poked the lion. I had set her off.

"Is it clear?" she repeated, her eyebrows rose upward.

I was dead silent. The cat had bitten my tongue and I became mute. I felt disorientation within my physical body. I was next to her, but I was not. I had never raised my voice at her. Was this the kind of abuse I would expect if we were married? No! Slowly, the stupefaction wore off.

"If we were together forever, is this how you will treat me? This whole thing is not new. You started this crap two years ago on the phone. You snap for no reason. I don't need this. Remember what I have told you: No one and I mean no one will ever cause me to suffer again. Not even you."

She was silent. She moved to the right side of the bed and lied there for about two hours. I was in the bed with her, but we did not exchange a single word.

In the late afternoon of the next day, I saw Sitsofe, her best friend. He was near the main road. I wanted to talk to him because he had told me that they were very good friends and that she always told him everything. They went to high school together. I asked him about Hawa's sudden bursts of anger.

"That's how the whole family is. Very stubborn," he said. I am sure he regretted having shared this with me, for later he would fight to keep Hawa and I together.

About two weeks passed since we went to the priest. In addition to trying to work things out with Hawa, I was preoccupied with the palpitations. Whatever the priest and his colleagues did show no improvement in my body. I was still complaining profusely to my oldest aunt about the discomfort and my lack of sleep. I was still sensing dark entities' energy around me, especially when I was in bed. She said that we should go see someone in Lomé to inquire about it. I agreed. She instructed me to put some coins under my pillow and to pray over the things that I wanted to know when we arrived there.

Later in the afternoon, I found myself in Agusta's house. She invited me to another dinner on Saturday evening. I told her that I could not make it because I had to meet family members that I had not seen for a long time. She sketched a knowing smile, probably unaware that I was registering every detail to be analyzed later.

"Where are you going?"

"Lomé. I'll be back in the evening. But I don't think I'll be back in time for dinner. Are you doing anything special there?"

I thought I had just answered that question. I could tell right away that she was being suspicious. She was brighter than her daughter. Perhaps, better words to describe her were "more wicked."

"To see old friends," I said as final words, then turning my head away as a signal that the conversation was over.

Amélino and I took a taxi to the capital. Then, we walked to a gas station where we took a "moto-taxi." Each of us was on a separate motorcycle. The guy riding my motorcycle was complaining. I asked him to hold the motorcycle with both hands and he was upset. I put my left hand on his left shoulder and firmly held the back metal piece on the seat. When we arrived at our destination, he expressed his disapproval.

"You were moving around too much. Haven't you ever written on one of these before?" he asked rhetorically in Ewe.

"You weren't holding the motorcycle with both hands. I did not feel safe."

I paid him and he took off, his face still disturbed. Amélino was in front of us. She had miscalculated the bokono's house. The streets of Lomé are nothing like those of Kpalimé or Kusuntu. They were larger and noisily bustling with people. Such was the current atmosphere. To our left were the gutters. We walked alongside of them for about two blocks before finding the house on the left side. My aunt was exhausted, and her knees, particularly the left one was killing her. She had to stop several times to rest.

Upon arriving at the house, we came upon a boy, a teenager, exiting his bedroom or perhaps a shared room.

"Is the boss home?" Amélino asked.

"He's not here now," he replied.

The house was a typical Togolese home. It had an empty center. Amélino walked inside. I followed. The boy led us to the left center of the house. He offered us a seat on a bench.

"When do you expect him back?"

"Maybe in forty-five minutes or an hour."

Amélino decided we should wait. She was sitting to the left of me. She made a phone call to Ameli. As she spoke I looked to my right. There was a little brick room with an opening in the center. A see-through curtain covered the entrance. I focused my gaze, but could see nothing but rocks. *Wait!* There above was a piece of wood. There was nothing moving inside. Months later after having met with a few more "healers" I would understand that this particular "voodoo" was an entity just like me and you Reader. This was his home, in that room. It could see us but we could not see It. This is because it resides in the in-between worlds. In other words, It is multidimensional. Those of us who are in-tuned with the "radio" frequency could tap into this so-called invisible world. It's all in the mind of the observer. By this, I mean accessing the frequency range was individual. The mind of each individual is like that of a computer, but much more advanced. One could give one's computer new information or change the program a little to alter such frequency range.

A tall, relatively young man, early 40s, head shaven and bald, entered the scene. My aunt greeted him jovially. They definitely knew each other.

There was a bench to the right of the entrance of the curtain when facing the door. The tall man sat down closest to the door. A hunched back old man sat next to him. My body was palpitating uncontrollably. I observed the bald, clean-shaven man. He seemed to be in an extremely good mood. I was absolutely impressed. He was so cool. It seemed that nothing could ever disturb him. He smiled. Amélino greeted him. They spoke for, recalling the past and inquiring about each other's health.

The man called out to the boy, whose name I have forgotten. He told him to set things up. He laid the hand woven thin mat-like bed on the dirt ground. He brought out different sorts of beads. He put them on the ground around him and sat down facing the bald man. The boy was directly facing the entrance of the being they worshiped. He had a necklace-like beads, which he was swinging to and fro his body. The inquiry had begun. The tall man asked my name and my aunt answered "Kossi." I had told my aunt not to tell them my real name. Besides, I was of the conviction that if they were any good, then they could read my aura and soul without much prompting.

The bald man asked for the pillow money and I handed the boy the coins. He put them on the ground. He asked me to tell the voodoo what I wanted to know. A thought occurred to me. He was referring to the being as voodoo. My aunt had assured me that it was not a bad thing, but she never called it "voodoo." However, here was one of the men who was serving it calling it this. I was not doing anything wrong I told myself. My distrust of nearly all creatures in the Universe was growing. This *being* whose presence I was in could not be completely trusted. I still had not fully digested the knowledge of the messages that I had received the previous months. However, I was reluctant to pose the voodoo my questions. Quick, brief images of the message of the nature of eternity flashed upon my mind. Then my mother's words "If they do something other than what you asked for, it will come back to them" resounded in my mind. I was alright to proceed.

"Is Hawa my soul mate?"

The bald man was laughing at the question. He was really enjoying himself. He was not really interested in what I wanted to know. He was having a good, almost child-like, jovial time.

"There was once a prince who asked his father for many things. He asked for a horse. His father gave it to him… Everytime he asked for something he received it…"

I turned to Amélino.

"I am not materialistic. I dress simply and–"

"Let me hear it," she said, very focused upon what the man was saying.

"The more the prince got, the more he wanted," he said, demonstrating by placing his hand above his head. His face and his shaved head shone brightly. He had very white teeth.

"He wants great things," he said, his face becoming more serious.

I was not sure what the man was talking about precisely, but months later, I would completely understand it without a shadow of a doubt. He was not talking about materialistic things. He was talking about my spiritual aspirations to reach the rest of the Purest, most positive part of Infinity. Not having understood this then, I thought I was being mocked, so I brought the session into focus.

"So, you're saying that Hawa is not my soul mate."

"She's definitely not your soul mate. She's trying to be the boss of you."

This was a confirmation of what my instincts and the last several weeks were telling me.

"Do you have any other questions?"

"Where is my soul mate? What continent is she on?"

There was no answer. Suddenly, I threw out a question that came out of nowhere.

"Did Hawa and her mother do anything?"

There was a pause, then I received a "no" answer.

I was not convinced that they were correct. I turned to Amélino. She knew what I was thinking and nodded in agreement.

"There is another girl, I just met in Kusuntu."

"That would be even worse," he quickly answered, "She'll leave you after you marry her."

Yeah, no doubt she probably just wanted to go to America.

"So," I said sadly, "I am back to where I started. I have no one."

"There is travelling in the near future. She goes abroad with you."

Hawa was going to America with me? That possibly was dimming. Nevertheless, the man was insistent.

"He says this one will work. She won't change right away. This one will work!"

"How long before she change? How long before she stops being angry all the time? Five years? Ten?" I said rhetorically.

"She won't change right away," the man repeated.

These were banal answers. I was not getting anywhere with them.

"Etro says that you need to pay attention to what you're eating. No cassavas, yams, or okras. Do not eat these things for fifteen days. The stomach problem you're having is due to these things."

I had not in any way hinted or mentioned a thing about my stomach problem. I was taking notes in my notebook.

"Focus on one job," the man said.

"What do you mean?"

"One job. Too many jobs!"

I understand this right away. As you know by now Reader, I was working like crazy. I was working several jobs to maintain my house, to pay for my student loans, car insurance, etc.

I was not exactly comfortable with the next thing he said. He said that my ancestors were being neglected. That is, they were not being prayed to or worshiped. There are many forms of worship. They include constantly thinking about something, going to church, a fixation in scientific theories or so-called truths, simple verbal prayers, verbal prayer with hard liquor, and animal sacrifice. I had witnessed the outcome of the latter as a child with my friend the ram. The bald man repeated the word "neglected." He even went as far as to claim that that was part of the reason why the negative things that were transpiring were happening. My stomach knotted and fear overtook me. I was visibility uncomfortable. I stared at him blankly as my aunt spoke to him about what to do. I was really uneasy with his pronouncements because I was the oldest male to carry the last name Epou. The responsibility had to fall on me. I was trying to give up eating meat, and now they wanted me to kill for my ancestors.

No! my inner voice cried out. *Ah! I don't even have enough money to do these things before leaving for America.* This was great, for it would give me time for the visions and messages to solidify, to trust my inner light and to be the master of my own decisions. *No!* I would pray to my ancestors with hard liquor, but I will never sacrifice any higher conscious beings for any being in any consciousness. *Not now, not ever!* The inner voice screamed out gain: *Beyond time, space, and to the stillness of all things, I am important and cannot be replaced. There is no hierarchy between the Most High and its Pieces. Love! Respect! No fear!*

The man had asked another man to go out to purchase hard liquor for the next session of the inquiry. This was our break time. My eyes followed the bald man.

"You did not give me concrete answers to some of the questions I posed you. Why should we pray or worship these spirits?"

"Because they protect us."

"But they are not greater than us. How are you able to hear what It is saying?"

He smiled.

"Can you please concretely describe what the soul is to me?" I was testing him.

He was smiling again, but had no answers.

"Have you ever seen your soul? The beauty of yourself beyond the physical?"

He was considering my questions. I launched some more.

"Do you know that you are literally a part of God? When I was out my body I—"

He cut me off in surprise, in awe.

"You have been out of your body?"

Amélino intervened.

"He questions everything. You will be talking to him for hours."

The bald man was excited, smiling and laughing.

"I like it. He wants every little point clarified. This is good."

He was obviously having fun, but my questions were not being answered.

"I came out of my body to defend myself. I had to. I was under attack. I still have these ticks all over my body." The bald man's brother had entered the scene a few minutes before and had been listening.

"Maybe it's some sort of annoyance."

It was clear to me that he did not know, but he claimed that the voodoo could help.

"How much?"

"100,000 CFA in America, and 30 000 CFA here."

These were hefty prices.

"Why so much for America?"

"The voodoo would have to travel all the way to America to help."

I was listening, but not really buying what he was saying. Isn't the whole concept of traveling different in the none-physical planes of consciousness? When the dark entity fled from my bed that night he was fast like the speed of light. The thought occurred to me that he and his brother were also in this for making a bit of money though they were helping people. His older brother chewed a lot of cola nuts. His teeth were not in the best of conditions like his younger brother. In fact, he was chewing cola nuts as he spoke to me. He seemed very nice.

"I am just here for help. The ticking in my body is too much. I don't want anybody killing anything or I can't go through with it."

He stared at me.

"What's your religion?"

"Catholic," I answered somewhat hesitantly. I really wanted to tell him that I had no religion, but I did not want to complicate things. In any case, I sensed he had a point to make.

"We do the same thing the Bible teaches..."

He did not need to convince me of anything. I was not on any particular side. For me, the most important thing was to respect the purest part of my soul.

Amélino motioned for me to follow her. She wanted some fresh air. We went outside. I continued my inquiries with her.

"Why do we, the world, worship? I don't get it? Why even go to church or have voodoos or whatever you want to call them?"

"We pray to our ancestors—"

"To help us. But, but if they were pure of heart, they would help anyway."

"We have to ask." Amélino and I were outside now.

"Understood! We go to church to pray. Words are important; for they reach the none-physical worlds. But yet, my questions are still without answers. Our ancestors, don't they belong to the Whole?"

"To the Whole?" Amélino asked a bit confused.

"To God," I clarified, "Why do we have these traditions throughout the centuries? I don't understand the worship, the killing of animals for these ancestors? These things take place all over the world. Why?"

"Our ancestors taught us."

"Where did they come from? If they are our ancestors, then they must belong to the Whole. How did they know to teach these forms of worships?"

"Maybe they came from outer space," I said, amusing myself as I laughed.

"The earth is alive!" my aunt said in all seriousness.

I definitely did not understand.

"Alive?"

"How?"

"You can pray to anything and overtime it can become alive. Let me tell you a story. There were a couple of young people out in the field having fun, calling spirits. One of them was praying to a stick. He prayed to it over and over again, asking for it to come alive, to do things for him…He became insane."

"What?" I asked incredulously.

"Young people now are practicing magic without understanding it. The stick, or rock can become your God if you pray to it enough."

"How?"

At the time, I did not understand, but I would a year later when I had the time to digest the information and my visions and out-of-body experiences as well as my Native American experience. Inside each person is a piece of God. A person who constantly prays to an object or anything that is either tangible or intangible is asking for something. This is a form of focusing one's energy on a desire. Sooner or later the different beings in the universe will hear you. An entity from another dimension may answer your request, though you may not be able to see it. What is happening is that you have invoked or given that entity permission to leave its dimension and to enter yours. If it is not possible to enter yours, then It can reside very close to your dimension.

We were sitting on a bench outside. The street was bustling with people and activities. There were people selling cooked food and all sorts of things in the street. Motorcycle taxis hunted for customers. One of them rode past me, and I turned to capture the image and the sound of the motor.

After the break, we were ready for the libation. The bald man poured some hard liquor into a very small glass, and prayed to his entity. First, he took a sip of it. Then with Amélino's help, he called my ancestors' names. Then he began calling my father and grandfather. However, he suddenly stopped, reflecting out loud:

"No, we can't call their names. They did not die peacefully."

Amélino joined in. Her voice was stern, grave, and her facial expression matched it.

"Let anyone or anything that seeks to harm your son Kossi, be pushed back. Let the bad turn on themselves..."

The man poured some liquor on the ground each time Amélino finished a major thought. So far, everything she had said was standard. She was asking my ancestors to protect me and the family, for my stolen car to be returned to me. What she said next, however, was totally inspiring.

"Let no one cheat by causing another harm. If I, Yawavi seeks anyone's harm, then may God All Mighty bring suffering upon me."

I was so elated that I joined the prayer. I took a sip of the hard liquor.

"The same goes for me. No intermediaries, no voodoos or entities! If I should ever be tempted to cause someone harm, may the pain be great upon me, so that I may learn quickly. No exception! I must learn, to elevate the purity within. Thank you father and brother for having been by my side all these years even when I was not aware of your presence."

I poured the liquor down the ground, wondering where the passion came from. We were finished. Now we could relax a little. The old man, who was sitting on the bench observing, was in good spirits.

"You should vary your accent a little," he said to me.

"But, I like my Kusuntu/Kpalime accent," I protested softly.

He seemed full of life. Before I knew it, he was talking about other things.

"How's life in America?"

"It's alright."

"Much has changed here in Lomé. Everybody keeps to himself nowadays. We used to go to each other for problems, but now everything is fast-paced."

"Sounds like America," I answered, "Would you say that things in Togo are changing for the worse?"

His answer was an immediate yes. However, he did not seem to despair. I observed him. Maybe he knew that his time in this consciousness was drawing close to an end, and perhaps he was secretly happy inside. That was a fleeting thought that I had, which was accompanied by an image of my soul watching its body on that auspicious night.

The ensuing day, something wonderful was beginning to happen to me. My mind was finally paying more attention to Its Light—my Light Self. One such manifestation of this was my determination to never eat meat again. In October of 2009, I also gave up fish. Oh my God, I used to love eating salmon. I ate it with red wine. A great weekend was when I prepared smoked or oven roasted salmon with teriyaki sauce. But now, as I write, I feel the need to stop describing such experiences, for the pleasure I used to feel now renders me weak in the stomach. My family was shocked to learn this. My brother was especially surprised. The look on his face was priceless.

"I can't believe you don't eat salmon anymore."

Like him and a lot of people who do not understand, my mind was less in control of my physical body. My soul was more in the driver's seat. I was aware that everything was alive. Though these feelings manifested in me right away, it took me time to digest the divine messages I received. As I have mentioned before if I had to do it over again with this great feeling, I would not have killed the cobra. That was the power of the message that I had that auspicious night. I am eternal and I cannot die. There are days when tears rush to my eyes, and I cry out of joy. I cry, for I know that the freedom that each soul possesses is immense. It is clear to me that salvation was a personal thing, only each soul can reach it through the acceptance of the purest part of him or herself. Furthermore, I feel a need to capitulate, surrender to my Lightest Self, the Universe, for I want to love this part of myself more. Love is an actual energy.

Presently, I was ready to exit the big red dirt road. As I turned, a wave of clarity as if it were an invisible energy struck me: *There is no god*[6]. This had happened just as I was considering the worship ceremony I was going to do for my ancestor before leaving for America. The message was so strong that I stopped short in the road.

Another thought wave ensued: ***There is no master. There is no hierarchy, no one or being or entity to be worshiped.*** Images of my childhood friend sketched upon my mind. I saw myself by the king's house. I had just returned from school. All around was blood. Assassinated animals abound on the ground with their throats cut open.

---

[6] This is not to be taken literally. It just means that there is no "superiority."

Among them was my friend. I bowed my head in sadness, resolved to sadness.

I brought myself back to the present, with a slight shake of the head. NO! *Thank you dear, dear old friend. I love you! There are no accidents in this world. Thank you!*

My eyes were slightly watery. *No one will sacrifice any animal in my name even if it means my death! I am more important than my culture! Animals are more important than false cultural belief systems!*

Two days after my aunt and I returned from the capital, I drafted the final version of the prenuptial agreement. Later, Hawa and I went to see a lawyer about the contract. It was walking distance, so we went by foot. The first office we entered was not the right one. The guy inside directed us to the right office. He was a few inches shorter than I was and was Kablé. His French was very good. He spoke with the jargon of a man who was well versed in the law. He explained to us how marriage works in Togo. Currently there are different types of marriage contracts. The most intriguing[7] part of this for me was the open marriage. This was where the partners elect to see whomever they want other than their spouse. In addition, the couple could elect to have a common possession or usage of their properties, or to keep their properties separate. Fortunately for me, the person who would take the document to Lomé was out of town and was not going to return for a good week.

"Merci monsieur!" I said, smiling and shaking his right hand.

Hawa and I left, and went to a very tall and big church. There was not anybody there. We sat on the pews and

---

[7] "Intriguing" here means "interesting or new." It does not mean that I agree with it.

talked. I was doing most of the talking. I asked her what she thought about all this. Her answer was an annoyed look on her face. I purposely waited in silence for her to speak. Still, I received no answers. At that moment, I had decided to break off the engagement.

"I think we need more time to get to know each other. Let's see how things go in 2010."

She was checking her phone now, looking at it with a detached, preoccupied concentration.

"You have to make the phone call?"

"Yes," she answered in a low voice. She had mentioned that she needed to make a phone call when we left the lawyer's office. She told me that she would see me later and I said alright. She was gone. I walked for a good fifteen minutes, heading to Amélino's place. Let me tell you Reader, those were some sweet moments. I felt as if a huge weight had been lifted from me. I felt light inside.

Amélino greeted me with a smile and:

"Hello big brother. How is it going?"

"I am doing very well. It's done."

"What's done?"

"I broke off the engagement thing. We'll see how things go."

"Agusta came by. She wants to see you."

Even before she could finish her sentence, I knew what Agusta wanted.

"Is she home now?"

"Yes," she answered.

Koku was next to me. I was walking away when he said that he would go with me. He was a little unnerved.

"What are you going to tell her?"

"What do you mean? Are you serious Koku?"

The look on his face implied that he wanted me to take the indirect approach, to choose my words carefully as not to offend Agusta.

"I get embarrassed easily."

"What do you have to be embarrassed about?" I said, trying to reassure him that we were in the right. "Here's a woman who is not taking her daughter's rage problem seriously. What I am sensing from her is sneakiness. There is no reason to be embarrassed."

"I am the one who is going to be here. You're going back to Yovode."

Yovode is where white people live.

Hawano welcomed us into her house with a smile. We were escorted to the living room. She sat in the sofa to the right and turned the television off with the remote control.

"How are you guys doing?"

"Good," I said, "How's Hawa? Where is she?"

She answered that she was in her room, and was very upset.

"Could you please explain to me why you called it off?"

"Well, I think we need to get to know each other," I said remembering Koku's facial expression as we walked to their house.

"But why?" she asked.

"You mean Hawa didn't tell you why?"

I knew she was playing the reserved wise "African" who did not volunteer information until the other person says what he or she knows. I observed her with my eyes and waited for her to answer.

"She did, but I wanted to hear it from you."

"Well, that's pretty much it."

I sensed Koku's discomfort and I was not happy about what he said next.

"Agbessi, that's the only reason you want to wait?"

"I haven't slept well in the last few days. Hawa gets angry easily. We have been fighting nearly the whole time I have been here. I am not sleeping well," I reiterated. The look of apathy that Hawano sent out would forever be etched in my mind. It was a frown and it transmitted so much meaning. I felt like she was blotting out my feelings, as if they were not important, perhaps because I am a guy, a man, who was supposed to be stoic, not sensible. She was being sexist.

"He has been very depressed, refusing to eat," Koku said, supporting me.

"Yeah, this has not been a good experience for me."

Hawano was not going to give up easily. She would employ several strategies—verbal and even a convocation of the chief of the village of Kusuntu. The verbal effort was personal, but futile in convincing me to change my mind. Nevertheless, it was good to hear about her marital hardship. She let out a mixture of a laughter and a giggle.

"There were times when…and I were at it. I left. I was pregnant with…"

I do not recall her husband's name. She was pregnant with one of her three girls. She had a fight with her polygamist husband and she left. He came to get her back, but she refused at first.

"You're going to have your difficult times, but you'll take care of each other."

She checked my face to see if the message was registering. Though I was quiet and interested in what she was saying, I did not really know what to say to her sad story.

"He died in my arms."

Now I definitely knew I wanted to leave.

"How long ago did he die?"

"Two years ago."

I waited for a few moments to pass so that it would not appear I was being rude, then I excused myself. Before we left, Agusta invited us to lunch the ensuing day. Deep inside of me, I did not really want to eat her food. I was a little paranoid, and thoughts of her putting something in my food came to mind.

While we ate that early afternoon, Agusta invited herself to my mother's house with:

"You haven't invited me to your house yet."

"It's not really mine, but alright. When do you want to come by?"

"In the afternoon."

We all ate peacefully, including Hawa. After lunch, Hawa and I once again found ourselves in the room that was being constructed. I asked her if she wanted her to accompany me to the airport.

"You don't want to go?" I asked.

"I'll think about it."

Agusta came by my mother's house and I gave her a tour. She seemed to like the house. After the tour we spoke on the front porch. She inquired about me returning in 2010 to marry Hawa. I did not give her a definite answer. I walked her out a while later. The conversation outside remained the same. She wanted to know what I was thinking about in 2010. Her every effort to inquire about my intentions were shutdown. She even gave me advice about how to treat a difficult partner in a relationship—her own daughter.

"You should find the appropriate time to talk to her, when she's not upset."

When we reached the main quasi-red main road, she said something that heightened the feeling that I had been set up since 2007.

"If she had been nicer, she would have had you."

I did not say anything to her, but her words and the smirk of a smile upon her face would sometimes come to me so clearly later on. Soon after passing her younger sister's tailor shop, I stopped at the second main road.

"She's a young lady. We'll work on what we've talked about. She'll wait for you next year."

"Bye-bye."

And with that I would never say hello to her again. I turned around to walk back to the house. I wondered if it is the responsibility of the other partner to tolerate the other's abuse, waiting for his partner to change. *Why should the responsibility fall upon the good-hearted partner?*

Upon returning home, I would have a laugh with Masavi.

"Guess what she said?" I asked, smiling.

"What did she say?"

"She said that if Hawa had been nicer, she would have had me."

Masavi laughed and considered the statement for a moment.

"That would have been better. I would prefer someone whose nicer," she said.

I appreciated her laugh. I was laughing too. Later, I told Amélino about it and we had more laughs.

"You got them," she said.

"Yeah, don't you think? They think they're so smart. Listen, I think I deserve a peaceful nap." I took one in her bedroom.

That same evening, I went out to the street to sell cooked food with Améli and Amélino. We sat at a bench. The street was lit by food stations; otherwise it was dark in the center of the long stretched paved cement road. A dog wandered near us. It stared at me. It seemed hungry, so I threw some "coon" to him. He took heavy bits at it and disappeared into the back, into the darkness. A man who was not "well in the head" came by to buy some food. After eating, he refused to pay and pulled out a knife. I watched him closely, my eyes surveying him. He was threatening the people who were there. He turned to me, menacingly showing me the knife. I offered him my silence. I was thinking about how to get the knife from him without hurting him. I thought that he might have to feel a bit of pain. As I stood in front of my aunt pondering this out, his brother, his keeper, entered the scene. They wrestled on the ground briefly. His brother punched him a couple of times with his right hand. Then he brought him to his feet.

"You were supposed to take your medication and to stay inside," he scolded him.

The *sick* brother was whimpering and indicating that he did not want to be beaten anymore. They both finally calmed down. The sane brother took the other home on a motorcycle.

Words definitely travel fast. In the evening of the next day, I learned that the engagement break had leaked out. One of the county chiefs told one of her family members about it. The woman came to see me in the evening. She had a proposition for me: to marry her sister, who supposedly was kindhearted, loyal, and did not get angry easily. Apparently, the town people knew Agusta's family pretty well. I told her that I would go by to see her, but something impeded me. In the meantime, the tall, slim girl from Kusuntu came by a few times to see if I were home. I did not bother with any of them. I was on the right path to keeping my eternal promise. Hawa and the other two girls would have caused me more suffering. I would go back to America and think things over.

CHAPTER 9

IN SEARCH OF A SPIRITUAL CURE

About two hours after returning to New York, I checked my voice mail and discovered that Lisa had left me a message. My telephone had been inactive the whole summer because I did not have a roamer, and therefore could not use it around the world. I never told Lisa the day I was leaving or coming back from Togo. Merely an hour later, the phone rang. I was in my brother's apartment in New York City. I turned around in the high chair table and frowned.

"Hello sweet heart," the voice said.

"Lisa," I said calmly, and firmly, "I know everything. I need the car back."

"Why didn't you tell me about your intentions this summer? You went soul searching."

"The girl, her family is wicked, and you didn't say anything to me about this."

"What was that stuff you were praying to? What kind of religion was that?" she asked in astonishment.

She was talking about our visit to Lomé, where I learned that Hawa was trying to be the boss of me.

"You should know. You practice Black Magic. You're lucky I did not do anything to you."

There was panic and fear in her voice.

"You could never. Your heart is pure—" she said.

"Enough of your crap! Are you telling me what I am capable of? Are you me?" I was frowning. "Now my soul is

281

bright?" I said sarcastically, "That was not what you had been telling me all these months. The car! Lisa, I need it back ASAP."

"The job is not done. I have some more mileage to do. What's up with all this business about the mileage? It never made any sense."

"I just need another week."

"You have until Friday, then we are going to have some serious problems."

"We don't want any problems. I'll do as you say."

"Friday, Lisa."

A few days later, I received two phone calls in the middle of the night at about 2 a.m. I was enjoying my sleep so I ignored them. In the morning, I listened to the messages. Lisa was begging me not to go to the authorities. I did not really question how she knew I would soon be going to the police. I was there when the police officer called her. She pretended to be someone else and said that she would give the message to Lisa. I asked the officer to file a police report, but he said that there was not anything that he could do until Lisa could be reached.

I returned several hours later only to come across another police officer whose first instinct was to accuse me indirectly of lying in so many words. I was explaining myself to him like a child who could not understand much of anything an adult was saying because he was not very smart. I knew he was doing it on purpose. I was tired.

"Listen, I have all the information on the car. Please look it up and give her a call."

He finally understood that I was not going anywhere until he did something. He took my license and gave it to his partner. His partner put the information about the Cadillac on his computer. I explained the situation to him, minus the psychic part. He wished me luck and told me that I had to lie before I could get the car back. He did not use the word "lie," but he specifically said that if I told the story like "that" they would never put it down as a stolen vehicle. He sent me to New York City, but I went to the place where I had originally given Lisa the car, where she used to live. I went to precinct 3. I parked on the right side of the street, facing the police station. They had me wait for two entire hours before an officer would attend to me. Meanwhile, there were officers shooting the breeze and laughing boisterously. At one point, one of them asked me to go outside for five minute while they took roll call. When I went back inside the station, I asked them how long before I would be seen. He told me that the officer who was supposed to help me was on patrol and that he would be back soon. They were supposedly busy. *With all those officers just chatting?* I frowned? I sat down and began doing my lessons for work.

After about twenty minutes, two officers entered the building. They had me fill out a form describing the incident. Then, they spoke to me about it. Their first instinct was to assume that I was making up the story. Both of them were standing. The one posing most of the questions had light red hair. He was firmly holding onto his gun-gear.

"You're looking a little nervous there," he said with an authoritative voice.

"Nervous?" I said, upset, "You have no idea what I have been through. With all due respect, I doubt you have the awareness to comprehend. You should not rush to conclusions. I am paying a ton of money for both vehicles when I should only be paying for the smaller one."

I paused momentarily. I felt I was about to waste my time, but what the hell, they were acting like everything is always logical, based on the left brain, and that I should have been smarter.

"Go ahead, tell us what happened."

I knew they would not understand, but a part of me wanted to see if it were possible for them to be open-minded.

"I was being attacked in the middle of the night by entities...I had never experienced anything like it before..."

They were taken aback. Their eyes widened and they were rendered to silence.

"As you can see, I had to find help. Lisa said that she could help."

Their demeanor had changed, more humane, and less authoritative.

"I'll give her a call. Maybe hearing from us will avoid the whole paper work. And so he dialed Lisa's cell phone number. The moment I heard the officer say "Kansas" in astonishment, I immediately said, "She's lying!" He turned his eyes toward me momentarily, then walked toward the entrance, still talking on the cell phone. He returned a few minutes later.

"She said that it's going to take her a few days to drive back to New York, and that she had moved..."

"She moved to Kansas? That's a load of bullshit. Don't you sense it? She's lying. I need to file charges."

"You need to go to precinct 4. Leave out the psychic stuff. Say that she was a friend."

Twenty minutes later, I was at Precinct 4. I explained the situation to the officer, showing him a copy of a ticket that I received in the mail. He smiled as he made a photocopy. That smile said so much. It said "your girlfriend pulled a fast one on you and now your car is gone." I saw this in his face. I tried to explain to him who she really was, but then recalled the other officer's advice. In any case, I could tell that this new guy was going to be useless. He too called Lisa. Lisa told him that she was in Kansas.

"She said to call her. She'll return the car."

"Yeah, everytime I do, she ignores my phone calls."

"Well, she's expecting your phone call now."

"You do understand that she lied to you about being in Kansas, right?" I said rhetorically.

He did not answer.

"You made a copy of the ticket. She got that ticket in August. We're in September now. Do you really believe she's in Kansas?"

"Give her a call."

This guy was being extremely difficult and judgmental. I wrote down his badge number and left the precinct without thanking him. He was a tall, skinning white guy somewhere in his early forties.

Upon exiting the police station, I called Lisa. She picked up the phone this time. As usual, she sounded convincing about her willingness to return the car. We even made an appointment to meet at Lehman College. I drove all the way from Upstate, paying toll to cross the Tappan Zee Bridge. I waited for her for about an hour. I even called to inform her that I was waiting. She did not pick up the phone, of course. I left a message. She never called me back. From that moment, I knew that I had to find another way to get the car back. I called her often, almost everyday to leave nasty messages. A typical message went something like this:

"You're an evil, awful person. Give me back my car you witch! I have always known that you are evil. I hope you live a very long time and that you suffer every step of the way because even with all of your witchcraft you probably don't know that there is no death. I hope you suffer deep within your bones. Physical death would be a release for you. I want the car you witch!"

Try as I might, the messages were futile, and this evil soul could care less about what I was going through. And so, I stopped going to the police. I saved the parking tickets that the NYC Parking Ticket Bureau were sending me.

During this time of feeling totally hopeless about recovering the car, I had to deal with Hawa and her friend Tsitsofe. The first couple of times Hawa had called, I ignored her. One evening, she called and I grabbed the phone and stared at it, battling with the decision of whether or not to answer. Finally, I had waited too long. The phone stopped ringing. I just could not answer it. What was I supposed to tell her? *I am not excited about you. I don't feel good when I am in your presence? You get angry too easily?* Nevertheless, fate would have us speak one last time.

A few days later, she called using someone else's cell phone. I picked up the phone, thinking that it could very well be her, but took the chance anyway.

"Hello?"

"Ça va?" she said in French.

"Ça va!" I answered.

"How have you been?" I asked her without emotion, "So what's new?"

I don't recall her exact words, but I do remember her telling me about her diplomat. I was not really interested in knowing these things, since I had her on the phone I had to be polite.

"So what are you up to these days?"

"I am heading North for a little while."

She was referring to the part of the country that was heavily populated by the Kablés, her father's ethnic group.

"I know this call is expensive for you. I'll call you when I can."

"Don't be a stranger," she said with a slight hint of laughter.

I hung up the phone. I had no intention of calling her. She should have paid attention to the words "when I can." Reader, if at this point you think I am being a little harsh, just wait; the story gets more interesting. This girl is definitely no angel.

A few days later, I reverted to my former weakness. I told myself that it was possible for Hawa to change for the better. So, on the 10th of September of 2009, I sent her an e-mail in which I told her that I had been thinking a lot about how we were going to get closer, and to make the relationship work. As I have already implied, my soul already knew that this relationship would not work for me, but now my mind and body needed to understand it. In this e-mail, when my body computer was still trying to decide what to do about the relationship with Hawa, I also shared with her the fact that Lisa had refused to give back the car. On September 11, 2009, I received an e-mail reply from her.

Hello,

You know I don't like your story with that lady, and I have clearly told you that in an e-mail, I believe. She's a manipulator and I have always told you that I don't trust psychics and their lot because it is the same thing here.

Please don't let her manipulate you once again.

I prefer being manipulated here than by a foreigner. In my opinion, it's insulting and appalling.

Later

I read the letter a couple of times, taking it seriously. *Whose manipulating whom? Are Lisa and her crew the only people manipulating me? And what about Hawa herself?* Suddenly, I stopped dead by my front door. I was near the kitchen. "If she were nicer, then she would have had you." Recall those were the words Hawa's mother uttered to me with a slick smile before I left Togo.

Less than a month later, I was speaking to my mother.

"Amélino said that you are still not protected and that you need to do something soon."

"I'll get paid soon. I'll send her the money then. But just for the record, you did say that she found someone who only uses plants, right?"

"Yes."

"No killing of animals?"

"I already told you no."

"I just need to be sure because intention is very important. If my free will is not respected, then I cannot take responsibility."

"Don't worry Agbessi. I have always told you that there is no force in this world that can make you go against your will. If you ask them to do something for you and they do something else, it will come back to them."

"Alright, I agree."

After carefully considering her statement, I decided not to wait until I was paid before sending my aunt the money. I used my reserve—my food money. I just had to be frugal for a week. I knew I could do it. I knew how to survive.

My mother called me a few days later. With a bit of research and patience, everything is clarified in time.

"Agbessi!" she said excitedly, "Agbessi! They prayed for you. Everything is ok. Guess what?"

"Please do tell."

"Amélino was crying because she learned that things were put in her body…They also said that Agusta and her older sister had been up to no good. They had been casting spells since they learned that you were looking for a girl."

"2007, since the summer when you went to visit," I said, interrupting her.

"They said that you would only marry Hawa and no one else. They set it up so that if you don't marry her you would never find anyone else."

"Ha, ha, ha!" I laughed, "Sounds like they think that they are the ultimate source of power in the universe. Each person's will is important. You see, I have suspected. I gave them the benefit of the doubt and it came back to bit me in the end. But that's alright. Now I know they were the ones who put whatever object or things in my body. I have to find a way to remove them."

"Don't worry. God is going to take care of everything," she assured me.

This piece of news was all I needed to get my mind to go along with my soul's decision. I never wrote to Hawa again. However, several weeks later, she sent me an e-mail. Every word was bold-faced, and the end was in capital letters. I sensed much emotional pain in it. The letter did not even have a salutation. She wrote:

Why didn't you have the courage to talk to me frankly?

It hurts to know that you are not sincere.

What I am wondering is how I could have dealt with this if I had been carrying your child?

Please stop thinking only about yourself.

No hard feeling.

MAY GOD PROTECT YOU
HAWA

"Get out of here!" I said aloud, laughing. Was she kidding? It was obvious to me that her first line about being frank with her had to do with the fact that I did not end the relationship by e-mail or phone. I simply stopped communicating with her. That was absolutely true. Since September I had ignored all of her calls. Whenever I received a call with a 228 number which I did not recognize, I pressed the ignore key. Reader, I hope you are not judging me too harshly here. Let us analyze what transpired here. Here was a girl and her family sending dark souls after you for over two years, would you have called her to break up "properly?" Ha, ha!

I cannot help but to laugh at the whole situation. She said it hurts. Wow! The audacity of wickedness! All these years she had refused to let me in her life, refusing to share her past experiences with me. And then, there was that statement she made in Togo: "I don't want it used against me." I was not frank with her? She is insane. I mean, she had been lying to me from the very beginning. What was she thinking? What if all those negative souls had been successful at gaining access to my body? I would have been totally possessed again by a lot of negativity. How would I have maintained my sanity? Did she actually think that one functions well while being possessed? I was possessed for eight years and I was utterly depressed. The audacity and the stupidity of these three women amaze me. She was just upset because she received a bit of what she dished out. As Hamlet would have said, "There's the rub."

On October 1, 2009, Hawa's desperation grew stronger. She sent me an e-mail with two poems. I assure you Reader, they are quite good. There is no point to translating them entirely here, so I'll just explain them. The first is called the "The Lake" by Alphonse de Lamartine. After the guy's name, she wrote: "to evoke precious moments of love. The poet asks time to suspend its course..." The author's pleas are futile. This is where Hawa should have paid special attention to the poem. The second poem was about two pigeons by Jean de la Fontaine, but was not as sweet as the first one so let us not discuss it.

Despite my great effort not to have anything to do with Hawa anymore, she kept trying. Several months later, before going to Togo again, my phone rang while I was at Costco. I looked at the name on the small monitor. It was Tsitsofe, her best friend. I pressed the "ignore" key and carried on with my shopping.

I was getting tired of dealing with Hawa. Much had been happening spiritually that I needed to focus on. In terms of the mundane, I was back to calling Lisa endlessly the next five weeks that followed. I left so many, many messages and was completely ignored. As I have mentioned, I had set my new phone on private. I knew that whenever she saw an unlisted number, she assumed that it was me and did not pick up the phone. However, after so many phone calls late one afternoon, Lisa finally answered her cell phone. We were at it immediately.

"Admit it, you've enjoyed our conversations," she said laughing. I wanted give her a good slap in the face, but, that was impossible, for I was on the phone with her.

"You're wicked, evil. Where's my car?"

"Listen, there's a reason why I haven't been able to get back to you."

"Lisa! Cut the bullshit. The car, Lisa! Focus! You're getting me very angry."

"You're gonna want to listen to this. Another curse was placed on you and I, but it didn't work."

"Lisa, you are a big liar. Enough of the lies!"

She was laughing.

"Then, how do I know your new phone number? It's 347..."

She was right. I was thinking hard about how she could have gotten my new phone number.

"Listen, a young woman with an accent called me some time back before the incident with the number beginning with 228..."

My eyes widened. I wanted to dismiss it because I thought it would have been possible for her to obtain the information on the internet, but I had a gut feeling that she was telling the truth. When I first returned to New York, I did send Hawa an e-mail with my new number, and she did call me repeatedly. And the 228 was definitely Togo's country code. Hawa and her mother had casted another curse. My mother was the only person whom I told about what occurred a few days ago. There was no way my mother would have told Lisa. I was now quiet, listening to her.

"She gave me your number...She wanted to join forces with me to hurt you. But you know, I would never do that..."

Hawa's frustration did indeed reach a new height. Though she tried to harm me, she afforded me another opportunity to have a glimpse of who we human beings are beyond the physical body. Furthermore, I also learned about technology and the futility of violence and war.

The incident to which Lisa was referring to occurred on November 6, 2009. It was a little after 2 a.m. in the still of the night. I was in bed, sound asleep. Suddenly, my soul rose above my physical head. At the foot of the bed was the tallest dark entity I had ever seen. It was a shadow being in semi-human form, and was negatively powerful in appearance. *Was I going to battle this thing? Who sent it?*

The entity approached from the foot of the bed, but then stopped dead on the spot. Had it continued, it would have probably been incinerated into stardust or something. Well, I do not really know about this latter point, but I was certainly impressed by my protector. A familiar soul who was very bright was at the center of the foot of the bed, unleashing and erecting some sort of amazing protective energy or force field around the bed. The dark entity's countenance was that of extreme bewilderment. It was just standing there—stupefied. He was caught off guard. My brother was not even looking at this being. It was powerless. It chose to leave. I found it interesting that Essevi did not choose to destroy the entity. It would have been so easy for him, but yet he did not. The great implication of this would dawn on me later—not only is war unnecessary, it can be totally avoided.

Unfortunately or perchance fortunately, the mind requires so much more time to digest information than the soul. It took me a year to completely absorb the major lessons of my brother protecting me spiritually on that night. After work one day, while driving, my mind had taken up the question of violence and war. I was near the post office. The concrete question that I had posed myself was: They say that violence is not the answer. If that is the case, then how does one protect oneself from harm? How does a nation protect itself from its so-called enemies? You see Reader, I wanted to know if there really is an alternative to violence. I had pondered these questions my whole life. And in only a few minutes in that auspicious afternoon as I went toward a traffic light, I had the answer. It was like an epiphany. It came to me in the form of pictures—my brother's force field. If my brother could protect me that night with spiritual technology without harming the negative entity, then what else is possible in this physical dimension of existence or the universe for that matter?

As I made a right turn, a strong feeling overtook my mind—war is absolutely insane. It is negativity on a large scale. Another wave of thought swept through my mind and I felt the words: "War is energy released to imprison us in this dimension. Energy, food!" I drove carefully. So many answers were coming to me that if I were not careful, I was going to have a car accident.

Everything is energy. Words and physical acts create positive or negative energy. There are different dimensions of existence. Hell and heaven are not a single state or place...The dark soul came out of thin air and became a physical person on top of me in that bed. Out of thin air! Then, it changed from a physical state to its weightless soul form!...E=MC²·

Oh my God! I just had a déjà vu from three years ago. I just saw myself writing these last couple of words!

If mass is part of energy, then the solid world is only a temporary or an ephemeral static view point of existence. It cannot forever hold.

The physical world is not what it seems. It's not physical at all. The clues have always been there. The "m" in Einstein's equation is everything that is solid in the physical world. *If the real nature of that entity was merely physical, then it would not have been able to change from one form to another.*

My mind quickly shifted to my science class in high school. The concept of condensation became utterly obvious to me. When you put some cold water in a glass, some of the water can seep out of the outer layer of it. The reason why this is possible is simple. The glass is not really solid. If it were, then some of the water would not have seeped through the outer surface of the glass.

I tried to focus my mind on my driving. I began to have an interior monologue. I asked myself for whom we kill on a grand scale. Who benefits? No, the economic and greed explanation of production is a superficial answer. *Energy! Food!* What is the difference? Food is a form of energy. Reader, please stay with me on this, and really consider what I am saying. First, magic (good or bad) really does exist. Entities in other dimensions can either enter or be summoned into our physical dimension. Secondly, human beings can be possessed without knowing it. They only feel the negative effects if the entity gives off negative vibrations. Thirdly, our food is contaminated with pesticides, chemical alterations and genetic modification. All these things hinder us from being aware of our none-solid true self inside our physical bodies. When most of our none-physical awareness is blocked, then other entities can feed off of our energies. The energy we produce is food, none physical food. Fallen angels or dark entities are without a doubt stealing our food. They certainly fed off me for years.

I am also absolutely convinced that these inter-dimensional entities have screwed up big time and are refusing to be brave, to face the consequences from having fallen from grace. Infinity absolutely requires them to return to the light, but they are afraid of the suffering they must endure to cleanse the darkness enveloping their souls. They use our energy to survive. I am absolutely convinced that this is the reason they have been manipulating our physical world for a very, very long time.

A few days later, my frustration with my lack of success at recovering the car increased. I lied in bed cursing out Infinity.

"God? Please," I said out loud sarcastically, "This is bull-shit. What was the point of that message? Why tell me that I am literally a piece of God, and then have everything taken from me when it was not my fault?"

I was upset and frustrated. The things in my body were still present. I was fed up. I could not get even with Lisa or the things in my body. The Infinity message was too strong. If a priest had expressed the message to me, I would not have believed him. Feeling the pain of Avon's life ending in that room compelled me that day to keep my foot on the path of positivity. I never, EVER want to experience such a feeling again. As a result, I did not do anything to Hawa, Lisa, Terry-Anne or anyone else in Togo who cursed me with the dark arts.

My concentration was now on healing myself physically, mentally and spiritually. More specifically, I sought to get rid of the things in my body. In such pursuit, I would not restrict myself to any particular culture, religion, and geographical location. I sought help from three sources: a Mexican friend, two American healers, and two Togolese healers.

One day, I was working on my lesson plans while listening to an interview of a well-known guy who said that he worked on secret malevolent mind control projects for the government. Stewart Swerdlow claimed that he could see people's past lives as well as their auras around their physical bodies. I was suspicious of him, but he caught my interest when he said that mermaids exist. He said that they were an experiment—a combination of a human being and a whale. I thought maybe he was credible, for I had seen one when I was a child.

I went on his website, carefully reading the services that he provided. The prices were really ridiculous. They were anywhere from $600 to $1,200 dollars. He was selling books, and participation in "rituals" as a way of deprogramming oneself. *"Rituals?"* I said inside my mind. *Could this guy be practicing witchcraft? Maybe he is a fraud, maybe not.* Well, I was going to give him the benefit of the doubt by scheduling a phone appointment to give me a reading. I sent him one hundred dollars, a dollar more than I was supposed to. I was three minutes late for my phone appointment.

Upon calling, I immediately apologized for the delay and asked him how things were with him.

"We're pretty busy around here."

Even before I had the opportunity to tell him why I had made the appointment he said:

"What we need is a full scan."

"My name is Agbe. You can also try Agbessi."

I walked toward the window in my classroom.

"Give me another name," he said.

"Try Kossi. I was born on Sunday."

"I see a lot of past lives."

"How many do you specifically see?"

"We have all had literally thousands of lives."

I could tell he was generalizing.

"What's your date of birth?""

"I was born in the latter part of the 20th century," I answered.

He sounded a bit puzzled. There was no way I was going to give him my date of birth, especially after how Lisa and her crew tricked me.

"I have three basic questions. The first is: When was my last incarnation? Please tell me about it."

"It was in the 18th century."

"What decade?"

"I am getting about the 60s and 70s."

"Are you sure?" I inquired, knowing full well that what he had related was not accurate.

"Are you sure that I did not incarnate after that?" I pressed on.

"No, that was your last incarnation."

"How did I die in that incarnation?"

"You were a young man in the United States. You were hungry. You stole food. You tried to escape. You were caught and made an example of. You bled to death. They cut off both of your arms."

"That's very interesting," I said giggling a little. Stewart Swerdlow pretended to be slightly upset.

"What I do is very serious."

"You just told me that my arms were chopped off and I bled to death. What do you want me to do? Cry? Next question. What do I have in my body? It's a sort of a palpitation or ticking. It's almost like an anomalous beating. It occurs all over my body—particularly my heart, biceps, triceps, and thighs. What can you tell me about this? Is it alive?"

"It's alive."

That was all he said. I was expecting an elaborate answer. I was taking notes on a piece of paper.

"Who put it there?"

"We need a full scan for that. Have you read my books?"

"I've read some," I answered, thinking that a few pages was enough to qualify as "some."

"I don't think you know much about what I do."

I was briefly silent.

"Where you are does not match your energy. There's too much negativity. You should be living in the southern states."

"Let me ask my next question. We can come back to that later. On November 6, 2009, there was a battle. A dark soul, very tall, stood at the foot of my bed. I only recall some of what happened. Can you tell me about it?"

Stewart was not specific.

"There are three people protecting you; one of them is from your maternal side."

He sounded sure, and I believed him.

"On that night, my soul rose above my head."

"The soul cannot completely detach itself from the body. The body will die," he immediately cut me off.

"Really?" I smiled.

He had made another blunder. Either he was unaware of his own soul's capabilities or he was simply putting forward his belief system or what he had been taught without actual evidence. I sensed manipulation in him. If this guy were to go up against me beyond the physical body, a soul to soul combat, he would not last fifteen seconds.

He was now desperate. He kept repeating the same thing: "You're dealing with some low, low stuff. Abandonment, low self-worth…"

This was again another big blunder. I have been abused and knew precisely what he was doing: He was trying to manipulate me. I became convinced then that to a good extent he was a fraud, though he is now helping *some* people. I wondered how much of his information was actually true and how much was false.

"So, you can't tell me when or who put these things in my body?"

"Normally rituals are done during the 2nd trimester of the pregnancy."

The next place I would seek help was Cuernavaca, Mexico. My superficial reason for going was to work on my Spanish, but the deeper reason was to find a cure for the annoyance in my body.

I took a plane to DF, the capital, and then took the bus to Cuernavaca. I arrived at about 4 o'clock in the afternoon. I spoke to the taxi driver in Spanish. He asked me if I were from Panama and I told him no. We had difficulty finding the exact address. After circling the house twice and not realizing that we had found the place, I gave my host mother's phone number to the cab-driver, who thought that I was going to call myself. I explained to him that I was new there and that I did not have a phone with which to call Carmen, my host mother. As soon as he called, he quickly found the place. Carmen helped me inside, and showed me to my room. They were eating when I arrived there. Her daughter, son, sister and daughter's work colleague and friends were also there. It was apparent that her daughter also loved drinking red wine. I was served a glass with my pizza. After about an hour, we killed nearly all of the wine.

The sun was beginning to die down, and I wanted to call my mother to let her know that I had arrived safely. Carmen told me to go to the Superama, the supermarket, where there were pay phones that I could use. I had on casual clothes and sandals. There were ATM machines near the supermarket. I stopped at one of them to withdraw some money. I purchased a few items at the supermarket, including a couple of bottles of red wine, and two phone cards. I then went outside to call my mother. A woman and her young daughter, probably about twelve years old, tried to help me but to no avail. I went back to the store to seek help, but still we were unsuccessful.

I decided to go home and to seek advice. The security officers at the gate opened the door for a car that needed access into the little neighborhood within a bigger neighborhood. I went to the right, where the security guards' small door entry was. I introduced myself and explained that I would be there in the city for several weeks. I looked straight ahead as I walked, thinking. At the house, Laura, Carmen's daughter asked me if she could open the red wine that I brought, and I said of course. I sat near the door to the back terrace. It was open. Below the ground was a river that passed behind the house. The sound of the water was wonderful. It was like a waterfall. I sat there in the living room, not talking, just listening peacefully, and savoring the ensemble of the experience—the sound of the water, the red wine, the pizza, and the amiability of my new family. Carmen was extremely nice. She was in her sixties, but was still very active. She got up at her usual time at about 5:30 or 6 a.m. and made me breakfast everything. She believed it was very important to consume fruit in the morning. She kept the house in a wonderful condition.

That evening, I slept on the second floor where my room was. The place was heavenly. The music of the river could be heard all the way upstairs. To top it all off, it started raining that very first night. The rain hit the roof rhythmically as the river whooshed. The synchronization of the sounds rendered me to sleep without much effort. Saturday morning found me relaxed and calm as I opened my eyes in bed. I took a shower and went downstairs to eat. Carmen was preparing enchiladas for me. They were good. After brunch, I went to the computer lab at the university to use the internet. The people were nice and the internet was free.

After sending a few e-mails, I took a little tour of the neighborhood. Everything looked alright. My mother, colleagues, and friends back in the States were wrong. There was not a hint of violence or drugs where I was. They were worried for nothing. I walked for a good hour. By then, I was tired and wanted to return home. I entered the gate. As I walked down the hill, a sudden feeling overtook me. I was having a déjà-vous. I recognized the street intuitively. There was no question that I had been there before in spirit. I looked at the jacket I was wearing. It was white. It was incredible! The dream that I had three years ago was not a dream at all. It was a glimpse of my future. I could not dismiss it. This was the third time that my visions or dreams had come true.

I had inquired about legitimate and honest healers. I was referred to a professor at the university. My excitement compelled me to register for his course. I sat at the center of the classroom. There was only a handful of us. This was a seminar titled "Voces marginales," which translates as "Marginalized Voices." He attempted to gain access to a website, but the internet did not work. He sought help. During this time we took notes on his PowerPoint presentation. He caught my attention with his first sentence:

"Everything is backwards."

He explained how native peoples in Mexico and Latin America were being silenced through lies and propagandas. In other words, the conquerors of Latin America have succeeded in belittling the native peoples. As a result, the world now sees the natives as primitive and superstitious. Science supposedly knows more than they do.

"They are backwards," he said, quoting the belief of mainstream people around the world. I posed him a lot of questions. I was dominating the discussion. He was saying fascinating things, things I knew to be true, things that I had lived beyond the physical level the last couple of years. After class was over, I asked him about his sister. He told me that she was indeed a "curandera," which is a spiritual healer in Spanish. I told him about the palpitations in certain parts of my body and if she could help. He said that he would let me know. I inquired about the means of the healing. I learned that it was a heat and plant healing.

About a week later, I was in Temixco. I was in his family's house. It was separated into sections. His part of the house was to the left. To the right was the oval sauna, which was to the right of his section of the house.

"This is Agbe, the student I spoke to you about. I'll let him tell you about what's going on," David said.

"He has a very strong story about his ancestors," she told her brother.

"You can sense this?"

"You just want everything to come to an end so that you can move on."

"More or less," I answered in Spanish.

We were standing next to the sauna. I went to David's section of the house as his sister heated up the sauna. A few minutes later, I was inside the dark room. I sat in the right corner. It was extremely hot. I applied the wet towel to my head and face as his sister had indicated. After about twenty minutes, she came into the tent and sat at the opposite end of me. I could not make out her face. But, I could see the shadow outline of her figure. She began the healing process by asking for permission from her ancestors to use the sauna. She asked them to see us as we are: Our strengths, desires, dreams and weaknesses. Then, she asked me to say why I had come. I was ready and knew exactly what to say in all of my acquired languages. I started with Spanish and then mixed it with the other languages.

"My name is Agbessi Ben Kossi Epou. I am fo Yema's oldest son. Let my family, current and past, ancestors be enveloped with positive energy, the purest part of the Most High, the purest part of the Ultimate Energy in the universe. I am here because I wish to get rid of any spiritual negativity in my body."

She said some more prayers. Then, she dipped the long herbal branches into the water bucket. She took them out and tapped my head and body softly. Then, she asked God to heal me spiritually and physically and for whatever negativity inside my body to leave. The session was getting very intense. The heat did not help. It was unbearable. I was sweating profusely. She asked me to repeat my request. I did with fewer words, but she was not convinced.

"I don't believe you!" she said with intense emotion in English.

"I don't want to feel any more tickings in my body."

"Say it with more emotion! Show that you've suffered! Show your anger!"

I could not. I did not feel or wanted to be angry anymore. I did not see the point. I was beginning to see anger as a negative energy, and wanted no part of it. Besides, the heat was overwhelming.

"How much longer?"

"Just a little longer," she said softly.

My feet took heat. They were extremely hot. I recalled this sensation. It was the same I felt night after night in bed after Lisa exorcised the negative entity from my body. My thoughts now centered on leaving the sauna. I could no more.

"I want to get out now."

"Alright. I'll lay sheets down for you at the entrance. Lie on it until you feel better."

This, I gladly obeyed. My body was physically exhausted and could not move. I lied face down on the thick cloths and covered myself with my towel. My face met the hard earth, but I did not care about how dirty the floor was. I was resting and that was all I cared about. I lied there for what felt like about half an hour, and then sat up. She brought me some herbal tea and I drank it slowly. Afterwards, I returned to David. David's sister's healing session did not remove the things or objects in my body. I felt the palpitations as he drove me back to Cuernavaca.

About a week and a half later, David invited me to a party. We arrived in his car with his ex-wife and co-worker. We went under the big open tent. I was introduced to a few people. I had a chance to practice a tongue twister, which I now do not recall. I was pronouncing it wrong because I had forgotten two of the letters. Several yards from us toward the left side of the room was a podium and some big speaker phones. A group of American women, young and old, gathered there. In the center was a very tall slender American white woman who appeared to be in her early thirties. The tall woman took the microphone and began speaking in Spanish. She thanked David's sister profusely for having given them a chance to have lived with her for a whole year to study traditional medicine. I was impressed. Her control of the Spanish language was quite good. Then a young woman in her early twenties also went to the podium to describe her experience with David's sister. According to the tall girl, who introduced her, when she arrived she did not know how to say anything in Spanish. Yet, as she stood there speaking, she was able to communicate in the target language very well. Next came an older woman, who nearly broke down in tears because she was about to leave the country. She threw her arms around David's sister.

"I'll miss you a lot," she told her. "You're welcome in our house in the States anytime. You're family."

She hugged her again. David's sister then spoke about her work, the importance of helping people. Then she pointed her finger to my direction.

"Enjoy yourselves."

I did not get up right away. I should have because by the time I went to the long table, nearly all of the vegetarian food was gone. Even the good red wine was gone. I took some rice and went to sit with David's ex-wife and her co-worker. We sat to the far right of where the big speakers were and began talking. The ex-wife took offense to my accent. She said that I spoke as if I were from Spain.

"Do you like them better?"

"I had a professor who was from Spain when I started learning."

They both observed me with steady eyes, unsatisfied with my answer.

"But you're in Mexico now."

"So? It took me time to acquire the accent. Why do you want me to change it?" I turned my body and head to the right, focusing more on the ex-wife.

"Let's get to the depth of this whole thing. Let's not hide. You will tell me if I am right or wrong."

"Bueno," she answered.

"You have a problem with the way I pronounce the 'y' because Spain conquered Mexico and enslaved you. Am I right?"

They answered affirmatively.

"Ok, that I can understand, but you know that we both come from conquered nations…To be upset is not going to do any of us any good. My stay here is short, and it will take a while to obtain a Mexican accent."

The conversation ended. The wind blew the rain my direction. I felt it on the lower portion of my legs. I had planned to take a bus back to Cuernavaca, but my professor was trying to arrange a ride for me. Another lady, with whom I briefly chatted, agreed to drop me off near the university. I slept most of the way back to Cuernavaca. Somewhere along the way, I woke up to a religious conversation.

About two weeks later, it was utterly clear to me that my Mexican friend's healing session produced absolutely no result. My sojourn in Mexico was quickly coming to an end, so I decided to try another healer. The person whom I was supposed to see was not available, so I was taken to another. She wore white clothes. She posed several questions, but I only gave her my first name. I wanted to know if she were authentic. I told her about the palpitations in my body and asked her if she could help. She said that it would take research and work. Given that I did not have the time or the desire to engage in such agreement, I accepted her offer to do a reading for me. She moved her tarot cards around asking me to participate. I observed her carefully as she moved her eyes from card to card. Then, she looked at me.

"You're firmly committed to your projects...Your determination to work with indigenous people is great. You have some things coming up here: a new job, new loves."

"Let's focus on the love aspect."

She instructed me to think about the girl in my mind as I touched a card.

"You have some past live issues here with this girl. Once you get past this, she will be totally devoted and loving and will give her best..."

She spoke about reincarnation as a matter of fact. What was even more shocking to me was the fact that I did not know this girl very well. We had only spoken on the phone. I began to think about the nature of existence. *There are really no accidents. Even the people we come across...the law of attraction. Interesting!*

"How can you live by so many rules," the woman said firmly, referring to the girl. "You're the opposite. You like your freedom."

I understood that this woman was onto something. The girl I was thinking about was very religious. In one of our conversations, she asked me if I were Christian. When I answered no, she was shaken up, and her hoarse voice manifested this for the rest of our phone conversation.

"Let's try another—"

"What you have to share with people is inside you, not out there," the Mexican woman declared suddenly and firmly and as she raised her eye brows.

Though she did not help me with the palpitations, she implanted questions in me: *What new job? What's inside?*

My next stop for healing was in Togo. As soon as I arrived, my aunt and I were at the capital. We stayed overnight at an old friend's house. I never met this particular guy before but I got to know him rather quickly. He and one of his friends came to visit in the middle of the night. My aunt was snoring so loudly that I had to leave. Besides, I had to use the restroom—to do a number 1. I decided to do it outside. All I had to do was find an isolated corner where there was not anybody. As I walked away north from the house, the guy whose apartment we were sleeping in started opening the gate. I turned back to talk to him. He came with a friend at the dawn of the night. We were conversing for the longest time. They seemed genuinely fascinated by what I was telling them about the United States of America and the so-called "developed" countries. They seemed extremely excited. I spoke about farming. I told them that there is nothing wrong with being a farmer, and that owning land is more important than working for a big company or being rich. Suddenly, they were extremely excited about being farmers. We laughed, conversed, and were lost in conversation and thought until my aunt came to greet us.

"I thought you went to the bathroom," she said.

"I got caught up in a very satisfying conversation. You snore really loudly. It was hard to sleep."

She smiled.

"That's ok. I still love you."

She spoke to the two gentlemen for a few minutes, then I lent my right hand to her for support. We went back to the room and I suffered through two more hours of sleep.

We arrived at the healer's house a little after 7 o'clock in the morning. Amélino turned to me.

"We came a little late."

There were nearly thirty or so people waiting already by the gate. A young bald man came out with a piece of paper for us to sign. He explained the difference between the first column and the second. I put my name under the first, which was for the newcomers (i.e., people who were visiting for the first time). We waited and waited for what seemed a very, very long time. Two hours passed before the bald man told everyone to go inside for roll call. The house was divided into sections, in three blocks. The guests gathered to the left section. There was an umbrella-like structure construction under which a lot of people were waiting. Some were sleeping on a sheet under this shelter. Others were sitting on the edge of the cement structure. Gazing upon their faces, it was clear to me that they had been there for a very long time. I turned my face to the right toward my aunt.

"They slept here last night?"

"Yes, they wanted to make sure they're seen early."

I looked around, trying to locate the lady everybody was waiting for. My aunt read my mind.

"She's over there to the left; probably sleeping."

The bald man called my name (i.e., Kossi) and I went under the bamboo structure to pay the fee. I was given a number to wait my turn to be seen.

"Come on, let's go outside. She won't see us for a couple of hours."

A couple of hours? I thought to myself. I should have brought the book La Casa en Mango Street that I bought at the airport before coming. We exited the main door, a gate rather. My aunt headed straight ahead, to the left, where a lady was selling veyi and hot fish sauce. She sat down. A little skinny, jolly poppy walked toward us. I wanted to play with him, so I grabbed him.

"Kayi!" my aunt said, trying to get rid of him.

"It's dirty Agbessi."

"That's ok," I told her. "He's liking it."

I was rubbing his head. My aunt offered me some veyi, which she bought from the lady. Unfortunately, I had to turn it down because the sauce contained fish. After my aunt ate, we both shared a bench, napping. I occupied the left side and she slept on the right half. I was not fully submerged in sleep. I heard blurred conversations between the guests, and my aunt's low snoring. Upon getting up, I wandered the north-west side of the healer's house. It was very bright and sunny. The ground was a red-brown color. A teenager was attending to very big cows in the field to the left. I stopped to observe them. I had never seen so many cows in one place in Togo before.

After a while, I became tired and returned to my aunt.

"Do you know what number we're on?" I inquired.

"We're still about two hours away. I decided to go for a walk again. I wanted to see if I could find the main road. I walked for about twenty minutes, keeping careful track of how I would get back. On the way, I saw motorcycle taxis and a few people exiting their farm houses. It was a vast open area. After a while, I decided to go back to see how things were going. It did not take me long before returning. The big, tall tree near the left entrance was a great way for remembering where the house was. I did not see my aunt outside upon returning. Immediately, I went inside the house thinking that perhaps I had missed my turn. My aunt was sitting on a bench, waiting. She was holding my place for me. She stood up, ceding me her place. I sat down and she prepared me verbally for the experience.

"Do you have the money?"

"Yes, in my pocket," I answered.

"You have to take your shoes off before entering the room."

I was ok with this, so I nodded in agreement.

"But, I will bring this video camera. I guess the lady will let me know if it's alright."

It was almost our turn. There was a woman, in her early thirties behind us. She smiled. A sudden spectacle captured our attention. An older woman with whom we had chatted exited the healer's room with bewildered eyes. She could walk now. Only a while ago she had difficulty climbing a few elevated stairs. She was in utter shock. I exchanged looks with my aunt and the woman. Suddenly, the long wait was over.

"Go inside," said the bald man.

My aunt was ahead of me. I went inside, taking off my pants, then pausing and seeking the healer's permission.

"May I?"

"Yes," she said, granting me permission for entrance.

I also had my shirt off. Only my boxers were on.

"May I record?"

She nodded affirmatively. She was a tall, big woman. She had a mirror in her hand, and was sitting on her bed. To the right of her was her table. I put the coin which was in a sheet of the paper on the table. She took the money out. The paper remained. My aunt said hello and not much else. I launched several questions at her.

"I have these things in my body. I want to know if they are animate or inanimate things and how to get rid of them."

She offered silence as an answer, and intently looked at the small mirror she was holding in her hand.

"You came straight from God. A lot of people want your harm, but only you can decide to take yourself out from this world. You don't want anyone's harm."

Straight from God. What is she talking about? Straight?

She smiled. I was too baffled to inquire further into this matter. She seemed so confident about her declaration.

"You came to have a different experience. You only want to be with one woman. In your last life, you liked women too much, and this time you chose differently. Your soul mate is white. One died. There is only one left."

"Really?" I asked in astonishment. Was she serious? I was not happy to hear those words again. That was how I was manipulated the last time.

"My soul mate? I really have a soul mate?"

I did not wait for an answer. I decided to focus on the dire element of my visit.

"Are you able to help me get rid of what's in my body?"

"We'll get to that."

She reached for the paper on the table. She grabbed it, aiming, for my right thigh. My eyes were intently upon her hand. My aunt was recording. She curved the paper with her hand and grabbed for something that could not be seen upon my thigh. She quickly threw it on the table. It was a snail. *A snail? In my body? Get the hell out of here! Impossible!* The snail materialized into physical form right in front of my physical eyes.

"It's alive," she proclaimed

"People are able to put such live things into other people's bodies?"

I laughed. *"Incroyable!"* my mind shouted out in French. The snail was merely the commencement of my astonishment. She also pulled out a piece of metal "wheel" from my chest.

"Naw! Get out of here!" I said in my native language.

I wondered how she was doing this. A thought crossed my mind. Was she a magician? And if she were, how was she materializing objects and living things out of my body? Perhaps, I should have believed it, but my mind could not wholly accept it as true. There were so many questions that I wanted to ask her, but what was transpiring in front of me was too baffling to pose them.

What she said next, to me, was simply dead on. My conscious and subconscious self were in complete alignment with this.

"You do not need to worship anything."

Those words resonated so much with me that my brows and eyes immediately seized her face. She had rendered me speechless. So, I was doing absolute right by refusing to have animals killed to protect me. I was following my path by not joining any particular religion. So, we all have different paths (i.e., different life missions) to take to reach Infinity. She had confirmed for me what I always sensed to be secretly true but rarely spoke to people about. People often insist that one has to be in this or that religion in order to get to "heaven." I have always challenged this belief system in my mind, though I have mostly avoided talking about it. This message was wonderful. It was wonderful because it means that we do have a say in the experiences that we have while we are here in this life. Dr. Brian Weiss was absolutely accurate: No "superior" power chooses for us. We are guided. It is absolutely up to us to decide. These were the exact things I felt that auspicious night when I was given the Avon-message about literally being part of God.

The healer wrote a note on a small piece of paper and handed it to me.

"Come back when more rises."

She was referring to the objects in my body. We thanked her and left the room. We had to wait again by the second door to be called for the medicine. Eventually, the bald guy gave us what appeared to be two litters of liquid plant medicine. I put the bottles in my yellow plastic string bag, and we headed out. As we reached the gate, I was feeling light headed, a slight headache. I was also dying of hunger. I told my aunt that I wanted to get something to eat across the street. The lady selling the food was in her late teenage years. She was selling cooked white rice and spicy red sauce. I inquired about the content of the sauce. It was safe to order. My aunt ordered the same thing, but with some fish. She made a face as soon as she put some of it in her mouth. She complained to the girl that the food was not good.

"Do you taste the rocks in it?" she asked me.

I smiled because the frown on her face was priceless. It was funny.

"Yeah, I am biting hard on pieces of rocks. I am going to get something to drink. Would you like something?"

She wanted a fanta, a coca-cola beverage drink. A few minutes later, she joined me on the terrace of the little bar. We sat down facing each other near the right side of the bar, when facing the entrance. A woman in her early thirties joined us. She sat to the right of my aunt who started a conversation with her about where she was from. I do not recall what she said. She was smiling, so I said:

"You seem to be in good spirits. Did she do a good job for you?"

She nodded yes.

"So why are you here?"

She explained to us that it was a family member who had done "this" to her. However, I do not recall whether she said it was her mother-in-law or someone else. My aunt had taken on a different Ewe accent as she spoke to the woman. She does this often. She could pretend to speak with a southern or northern accent, and could fool people in thinking that she was from a different part of the country. My mother is particularly good at switching accents when she speaks Ewe and Kablé.

Finally, the drinks arrived. The server took the caps off with a metal opener, and brought each of us a glass with brown coverings to put over the drinks when we were not drinking them. This was so that flies could not get in them.

My aunt and I went home in a crowded bus as soon as we finished drinking. I did not enjoy the ride at all. We were squished together like sardines. Recall that all taxi and bus drivers in Togo do this in order to make more money. For instance, if a car has a sitting capacity of four, the taxi driver would find a way to have seven passengers fit inside. This is how they make their money. So, I was squeezed between a woman and a man whose buttocks I could literally feel. I could not even move my arms. This is insane, I told myself silently. To pass the time, I started thinking about how to avoid this problem the next time I came. I first considered purchasing a car. Then I changed my mind because of the cost. I thought for a while, then I had it—a motorcycle. I would save money to purchase a motorcycle the next time I came to Togo.

The ensuing day after I returned to Kpalimé, the ticking in my body continued. I drank my herbal medicine daily. It was very bitter to my taste buds and it was with great difficulty that I swallowed it.

About a week later, we returned to the capitol. We went to the same apartment that we slept in a week prior. My aunt searched for the key where she had left it near the vicinity of the door. It was not there. A nervous look appeared on her face.

"He must have taken it."

She was talking about the guy who owned the apartment. She knew a relative who lived in the city, but she did not have her phone number. She dialed the apartment guy's cell phone number, and left two messages. We sat near the stairs of a tall building, a hotel. After about forty minutes of waiting and not hearing from the guy, my aunt decided she wanted to find the relative's house. The woman received us very well. I was introduced to another "aunt," whom I had never seen. She was older than my mother, and was one of their sisters, a sister from another

315

mother. We were in their living room. The woman's husband was in his own world, listening to the news broadcast on the radio in Ewe. It was very loud, but the conversation continued between my aunt and my half new aunt.

A little over forty-five minutes later, we were in bed. I slept on the couch while my aunt slept on the folded bed. I recalled that it was a really long night because of her way of sleeping. She snored so loudly that it was impossible to sleep. At one point, I put my index fingers in both of my ears as I slept. This worked until a mosquito started buzzing in my face. I quickly slapped my hand around in the darkness aimlessly. A few minutes passed and the mosquito returned, this time near my left ear. I slapped it, but again was unsuccessful. I put my shirt over my ears. There are two things I find most irritating in living quarters: flies and mosquitoes.

Morning found me with a smile. I was up before my aunt. I was smiling, for the awful night was over. We left at about 6 o'clock in order to get an early start. When we arrived, there were a lot of people already there. We were put on the list of patrons. If my memory is not deceiving me, I was the eleventh person on the list. About twenty minutes later, my luck had changed. The bald man came to inform me that he was putting me earlier (i.e., changing my number to 7th place) because a man had left, thus leaving an empty place. He told me not to say anything about it to anyone because they may have become upset. I agreed and kept quiet.

Like the last time, we waited for hours. I went out for several walks, and even read my Spanish book. Finally, it was our turn. We went into the room. I sat down, shirtless, and was expecting the session to last for at least five minutes. The healer advanced toward me with a piece of curled paper in oval form, and with a sudden touch at my chest, she pulled out a piece of metal that looked like a wheel and with a leg. She called it by a certain name. She explained its function and I listened attentively with interest. My aunt was recording everything. I learned from the healer that the little metal was for "bad luck."

"It's responsible for bringing you bad luck in your life."

"Who put it there?"

"That would require research," she said.

I did not have time to go back. I waited for the lady to pull out more things from my body, but she did not.

"That's it!" she said.

"That's it?" I asked, perplexed. I felt movements within my buttocks and thighs, so how could that have been it? She saw me staring at her.

"That's it," she repeated.

I began putting on my clothes. I could not verbally fight her. It would have been futile. We left the room and walked outside. I was wearing my new necklace, one with the third eye dried seed. To the left of the gate were people chatting. I was ready to go. My aunt was saying goodbye to them.

"Will you marry me?" a young woman sitting on the cement ground with a group of customers asked, looking at my direction.

I looked around to figure out to whom she was speaking. I saw the smile on my aunt's face.

"Will you marry me?" she asked again.

I turned to her. She was staring right into my eyes. I asked myself if she were joking, but the look in her eyes was quite firm. She was serious. I had never seen her before. Given that I was flattered, I walked to her and kissed her on the cheek. She smiled. If my skin complexion were white or lighter, they would have seen me blushing.

"We have to go back to Kpalimé," I said feeling a bit nervous.

The next day after returning to Kpalimé, I began to feel a great disappointment, for the ticking in my body had not ceased. In fact, as I sat on the chair that day talking to Améli as she cooked, it was as if the lady had not removed anything. I was frowning as I made sketches of geometric figures on the ground.

"Da Améli, why is the ticking still in my body? She was supposed to have completely cleared it. What did she do? She didn't do her job."

I looked at her.

"I don't believe in that stuff."

I was surprised.

"You don't believe it? Why didn't you say anything about it."

"I didn't want to discourage you and my mother."

"So, what do you think? Do you think she's a magician or something?"

She answered yes. I listened to her explain. She believed that the healer was there to make money.

"If she removed everything then she would not have a job?" I said.

"That's possible," she answered.

"Who am I to trust? Lies and deceptions everywhere. Lies in America! Lies in Africa. Everywhere I turn, I fail. I can't get any help anywhere. Will these things be stuck in my body forever?" I spoke out loud, but Améli did not answer, for she knew I was being rhetorical. I was quiet for a while. Though I was not sure about the healer at the time, I would learn in the summer of 2011 that the lady did indeed remove things from my body.

A few minutes later, Améli started talking about her children's education. Her husband was refusing to relinquish her two oldest daughters' school records. This was because he did not want the children to go to school.

"Why is he doing this?"

"He wants to punish me for leaving. Koku went to get the papers a couple of times, but he claimed he could not find them."

"What's wrong with this guy. You told me before that he bit you at one point, right?"

She removed the upper portion of her shirt showing her big scar on her right shoulder.

"That's huge!" I exclaimed. "This guy is really sick. What in the world happened?" I inquired.

She was about to speak when I made a joke, my good mood returning.

"What happened? Was he hungry? Did you not cook for him?"

She laughed a little.

"Sorry, tell me what happened. I really want to know.

"He wanted to take a shower, but there was no water. He had already eaten..."

About two hours or so later, Amélino came home. She told Améli about the woman who had asked me to marry her. She told her that she did not think I understood who the lady was.

"She's a voodooist," Amélino said.

"A voodooist!" I said in shock. That meant that this woman was more or less married or permanently tied to the voodoo she was serving.

"A voodooist asked me to marry her? No way! Imagine that, being in bed with two people—her and her entity. Non merci."

The next place I would seek help was Ewomé, which was about forty-five minutes from Kpalimé. The day before my departure for this city, I went to the store near the mayor's office to get some change. In order to do this, I had to first purchase something. I bought two litters of red wine in juice-like plastic containers. After returning to Amélino's house I considered going to Kusuntu to remind Yawavino about the trip, but Amélino reassured me that fo Bernard would remember to give her a ride on his motorcycle. Thus, I stayed to chat with Amélino. She was listening to the radio. She told me to think about the questions I wanted to ask.

Koku and I woke up very early that morning—at about 5 a.m. It must have been about 5:45 when we took off on the road. On the way, I told him to stop to see if Amélino had already left. He was sure that she had, but he was wrong. In fact, she was not even dressed. Koku scolded her a little and we left. About eight minutes later on the road, the rain started pouring as if there were no tomorrow. Koku pulled over and we hid under a store's door step and waited. Several other Zémija drivers had stopped there as well. One particular driver was completely drenched. Not much later, the rain had nearly ceased and we continued. Another fifteen minutes later the rain returned. I put on my goggles for protection from dust and bits of little rocks in my eyes. The road was somewhat reddish-brown, and was mostly unpaved in Ewome. It had been paved mostly all the way until we reached the big village. My brother Essevi was around my head and left arm area. I knew he would accompany us. I did not say anything to Koku about this. I had stopped discussing such things with most of the family. It went in one ear and exited the other without much comprehension.

Upon arriving, I looked around, trying to remember this town I had not been in over ten years thither. Eméfa's name came to my mind. She was gone now, in Germany with her husband. I stepped in a pool of mud, not paying attention to where I was going. We had apparently arrived at the house. An older woman in her fifties came out. The woman greeted us with a long Ewe salutation.

"Welcome!"

"Alright," we said.

"So, how are you guys?"

"We are doing well," we answered in unison.

"And the kids?" she asked.

At this point I was quiet, for I knew that the greeting would take about another two minutes.

"They are fine," Amélino answered. The lady then inquired about the health of specific family members.

What made this particular greeting long was that my grandmother had not seen this part of her family in a long time. This was where she had grown up.

Finally, for the love of Christ, it was over. I was tired of shaking people's hands. A little girl who had been standing in the corner offered us some water. More water was offered to everybody. It is customary to offer water to guests whenever they came over to your house in the Ewe culture. At that particular point, I had a wonderful thought: *Wouldn't it be nice if it were a glass of red wine?* I would not have refused it if they had offered it to me that morning.

It was now time to discuss real business. The woman asked about the purpose of our visit. Yawavino, being the oldest, took charge of the conversation, explaining that we wanted to talk to a few people who have passed. She motioned with her hand, introducing me to the older woman of the house. She shook my hand.

"Would you like to offer them something to eat when you go?" she asked, looking at me and my grandmother and my aunt.

"Sure," I answered, thinking that my brother and father would receive the food in thanks, gratitude, and not the actual consumption.

"That's fine as long as no animals are killed," I added.

"It'll just be chicken," she assured me.

"No chicken, no meat."

"You want to feed them empty food?"

"I eat it everyday," I answered, purposely implying that if it was good enough for me, then it would be good enough for them.

My aunt told her that I did not eat meat anymore. The lady's eyes widened in stupefaction. With the exception of my aunt who remained silent and neutral, they all attacked me with their disapproved stares and comments. A man standing to the left reproached me with:

"If they ate meat while they were alive, what makes you think they would not eat it now?"

I did not say anything to him.

"Just because you don't eat meat doesn't mean that you have to impose it on them," Koku said. The intensity of his conviction was palpable. It was as if I had done something wrong, as if I were his little brother. I did not even have the opportunity to answer the question when another grenade was thrown at me by Yawovino.

"Then you won't get a chance to talk to them."

I felt frustrated. They were all against me because I wanted them to do things a little differently for me.

"Then, I'll go. I will find another path. I always do." I said with firmness.

She stared at me in silence. Koku was taken aback.

"This concerns me, not you. I am the one you're here for. It's under my name they would be killing the chicken. I have the right to decide for myself."

"But it's for them," Koku retorted.

"They'll eat it. I know a little about these things."

It was clear from the dubious expression in Koku's face that he did not believe me.

"What we have here is more than a difference in cultural practices. They will accept the food without meat."

Koku, ignoring me, turned to the lady of the house for guidance.

"Will they accept it?"

"I don't know," the woman answered truthfully.

She went to check to see when the old woman and her assistant would see us. A while later, she returned, offering her apologies. It turned out that we came on the wrong day. Apparently, spiritual inquiries, visits and ceremonies take place during certain specific days of the week.

Yawavino was now talking to me about the past, as if nothing had just happened. I was pretty much ignoring her. The lady of the house brought a very large plate of akple and adema detsi for us. I did not eat it. Koku, Amélino and Yawovi were busy at work. It was time for them to have a little fun at my expense. Amélino told him about me being upset the previous night because Améli put fish in my food. They were fried ground little fish in the sauce. Koku was smiling. He looked at me, and said "Ah!"

It was time to put him in his place. Words were flying out of my mouth a thousand miles an hour in Ewe.

"Don't do it again...It is completely disrespectful..."

His mother seemed surprised at the lecture I was giving him about respect. She seemed to be enjoying it.

When it came time to leave, Yawavino said that she would remain and wait for us to return. Amélino asked me to give her some money for food. I gave her 1,200 cfa. Koku and I walked out. About a minute later, we were on the main road. It took about forty minutes to return to Kpalimé.

When we returned to Ewomé a few days later, we did not have to wait long before being seen. When one entered the room, one saw a curtain to the right. There was a family already in the room. To the left of the curtain was an Ewe woman relating information to the guest who sat in front of her. Behind the curtain, one heard an old woman's voice. We sat in the living room quietly. At times when the woman spoke, she took on different accents and intonations, which were usually very high-pitched. Her voice was peculiar to me. It was scratchy, and at times nearly incomprehensible. I easily understood that the woman behind the curtain was possessed by the spirits she was serving. They were speaking through her. The woman in front of the curtain was explaining what the possessed woman was saying.

"Her death was not an accident…"

The family had not even buried her yet. It appeared that the deceased woman was relatively young. From what I gathered, she might have been in her thirties. The curtain woman turned her attention to Koku.

"Don't cross your legs in here."

She seemed quite serious about it. I wondered why she was absolutely against us crossing our legs or folding our arms. My concentration was strong now. I focused on the voices I was hearing behind the curtain. Suddenly, I had the answer. These beings were inter-dimensional entities. They exist in close proximity to our visible world. They are souls just like us. I was really applying the knowledge I had acquired from my spiritual experiences. The woman behind the curtain came out with an empty hard liquor bottle and a big empty cup. She seemed genuinely confused, and was worn out. It seemed as though she had woken up from a deep sleep. Her speech was irregular.

The other woman sent someone to purchase more hard liquor. Since my childhood, I had noticed hard liquor being used when people prayed. The man returned with a sizeable bottle of whiskey. We all took a small sip of it. The logic behind the sipping was to assure the receiving spirit that it was safe to drink it.

The old woman walked to the room behind the curtain again. I sat in the center of a wooden chair, facing the woman in front of the curtain. Amélino was sitting to the left of me. My shoes were off. I turned my video camera on to capture the entire conversation. I placed it on the ground and took out a notebook. The woman inquired about me. I told her that I was there to speak to my brother Essevi, my father, and my paternal grandparents. The curtain woman related this to the old woman. The old woman said that she would go find them and bring them to where we were. I smiled inside, aware that I was being fooled.

"Where are they from?" the curtain woman asked.

My aunt told them that my father, brother, and grandfather were from Kusuntu, while my grandmother was from Kpelé.

"It will take her a few minutes to go to both places," she said, referring to the old woman.

"The rain also makes it hard."

What she was saying made absolutely no sense. All I knew was that we were being deeply manipulated. I did not for even an instance believe that the old woman was travelling spiritually to two different villages to find my deceased family. I knew for a fact that my brother was already there with me because I felt his presence on the way to the village. Furthermore, I had just felt his presence on top of my head prior to entering the room.

The old woman mumbled a few things out in Ewe. They were mostly incomprehensible because she spoke through her nose. Apparently my dead aunt Lisa, my grandfather, Essevi, and another maternal grandfather had arrived. Yawavino was delighted, for she said, "Kuteto is also here?" This was his older brother who died over ten years ago. My deceased family all supposedly spoke through the woman. They were so vague. They did not say a single thing that

325

would have convinced me that it was indeed them. I wanted to test them further.

"Ok, let's go with some specific questions. The first is this: On the night of November 6, 2009, a dark soul came to attack me. Could you please tell me about this?"

"Your family is protecting you…When they come to see you in America, they don't like the way things are. They know that you are aware that they are there," the spirits said through the woman behind the curtain.

"I am sorry, but you're not answering my question," I said.

Amélino intervened, paraphrasing and expanding upon what I had said. Still, the spirits could not answer the question, so I let it go.

"I have some things in my body, moving about, palpitating, particularly in my arms and chest. What are they, who put them there, and how do I get rid of them? "

"You have things in your body?" the spirits answered in surprise.

What was going on? I was told that the old woman had the gift to see such things. The entities working through her pretended did know either. I was suspicious of them. I wanted to challenge them, to ask what dimension they were from, but the quiet voice inside silenced me. Without being aware of it until several months later, I realized that I was developing a distaste for these inter-dimensional entities. They are manipulators, telling lies and half truths.

I listened attentively to ascertain the half-truths.

"White people brought written language to Africa. It will help you…"

"*Ah!*" I exclaimed inside my head. So, they can see a bit into the future. They already saw me as a writer. I did not say anything to them about it; just as I did not say anything to them about my ability to sense beyond the physical to a certain extent. They must have sensed these things about me and were merely reporting them. No, my deceased family was not speaking through them. The entities themselves were speaking through the old woman. They were pretending to be my family members. I had them! I was jotting down notes about their deception, when I suddenly found myself lifting my head up.

"He has forgotten the African way. You must teach him."

There was no way I was going to let this last comment go. I sensed that they wished for my perception to be limited to one culture.

"Please explain this."

It was incredible. I was sitting right there and talking to them directly, but yet they were choosing to speak to me in the third person.

"He goes around sharing personal things with strangers."

This was absolutely true Reader. I no longer believe in hiding. I have been telling my West African people that the use of Black Magic is more rampant throughout the world than people realize. I usually follow it up with general examples of how it was used to try to kill me. I even shared my insights with a mixed Togolese-Congolese Ewe-speaking young man who I met on my return to the United States in 2009. If these entities disapprove of me sharing personal information with strangers, wait until they see what I have planned—hence this book. They ain't seen nothing yet. We are supposed to share knowledge with each other. To help each other grow as Light Beings. We are not are culture, and I certainly am no longer interested in being "African" or "American." I want to be myself beyond the superficial appellations such as African, American, Black, Ewe, and a teacher. *Enough of the superficial!*

I was finished asking questions. My aunt continued. I was slightly aware of something through my conversation with these entities—they had recognized that my awareness was greater than the typical person who comes to them, filtering ideas and views of existence through the superficial (i.e., African, skin color, etc.). This limited way of viewing existence is helping these entities keep us in ignorance of who we really are beyond religion, culture, and the fake science that we human beings worship. They are manipulating humanity in the shadows for one simple purpose—food! Energy! These entities are benefiting from us worshiping them. As I mentioned before, worship comes in many forms—constant thinking about something, praying, and the offering of food such as animal sacrifice.

The old woman came out of the room. She was exhausted again from her session. I wondered how long an old lady could endure such intense spiritual exercises. She must have been at least in her late 80s. I asked her what I could do to get rid of the things in my body. She said that I had to return another day for my soul to be called and I could talk to It. I was confused. How could one talk to one's own soul? I mean the soul interacts and interfaces with the less fluid consciousness which is the mind, but I did not understand the mechanism of how the mind could talk to the soul. Later, I realized that I was being too literal with the word "talk."

As I reached the door, the old woman's eyes seized my necklace.

"May I have it?"

I smiled.

"Do you like it?"

"It's very nice."

"I'll get one for you from Latin America."

We went back to the main part of the house. I provided physical support to my aunt. The ground was muddy, so we had to walk on the grassy part. Amélino sat down with my grandmother to begin discussing the session with the lady of the house. The man who had gone out to purchase the alcohol told me that he knew of a man not too far away who could help me with my body problem. I decided to give it a try. All three of us mounted the motorcycle and Koku drove us there. When we arrived, we could hear his voice emanating from his office: a somewhat of a rectangular structure built out of wood and bamboos. A young, tall, and physically fit man came to tell us that we would be seen shortly. They brought us wooden chairs to sit in the open area of the house. The wife had a pot on the fire cooking something. It was a bit chilly, so I was grateful for the fire. The children were near the fire, taking the skin off the cassavas. A man exited a room. I stared at the house. The cement was old. The young man was now carrying a machete.

"Please follow me," the man who would see us said.

Inside his office were plants and a desk, and a bench, on which Koku and I sat. He greeted us and then asked why we had come. I explained my body problem to him.

"I could call your soul but you would be sick."

He told us to go to the old lady. We told him that we had already seen her. We went back to the main house. My aunt and grandmother did not want to leave right away, so I gave Amélino food and taxi money, and Koku and I left the village.

The next morning, I headed toward the internet café as soon as I woke up. I often went to write to friends and loved ones. At the intersection, I went out toward my younger aunt's street corner where she had her food stand. I looked to my left. She was not there: I was too late for breakfast. I went to the internet café. After about forty-five minutes, I felt.

I was in a state of placidity. However, as soon as I went out of the door that would change. To my right was Hawa's mother coming from the right side of the road. She had that retarded slick smile on her face. I needed to turn right to go to Kusuntu. A frown overtook my face. She stopped to greet me.

"Hello Ben."

Hello Ben? I thought to myself. I was wearing my dark sunglasses. I stopped right in front of her. My left hand immediately went up, almost instinctively, blocking her face from my view. A mental image of my hand smacking this lady flashed before my inner eyes, but just as quickly my inner voice said no. An astonished look sketched upon her face. Her eyes widened. I walked away toward Kusuntu. I stopped at my cousin's barbershop to say hello.

"Where are you going?"

"Kusuntu to see the house."

"Why?"

Why was he asking me why I was going to see my own house?

"This is my village too. My house. Do I really need to explain my every move?"

He looked at me, wondering what I was up to. I smiled and took my leave. I was close to Kusuntu now. On my left was the cemetery. I stopped, walked toward it, looking for my brother's tombstone. For some reason I decided not to pursue the search. A few minutes later, I was in front of my old house. Instead of going in, I decided to sit directly across the street. I sat on the same big rock I once sat upon as I waited for my father's return when I was a child. This was the same place I sat years ago and where a little girl was hit by a car, her skull cracked open. I recalled seeing so much blood.

I sat across the street now. Memories of my grandmother's fake-crying popped into my mind. I smiled. Some passersby looked at me, not recognizing who I was. I recognized quite a few of them. I went to Kusuntu several other times during my sojourn for one reason: to show the people of the village that I was not going anywhere no matter how many curses they launched at me. I was there to stay. I returned to my aunt's house that day. As usual, we chatted about everything and nothing as she helped her daughter with the evening meal that they were to sell in the street. A few hours later, we exited the house, making a right turn. Améli and the girls and I walked to the street. The children carried things to help their mother. Amélino took a motorcycle taxi because of her knee problem. Améli had a big, oversized bowl on her head. In this pannier was the food she was going to sell for the evening. She had prepared "coon," which is made from ground fermented cassava. One eats it with hot sauce.

It was dark now. The street was not well-lit. There were a lot of food sellers in the street corners that night. They brought their kerosene lights as well as their very bright flashlights. We talked and laughed as they sold the food. There was a bowl for the customers to wash their hands and another bucket-like structure full of water for them to drink clean water. Between intervals of inactivity, my aunt and I engaged in conversations of our possible future lives.

"What would you like to be in your next life incarnation?"

She paused, reflecting.

"Black American," she answered partially in Ewe and in French.

"Interesting," I said.

"What would you like to be?"

"To be?" I laughed. "I don't want to come back to this planet. There's too much suffering here. I am not coming back if I can help it. To come back and not know who I am? Such slavery! We are slaves. I don't want to be a slave anymore. I want my ultimate freedom."

I stood up.

"Give me liberty or give me death!" I roared in English.

"What does that mean?"

"It means that I prefer death to being a slave."

She smiled, her teeth shinning.

"There are people who envy your position."

"Why?" I asked rhetorically, "I am miserable."

"You are better off than they are."

She was right about how people around felt. I excused myself to go urinate in the bush. A dog accompanied me.

Upon returning, my aunt called me over.

"You just missed it. Your Elomevi just walked by, swaying his broad shoulders."

I stayed with them until about half past 9 p.m. Then, I took my leave.

The next day, early in the morning, I headed to my older aunt Amélinos house. I stopped at my younger aunt's breakfast corner station. I asked for some akacha and botokoe. The botokoe was sweet, but not too sweet. It was good with the akacha. Suddenly, my aunt started giggling and smiling.

"You just missed Hawa going by. It was about a minute ago."

"Yeah?"

"She had her suitcase, and was on a motorcycle."

"How lucky she is. I missed my chance to slap her. That's alright, I still may get a chance. Darn it! I could have thrown a rock at her or something. Some positive force must be protecting her," I said smiling. My so-called "crazy friend" came out of nowhere.

"Hey baby."

He was talking to my aunt's daughter. She was seventeen years old. He was fifty-something and only a few decaying teeth remained in his mouth. He drank and smoked a lot.

"Hello," I said to him.

"How are you?" he asked in English.

"What language is that?" I asked smiling.

"You never speak English for French to me."

"I speak English and French all year. I need a break. I think your chèrie wants to give you a kiss. She was talking about you earlier."

"I am going to marry her. I swear!" he said, his left index finger going up in excitement.

"Yes. That would be cool. I can be the priest who marries you two. Listen, I brought my Bible. When can we do this?" I was smiling, having fun.

"Fo Agbessi, stop! You're disgusting me."

I slapped her thighs with my right hand.

"Have you guys French kissed yet?"

"Oh, fo Agbe!" she cried out shaking her body.

"You marry him."

"I can't. I am a guy."

She smiled.

"Yes you can. Men marry each other in your country."

"So, do you want me to find you a nice white girl in America?"

"You're being disgusting."

"This is going to be so cute," I said, taking out my video camera.

"Please come closer to her so I can take a picture."

I looked up and she was gone.

"Akpene! Where are you going?" I inquired with a smile. "Is this how you usually treat your husband? You did not even say hello to him."

She was across the street giggling and smiling. I crossed the road to get to her, but she ran to the house which was directly across from where her mother was selling the food. My fun was gone. Where to now? Amélino's house! She was not there. The goats greeted me by coming to the door. They were always hopeful. Every time someone opened the gate, they thought food would be brought to them. Améli greeted me. I gave her a kiss on the cheek, and she offered me a seat. She had already started cooking for the street for the evening. She fanned the fire with the hand-made fan. I watched her. The sparks flew upward, the big heavy silver pot sat on the pointed reddish earthen stove. She pushed the woods farther inside where the fire-action was taking place. The intensity of the fire increased. My body began palpitating. The movement started in my left biceps, then another in my right biceps, then in my heart area. They increased, simultaneously throughout my body, rendering me uncomfortable, and very upset. I frowned.

"You're quiet. What's wrong?" Améli inquired.

"I'll be back."

"Where are you going?"

"I'll be back," I said almost in a whisper. I was at Hawano's house now. I knocked on the gate very firmly. The video camera poised to record, my eyebrows gathered into a frown—I was ready for the confrontation. I knocked on the door again. I waited. No one! I tried to force the door open. Finally one of Hawa's male cousins more or less my height opened the door.

"Where's Agusta?" I demanded as I recorded the conversation.

"She is not here. She is on a trip."

"And Hawa?"

"She's also gone."

"When are they coming back?"

"I think Thursday or Friday."

"Tell Agusta she has until Friday to get rid of whatever they put in my body."

I magnified the image on the video caption. The boy appeared confused.

"The curse she put on me. She'll know what I am talking about. If the thing is still in my body when on Saturday morning, tell her I am coming to beat the crap out of her."

I took my leave and went back to Améli. I sat down.

"Where did you go?"

I was sketching pictures on the ground.

"I went to pay Agusta a visit."

"What! You should not have."

"She was not there. I left her a message."

"Why Agbessi?"

"Because I am tired of this thing in my body. I am trying and trying, but my efforts are to no avail. Why should I be paying to take care of this?" I was very upset.

"Let her remove it since she put it there. Did I do this to myself?"

She did not answer.

"Well, why should I be running around trying to fix it then?"

She looked at me compassionately, and then returned to her cooking.

"I am going to the internet café. I'll be back in about an hour."

I sent a couple of e-mails to a friend, in which I described my state of mind to the same dear person; then I left.

As I walked out of the internet café, I considered what I had done that morning. I have indeed shown Hawa and her family a lot of mercy since I have discovered and become more aware of who I am. I was calmer now. Knowledge must be digested. The super computer (i.e., the mind) and the soul that is animating it do not always share the same perspective on the experience one is having. The soul's access to knowledge is far greater. In the physical body, it is extremely limited. As I walked out of the café, a though became stronger within my mind's eye: *All pains are healed in time. Must work on mastering oneself. I am already tired of this place.* Kusuntu and Kpalimé reminded me of the bad things that have transpired. Though I was enjoying the time I had with my family, I was ready to take a break, to leave.

I returned to Améli nearly two hours later. I helped them with the cooking, then went back home. I took my malaria pill, turned on the fan and went to bed. I woke up late in the evening, at about 6 p.m. I went to the street where Améli was selling food. It was bustling with music and people. To the left of Améli's food station was Carnet's liquor and beverage bar. Bob Marley's music roared out. Memories of calm came over me, and I remembered listening to "Red Red Wine" in my Harlem apartment in New York City during the times of my bodily torture. I leaned my head against the tree. I was sitting with my three nieces. Calm thoughts filled my mind. *So ordinary, but yet so extraordinary we all are. The beauty of us is Infinity. So, I must work harder on letting go of the pain, the past, to accept all possibilities. Only then will I be able to draw in more positive things in my life. I cannot descend. It's not an option. Though this time period may be difficult, I must let the beauty of the ordinary shine through. Only then can I reach my extraordinary Self. That is my ambition—to know my ultimate pure self.*

I felt confident that I was on my way. After all, I did not strike Hawano. I saw her several times on the street, but I did not hurl violence upon her. Yes, I was on my way.

Two days later, I was chatting with Navi Eddie in the street where she sold food when Hawa's little sister walked by us. I waved to her. She said hello. I was sure she was too young to have anything to do with the whole affair. My aunt was smiling now.

"So you went to their house. You shouldn't do that again."

"Why not?" I said sarcastically.

"It's like messing with the lion."

"Yeah? I AM the lion. She has woken me up. Are you afraid of her?"

"You don't know what she might do."

"I don't care. Death? Give me death! A gift! Been there, done that."

I spent the evening with my older aunt. She had difficulty walking to the street. Her knees were hurting her more and more. Right outside, to the left of the gate was a small attached room where she sometimes sold food. It was about 7:30 p.m. in the evening and she was selling veyi. One of my male relatives, who is very tall and slim approached us. After a long salutation he ordered some food. It started raining. Two customers were caught in the rain. One of them sat on the bench with us. The other one took a tall stool and sat down.

"It's coming down hard," I said, enjoying the sound as it struck the sheet metal on the roof. Beautiful! What a beautiful peaceful evening! The music of the rain was soothing. It rained for a good ten minutes before subsiding. The two customers left, walking fast, without an umbrella. Sleep was calling for me. I put my head down on my aunt's lap.

"May I?"

"Bien sur!" she answered.

"Doesn't it hurt your legs?"

"Let's move inside the room."

The rain was strong again. I pulled the bench back in and my aunt closed the door. I positioned the bench away from the little hole above. Water was trickling down. I put my head back down. I was enjoying the time with my aunt and the beat of the rain. I have always loved the rain.

When it stopped I went home. Tomorrow is another day. Maybe it would bring something wonderful. To my chagrin, nothing exciting happened. But, I was wrong.

Something wonderful did transpire that day. My aunt just did not tell me until the following day. I was sitting with them as they cooked.

"You frightened Agusta," she began.

"Please wait. Let me prepare for this. This is going to be sweet. Don't leave any details out!"

My eyes dilated with anticipation.

"Hawano went to talk to Eddi about the message you left her during her absence. She was afraid to come to this house because you would be here. Eddi related the story to me. She really wanted to talk to me."

In Togo, as it is in much of the world, I think, one approached the oldest person first. In this case, it was my aunt, but given Agusta's fear, she went to my younger aunt since to her knowledge I was always with my older aunt.

"So you went to see her?"

"Yes."

"What did she say?"

"She said you had gone mad. She asked me if you had heard something negative about her from anyone."

"What did you tell her?"

"Let me tell you about her initial reaction. She said that as soon as she heard the message, she rushed home; she had to take her pills because her heart was beating out of her chest. She then asked me how long you had planned to stay in the country. I waited. Then she said that they were waiting for you to come back and to marry Hawa. I emphasized that you didn't come for girls. She looked even more worried. She even closed the door to the living room and was speaking so that no one else would hear—"

"When did she close the door?" I interrupted my aunt.

"At the beginning of the conversation."

"You said she was afraid and took pills?"

My aunt confirmed this with a smile.

"Sweet Jesus!" I exclaimed, taking my little niece's hand to dance.

"Ahhh leluyah, ahhh leluuuyah...."

I swung Jacqueline around a couple of times.

"I knew you were going to enjoy it."

"You see Amélino, this is how you know God really exist."

She laughed.

"I thought you said it's because of women and red wine," she said jokingly.

"You've got it."

I enjoyed every word of my aunt's report. A few minutes later, my mother called from America. She had already been informed of what I did. Améli passed the phone to me.

"That was a really stupid thing you did," she told me. She sounded very upset.

"You don't know what she might do."

"Please," I said, brushing off her words of fear. "She'll think twice before casting another curse on me. I know that the African way is silence, but why should I keep quiet?"

Despite my lack of success at finding a suitable healer, I never gave up. Though I planned a trip to Latin America, my impatience compelled me to seek further help in the United States of America. I was on the internet again. I found several people. I called a couple, and left a few messages. The first person to call me back was Jonathan. I asked him a few questions about his background. It turned out that he studied with a shaman in Brazil and feel presences himself. He posed me some questions. I explained to him the basic problem of the things in my body, and recalled him saying something to the effect of "Inviting them in." Stewart with whom I had the phone conversation had said the same thing. This was a standard response, which to me did not fit all possibilities. Besides, one does not "invite negativity" unless one is worshiping dark souls. He asked me questions about alcohol and drug use. I felt like he was trying to guess the root of the problem instead of actually listening to what I had to say. I decided to be a little funny.

"Well, I do drink red wine in the evening before going to bed."

He did not laugh. We made an appointment for December 27, 2010. However, the date was no good because of the snow blizzard. We met on the ensuing day. I drove to Lehman College, took a train and headed to Lower Manhattan. Finding his place was not difficult. I rang his door bell from downstairs. He buzzed me in without asking who it was. I headed to the fifth floor. As I mounted the stairs, I said a prayer inside my head which went something like: *I come in peace. I wish to receive positive healing. Anything that Jonathan should do against my will be his karma, so that he may learn…*

Jonathan and I spoke for about fifteen minutes. He asked me about my age and where I worked. I refused to answer them fully. I gave him general answers. I told him that I live in New York and was a teacher. He also asked about my relationships and whom I went to for healing prior to coming to him. I gave him specific and detailed answers to these questions. Finally, he asked me about drugs and alcohol use again. I was beginning to think I had wasted my time coming to him. After the conversation, he had me lie down on what looked like a massage table. He used his hands to perform the healing. After about forty-five minutes, he said:

"Get up slowly, and have a seat."

I got up slowly. Jonathan was in the kitchen or somewhere out of sight.

"How did it go? How do you feel?"

"Ok, it was a bit cold. My feet, that is. I felt the heat in my face."

"It can get a bit cold here."

"I just felt a tick in my left feet," I said. "Is it alive?"

"Yes, but not like in the way you think."

"What do you mean? There are living and inanimate objects."

He looked at a cup of pencils, pens and markers on his table, which was to his left.

"The cap of the pen over there exists…" He had raised my interest. His earlier comments were making sense.

"If the cap were in the body, it would be alive, but not in the way you think." These thoughts had dawn on me before. He was right, but could not explain it in simple terms.

"Your crown chakra is way up there," he said raising his hand. He explained that my moral sense of what is right was extremely elevated.

"The problem is in your heart chakra. It's not due to a curse. I think it was easier for you to call it a curse. Before you met the lady who gave you the reading, did you ever think it was a curse?" To me, this was a silly question because before I had the psychic reading from Linda and Lisa, I did not believe in curses nor was I aware that I had a soul.

"How could I?" Once you used the word curse, the people in Africa grabbed onto this."

I was taken back. Was he insinuating that I had made all this up? I was speechless.

"Your relationships, there are always long distance."

This was mostly true.

"That's because I know what I want. I have no intention of remaining in America forever."

341

Intuitively, I knew he was partially right about the relationship thing, but he was dead wrong about the curses. I could not understand why he simply could not say that he could not read my soul. He changed the subject.

"And what you say is a lot of money stolen from you—"

He made a hand signal as if he were quoting me "And the high fee you talked—"

"They charged a lot of money," I said, cutting him off. Why the hand signal? Was this a personal thing for him? He did not tell him that I lost over twenty thousand dollars, but yet he made such comments. As I thought about it, I understood that it was indeed a personal thing, for he too charges his customers for healing sessions, and so in his eyes the money stolen from me was legitimate. If I were in his shoes, I would not have reached a conclusion so quickly without having more information.

As I was listening to him, I sensed my brother's presence. I thought about Avon, like I have done so often. Was I still angry with him? I did not sense this. What I sensed was a huge longing for my brother, feeling unhappy for not having done my very best to keep him alive. How was I to know that he was going to die? Even as I write these words, I cannot help but to hold back my teary eyes. I had felt his physical presence a thousand times over, during sleep, while awake, and I did not need someone with a limited spiritual access telling me partial truths about what he was able to sense. I listened attentively as Jonathan spoke. He was choosing his words very carefully. He saw that I was not buying what he was saying, for I had a blank stare in my face.

"I know you don't like it but—"

"I don't have to like it," I said, supporting what he was saying. However at the same time I could not help thinking that the facts were not fitting. I purposely did not tell him all of the story because a really talented psychic does not need to pose a lot of questions before giving you a reading. If I wanted psychological healing, I would have gone to a psychiatrist.

I decided to offer him my ears out of politeness. I leanedmy body forward to listen attentively, but he had stopped talking. We were both silent for about two seconds, each questioning the other with our eyes. Suddenly, to my surprise, he decided to open up to me.

"Let me tell you a story. I am gay..."

I do not recall his exact words here, so I will paraphrase what he said. At this point, I should also mention that I do not recall precisely whether or not he said that his partner was a current or an ex-boyfriend. In any case, he said that he was in bed when papers and other objects were flying around.

"I asked myself what's going on here. This place is well protected..." He was really getting into the conversation. He stood up, using hand gestures to explain. He gestured his hands to the right window.

"There was no way anything that does not belong can get in."

"So, what happened?" I inquired.

"He was lying in bed with me," he said. He said something about a street lamp, then explained how he and his boyfriend were having the exact same dream. Furthermore, he said that such manifestations were coming from his boyfriend, and that it was his partner who was manifesting these things."

"It's very possible," I said. I believed him. The soul is that powerful. It can do whatever it wants. It is Infinity. Jonathan's basic premise was that the negativity that surrounded his boyfriend were real and, tormenting him, showing up in dreams. However, I did not see the correlation between his story and mine. Suddenly, I was completely confident and excited. I too stood up, smiling.

"But you were asleep, right?"

He answered affirmatively.

"I was not asleep. I was not asleep when my father came to visit. I was not asleep when the entity materialized in my bed…"

This gave him pause. He was listening intently.

He was operating in the realm of theory, looking at a piece of the picture and trying to come up with a plausible reason that would fit. We human beings do this all the time. When we have a problem, we think of possible reasons for the cause of the problem. It is called guesswork. Theories can be tested; in this case it can be absolutely analyzed with the data one possessed. He was making only partial sense. My gut instinct told me this, and I had so much evidence that my physical mind could not deny.

"Do you believe in curses?" I wanted to make a point.

"Yes," he answered verbally and with an acquiescence of his head, up and down.

"Are you aware that physical objects and livings can be put into your body?"

"Yes."

"So you believe in curses, but not what happened to me. You see, this is where I absolutely disagree with you. According to what you're saying even the vision I had of who we are is not accurate."

Thitherto, I had not told him about this. I was no longer having a discussion with him; I was telling him what is.

"Do you really know who you are? Do you know that you are literally a part of God, the Whole?"

"Yes!" he answered again with the same bowing of the head.

I did not really expect him to agree with me, for I was beginning to think that he was not as aware as he thought.

"Really, truly?? Not children of God! Literally a piece, a part of God. Yes, you are. God can do whatever It wants.

344

It has no sex. It can take any form. I *can* take any physical form."

"I believe you," he said, even more convincing.

"Have you ever been out of your body? Not projection. A complete detachment."

"Yes, I have," he answered, getting up to buzz someone into the building. A minute or so later, the person was at the door. He opened the door.

"Please give me a few minutes." He left the person at the door to conclude our session. Two hours had elapsed.

"One more thing before I leave. Do I have your permission to write about this in my book?"

"Yes."

I opened my book bag and handed him a $150, five dollars more than what I was supposed to give him. I put on my necklace and shoes, thanked him.

I walked out of the apartment reflecting on what I had learned. By the time I arrived home, my thoughts were clear. The session with Jonathan confirmed what I believed about the dark entities. Words are not merely words. Verbal abuse can be as detrimental as physical abuse. One literally accumulates negativity in one's soul. Verbal abuse for instance can reduce one's inner light if one allows it. This is easy to visualize once one acknowledges that the soul is not a solid object. It is fluid, intangible. This was my evidence. I was the subject and the scientist all at the same time. I believed him when he said that some of the ticking in my body were manifestations of accumulated negative experiences in my past.

On the way home, I stopped at the store, an organic supermarket. I texted Joyce, a friend. The message read:

"You're not going to believe what I did today…"

She texted me right back with the words "call me."

About fifteen minutes later, I called Joyce from the car. After our greetings, I started telling her about going to see Jonathan, but before I knew it the conversation took a different turn and I never finished telling her about my experience. On New Year's Eve I called her again. I did not expect to be able to reach her since I had sent her a text message and she did not answer. To my pleasant surprise she picked up the phone.

"Hi Agbe," she said, the tone of her voice indicating that she was happy to hear from me.

"How are you?"

"I am doing well."

"How about you?" I asked. She was not doing well. She was feeling down. After she told me why she was not doing well, we returned to discussing my visit with Jonathan.

"You have to stop going to Americans. He could not read you. He took your money."

"That's what I thought."

"You come from a place that he was not able to reach." By the way Reader, you should know that Joyce has psychic abilities.

"Go see someone who is Cuban, African, Brazilian or Peruvian."

"I am not going to see anymore Americans or Africans. I don't trust them."

Joyce laughed.

"That pretty much leaves you with Brazil and Peru."

"Have you started your book yet?"

"I have the first line."

I was happy to hear her say this because she had been procrastinating or rather should I say "being blocked" and cannot get started.

"Joyce, he did not do anything bad, right? What are you sensing?"

"No, but he also did not help you."

In the summer of 2011, I would learn that I should have trusted my instincts about Jonathan. That is, the entity in his apartment is a fraud, and he should have kept his mouth shut instead of guessing and letting his entity mislead him.

CHAPTER 10

A GLIMPSE OF THE GLOBAL SLAVE SYSTEM

Why are the oldest libraries in the world secret libraries? What are people afraid of? Are they worried that the truth…concealed for so many thousands of years, will finally come to light? …the delusion still prevails that a thing must be proved before a 'serious' person may—or can—concern himself with it" (29).

Erich von Däniken

As the weeks passed, my mind would not leave my Lighter Self alone. It was completely now aware that on this dimension It was literally a being within a being. That is, my mind was aware of the different layers of Infinity. An example might be the peeling away of an onion. The outer layer of the onion is the solid, dense world. As one peels away, one gets less and less denser, finally reaching the Most Light. This is the basic essence of each human being that is completely aware of the purest part of Infinity, from time immemorial. This is the part that my "mind" wishes to understand. My mind wishes to become the Lighter Self within the physical vehicle, for It too knows that deep within It cannot die. In the pursuit of this awareness, questions of days of old kept coming to me. The first of these was reincarnation.

I decided to revisit Dr. Brian Weiss's book: <u>Many Lives, Many Masters</u>. Recall that Dr. Weiss, M.D., used to be a none-believer in life after death. It is important here to understand a little about Dr. Weiss's background before discussing history and reincarnation. Although his earlier religious training taught him about some kind of vague existence of the "soul" after death, he was not convinced about the concept. He was the oldest of four children, and his family belonged to a conservative Jewish synagogue in Red Bank, a small town near the New Jersey seashore. His father had a good job as an industrial photographer, and although they always had plenty of food, money was very tight. All six family members slept in a small two-bedroom garden apartment. Life in the apartment was hectic and noisy, so he sought refuge in his books. He read endlessly when he was not playing baseball or basketball, his other childhood passions. He knew that education was his path out of the small town.

He was always first or second in his class. By the time he received a full scholarship to Columbia University, he was a serious and studious young man. He majored in chemistry and graduated with honors. He was interested in science and was fascinated with the workings of the human mind. He performed well in school and fell in love. Everything seemed to be falling into place for him. However, he did not realize that part of his soul's awareness was being closed through the formal education system. On page 37, he says:

"Few young men worry about life and death and life after death, especially when things are flowing smoothly, and I was no exception. I was becoming a scientist and learning to think in a logical, dispassionate, 'prove-it' kind of way."

Medical school and residency at Yale University further "crystallized this scientific method." He wrote and published many scientific papers, lectured at national conferences, and became quite renowned in his field. He was "a bit obsessive, intense, and inflexible, but these were useful traits in a physician." Then he met a patient called

Catherine who shattered his limited awareness of the various tools souls use to experience different forms of Infinity. Through regression therapy, he was compelled to consider the concept of reincarnation. He had never believed in reincarnation, and had never really spent much time thinking about it.

Despite this belief, he was a caring and compassionate medical doctor who was resolute in finding a way to heal his patient. As he helped Catherine, he discovered that Jesus's teachings were compromised. On page 35, he writes:

> During the week I had reviewed my textbook from a comparative religions course taken during my freshman year at Columbia. There were indeed references to reincarnation in the Old and the New Testaments. In A.D. 325 the Roman emperor Constantine the Great, along with his mother, Helena, had deleted references to reincarnation contained in the New Testament. The Second Council of Constantinople, meeting in A.D. 553, confirmed this action and declared the concept of reincarnation a heresy. Apparently, they thought this concept would weaken the growing power of the Church by giving humans too much time to seek their salvation. Yet the original references had been there; the early Church fathers had accepted the concept of reincarnation. The early Gnostics—the Clement of Alexandria, Origen, Saint Jerome, and many others–believed that they had lived before and would again.

I had read those words in 2000, but they did not mean much to me. However, after experiencing three of my own past lives in 2007 and having been out of my physical vehicle in 2009, I had to take it seriously.

I searched for other sources of information to substantiate Dr. Weiss's statements about the purposeful deletion of reincarnation from the Bible. I found this on page 148 of The Gods of Eden. William Bramley writes:

By the middle of the sixth century A.D., the death penalty came into use against heretics and pagans. A campaign of genocide was ordered by East Roman emperor, Justinian, to more quickly establish the Christian emperor, Justinian, to move quickly establish the Christian orthodoxies. In Byzantine alone, an estimated 100,000 people were murdered. Under Justinian, the hunting of heretics became a frequent activity and the practice of burning heretics at the stake began. Justinian also introduced more changes to Christian doctrine...At that time, in fact, many of the changes to Christian doctrine in the eastern Roman empire had not yet reached the Papacy, although they eventually would. The Second Synod issued a decree banning the doctrine of 'past lifetimes,' or 'reincarnation,' even though the doctrine was an important one to Jesus.

After reading such statements about reincarnation, I was compelled to accept the fact that the church did indeed eliminate this piece of knowledge from the Holy Bible. It was at this point that I understood myself better in terms of my feelings about Jesus Christ. Unlike the Pope and other high status religious figures of whom I have been extremely suspicious, I have always secretly admired Jesus. I am not talking here about the Jesus Christ of whom we have created religions. I am talking about the part of Infinity that was brave, who allowed his infinite positive light to shine through the world by sharing knowledge. Reincarnation was a part of his knowledge base and it has unfortunately been put in the category of a "belief" system. To me, this was a tragedy and an injustice to humanity. If people really knew that the religion or culture they are in is merely an experience, they would not hold so firmly to the ephemeral. Deep hatred and racism would no longer make sense. It would seem not only ignorant, but crazy. People would see that we can be anything: a Catholic, a Muslim, a Christian, Jewish, a Hindu, a Buddhist, a scientist; Black, White, Japanese, Haitian, poor, rich, and disabled. It only matters as far as the experience. Furthermore, common expressions such "I am only human," would no longer make sense.

My appetite for rediscovering the truth within me was highly stimulated. I knew there was more to the story of humanity's spiritual enslavement than what the basic, limited five senses were telling us. I wanted to know what else Dr. Brian Weiss knew about none-human entities. I found my answer in <u>Same Soul, Many Bodies</u>. In chapter 9, he describes a unique soul that matched my own experience. Patrick, his patient, was an insecure young man who sought Dr. Weiss's aid to uncover the source of his unhappiness. Dr. Weiss states, "...This was a man whose self-esteem was as low as that of anyone I've ever encountered."

Before meeting Dr. Weiss, Patrick had no idea that reincarnation was real and that he had lived before. During one of their regressions, he encounters a life time where he first came to this third dimension.

"I'm a male," he said, "but not exactly a man, not exactly human."

According to Patrick, this was 60,000 years ago. Apparently, he was born on another planet, which had no name.

"Maybe it existed in a different planetary system or a different dimension. Anyway, I'm part of a migration from my planet to Earth. When we arrive, others greet us, descendants of beings from earlier migrations from different start systems. They've mixed among an evolving sub-species, human beings…" he said.

According to Patrick, they had to stay on Earth with human beings because their planet was dying and Earth was new.

"True, we needn't have physically come here. Our souls could have been reincarnated into the humans around us or into the beings from other worlds. But we are a proud people. Our technology is advanced—we have travelled vast distances—our culture is sophisticated, and our intelligence is acute. We want to preserve our knowledge and our accomplishments. We want to join the others and through reincarnation aid the evolution of these new human people."

Upon reading this, I immediately thought about the auspicious night when I exited my body while awake to battle the dark soul. I also thought about the time when I was above my body arguing passionately with my father in a strange language that was out of this freaking world. Given these experiences, I understood two things. First, I knew intuitively that there are an infinite number of planets out there that are similar to our own. Other planets are habitable for human beings. Second, I knew that the physical human body is just a vessel and that we are the aliens. Other "aliens" can look similar to us. I had thought this, but up to that time, I had never heard anyone else say it except Patrick.

As usual I wanted to find other sources that would substantiate Patrick's statements. I found it in a very popular book Chariots of the God, by Erich von Däniken, a scientist. He states:

The idea that life can flourish only under terrestrial conditions has been made obsolete by research. It is a mistake to believe that life cannot exist without water and oxygen. Even on our own earth there are forms of life that need no oxygen. They are called anaerobic bacteria. A given amount of oxygen acts like poison on them. Why should there not be higher forms of life that do not need oxygen...In fact, the assumption that life can exist and develop only on a planet like the earth is untenable. It is estimated that 2,000,000 different species of living creatures live on the earth. Of these—this again is an estimate—1,200,000 are 'known' scientifically. And among these forms of life known to science there are still a few thousand that ought not to be able to live at all according to current ideas! The premises for life must be thought out and tested anew...Teilhard de Chardin, the epoch-making thinker, suggested that only the fantastic has a chance of being real in the cosmos! (3-4)

"Our bodies are not too different from the humans', but our minds are far superior...Earth is far more beautiful than the place from which we came. There are trees and grass and water, rivers and oceans, and flowers, birds, and fish of every color...Eventually I die, but long ago my people learned to detach their souls from their physical bodies at the proper moment so they can move with ease, to levels of higher consciousness...," Patrick said.

Dr. Brian Weiss also substantiates Patrick's experience.

"Souls are the same, I believed, whether they come from different dimensions or galaxies or from Earth. New arrivals to our world quickly enter the reincarnation cycle and then tend to incarnate here, in part because their mission is to assist in the evolution of the human race. Souls can enter earthly bodies as any 'alien' body."

When I read these words, I thought that Dr. Weiss was accurate. In 2010, when editing the first draft of this book, the line between a human being and an alien or any being in the Universe began to blur for me. What Patrick said next was not only exquisitely delicious, but would reinforce this blurry distinction for me.

"The distinction between God and humans is minor. One of the pieces of knowledge that remain hidden where I have had it stored is how to master the art of separating consciousness from the physical vehicle. Someday soon your culture will learn how to do that, too. When that happens, you will find that the separating awareness can assume other, less 'solid' bodies as it wishes..."

His statements correlated perfectly to the message that I received that evening about being literally part of the Whole or God. I was impressed with his level of awareness of the nature of the soul. Given my experience, I knew without a shadow of a doubt that Patrick was telling the truth. *Extra-terrestrials coming to planet Earth thousands and thousands of years ago.* As usual, my mind started connecting the dots. *There are beings who inhabit human bodies that are from other dimensions. Some of these being are not benevolent. They are infinitely intelligent but spiritually drained of positive energy. Unlike most human beings, they are aware of their God-like status and are abusing it.*

The truth of this quickly came to me. I recalled the morning while driving on the bridge when I felt the negative entities' hopeless fear of never reaching Infinity. They may possess very little positive light, but they are absolutely aware that they too are Infinity. The vast majority of humanity is not aware of this fact.

Patrick's past life experience as an extraterrestrial on planet Earth is an indication that these beings were once upon a time out in the open for human beings to see, and most of us perceived them as Gods probably because of their so-called advanced technology. They are not more evolved than us! Before Infinity, there never can be a hierarchy no matter how technologically or spiritually aware one's soul is.

It is evident to me that some of these "advanced" souls who came to Earth a long time ago had manipulated and reduced our spiritual awareness, and they are still doing it today. They are far smarter than us in our physical form, but devoid of wisdom or positive spiritual growth. During the four months I fought them, I learned that they were intellectually brilliant *beyond* the human imagination.

People who are aware that there is something terribly wrong with the world usually stop at what they cannot see, hear, or touch. This is a mistake. We cannot measure what they are capable of by our standards. How could one see a manipulation that is hidden beyond his or her perceptible field of awareness? One cannot if one does not have more access to one's five senses. I submit to you therefore that it does not make any sense for us human beings to have lost the vast majority of our memory. For crying out loud, why in the hell is the typical human being only able to use less than ten percent of his or her brain? *This is absurd!*

This absurdity was clarified for me by Erich von Däniken, a scientist. On page viii, of <u>Chariots of the Gods</u>, he writes:

> The gods of the dim past have left countless traces which we can read and decipher today for the first time because the problem of space travel, so topical today, was not a problem, but a reality, to the men of thousands of years ago. I claim that our forefathers received visits from the universe in the remote past even though I do not yet know who

these extraterrestrial intelligences were or from which planet they came. I nevertheless proclaim that these "strangers" annihilated part of mankind existing at the time and produced a new, perhaps the first, homo-sapiens.

I knew most of his claims were true, but I could not be sure for myself about his latter point about humans being created by extraterrestrials. I knew with absolute certainty that human beings' infinite perception has been genetically modified to restrict their awareness. Besides, I knew for sure that the Light or soul within the human body cannot be "created" or destroyed. It can only change form—either from liquid to solid or fluid or in any order It wishes.

As my research progressed, I came upon numerous mainstream scientific and none mainstream authors who further helped me to connect the dots about humanity's enslavement. By far, the most controversial is David Icke, a once very popular British sports presenter. He is originally from England, and has been exposing how the human race has been and is still being manipulated by our world leaders and secret societies through none physical alien entities. He basically states that Reptilian aliens have been ruling the world for thousands and thousands of years. At first I did not understand this, for the minute I heard the word reptile I thought of a physical entity. However, it soon became clear to me that he was talking about inter-dimensional entities who are the ruling elites.

Sometime in mid-February of 2011, I came to an inevitable conclusion: My "mind" and my Light Self are still not in complete accord. Though my mind may from time to time ignore the intuition of my soul, It now knows with absolute clarity that my Light Self knows better. This became absolutely clear to me when my last relationship came to an end. Several months before our encounter, I had a very vivid and lucid dream about her. However, when the relationship came to an end seven months later, I quickly accepted the vision.

Like the relationship, something similar occurred with food. Without doing absolutely any research, I stopped eating none organic food. This was about eight months ago. This was purely based on my intuition alone. Recall that about a year and a half ago I stopped eating meat and fish. Even though my intuition was sure of this decision, my intellect pushed me to prove why this was a good decision. Hence, I decided the best way to do this was to be both the scientist and the subject. As I mentioned earlier, my intuition communicated to my mind that energy is food, and food comes in different forms. Given this awareness, I wanted to explore the extent to which we human beings are being energetically poisoned through the food we eat. I had heard about chemically and genetically altered food. However, up to that point I did not understand the gravity of this. Through my research, I learned that only two or three corporations control our food supply. They have been successful at obtaining patents from their governments across the world to spread their genetically altered seeds and food. They have also influenced the recommendations on the food pyramid. I hate to use the word "evil" because it may imply judgment, but that is precisely what these corporations are. They are extremely dark and negative. Food affects us in many ways—physically, emotionally, mentally, and most importantly spiritually. Polluted food via pesticides and genetic alterations hinders the soul's awareness of what It really is beyond the physical, solid body.

Since I started eating only organic food, I honestly cannot recall the last time I have been depressed or sick. Well, that was because warm up the vegetable marinade before eating. Even then, I only had a stuffy nose and a scratchy throat that lasted for a few days. I believe it is a travesty of justice that restaurants do not serve organic food. I have only found one restaurant that serves none poisonous food in the State of New York.

In February of 2011, I wanted to find out the results of my experiments, for much time had passed since I became food conscious. Presently, I was at a clinic in Upstate New York, waiting to see the doctor. It was about 12:30 in the afternoon here. I was in the waiting room. It was amazing how everybody was trying to save money. I could feel the cold in my feet. There was absolutely no heat in the waiting room. The lady at the desk asked me for the reason of my visit. I told her that it had been a while since I had had a blood test. Besides wanting to know if I were physically healthy, I also wanted to know if the doctor could detect the cause of the palpitations in my body.

I arrived at the clinic at 3:30 in the late afternoon of Friday, February 18, 2011. Fifteen minutes later I was called. This was it. This was the verification I was waiting for. A bald Indian American older man walked into the room. He brought a set of three stapled sheets with him.

"I need you to have a seat over here," he said, pointing to the bed-like structure in the center of the room. I sat down and observed the yellow papers in his hand.

"Did you find anything?"

"No, it was alright."

"You found absolutely nothing in the blood?"

He was writing.

"Let's go over the results…"

He mentioned a few technical words, which I did not understand, so I stopped him for clarification.

"It is your liver. The number is slightly high. Nothing to worry about! It's just a little above normal. Avoid eating less meat, especially red meat, eggs, and ice cream."

"But, I don't eat those things now. What's causing it?"

"Your body is producing too much bili rubin..."

"So, basically you didn't find anything?"

"What were you expecting?"

"It'll take too long to explain," I said.

I sensed he was too steep in his left brain to understand any of my spiritual experiences, so I did not explain.

"Wait a month and go back to do a follow up. I'll give you a prescription."

"May I get a copy of the report?"

"Yes, you can have the front desk make a copy for you."

A young white woman who looked like she was going to give birth any minute made a copy of the report for me. She had a white protective mask around her mouth and nose. She handed me the paper, which was completely incomprehensible—filled with so much jargon. The numerical chart was much more comprehensible. I focused on my protein level. It read 7.2 g/Dl. The range was from 6.0-8.5. This was really good considering that I gave up eating meat and fish. When I gave these things up, I was concerned about not consuming enough protein. This concern only came up when people around me kept saying that vegetarians put themselves at risk because they do not consume enough protein. I mean, strangers, colleagues, friends and families have said this. Despite this, there was no way I was going to give up the good fight. This blood test was the proof that the food pyramid is completely wrong. Worse yet, further research proved to me that it has been manipulated and falsified by two or three corporations that are controlling and polluting our food supply. Reader, if you want to explore this issue, a good place to start is the film <u>Food Inc</u>.

I am aware of the fact that the poisoning of the food we eat is part of a larger agenda. As you may recall Reader, I have said in earlier chapters that the world is sick and it is not a mistake. I have also said that it was intuitively clear to me that the none-physical entities that I had battled for four months are absolutely part the chaos. Originally, I was going to omit this last chapter, but then realized that I would have been remised in my spiritual duty if I did not include it. At some point, I realized that this story is no longer just about me. It is about the whole of humanity. Perhaps some of you Readers are able to connect the dots between what appears to be unrelated global events and the turmoil in the world. Perhaps some of you have not. This latter possibility gave me pause and compelled me to do more research. I became deeply serious and involved in it. I researched everything from drugs, the CIA, reincarnation, religion and its symbols, and quantum physics.

After having done all the research, I realized that it might be too far out for some people. Thus, I decided to use the "mainstream" knowledge via the five senses to help those Readers connect the dots. When I employ the words "mainstream" I am referring to accepted science as well as to the source of where most people obtain their news. In terms of the news, I am talking about media outlets such as CBS, NBC, MSNBC, and so forth. These sources are important because they are the "norm," which shape and control most people's awareness of what is happening in the world. My logic is simple: to use evidence in the accepted belief systems to point out that even with the limited five senses one could connect much of the dots.

I started with the dark arts and quickly found evidence that witchcraft has indeed penetrated every aspect of our world community behind closed doors. One of the videos that I found was Tim Russert of MSNBC, Meet The Press, interviewing George W. Bush and John Kerry. This video can be found on the internet under the title **George Bush and John Kerry Skull and Bones members 322.** The following is the transcript.

> TIM RUSSERT: You are both in Skull & Bones, a secret society.
> GEORGE W. BUSH: It's so secret that we can't talk about it.
> TIM RUSSERT: What does that mean to America?

George W. Bush is momentarily silent.

> TIM RUSSERT: The conspiracy theorists are going to go wild.

George Bush laughs boisterously.

> GEORGE W. BUSH: I don't know.   I haven't seen...
> TIM RUSSERT: Do you remember?
> GEORGE W. BUSH: First of all, he's not the nominee and the...I look forward to, and the, but uh
> TIM RUSSERT: Are you prepared to lose?
> GEORGE W. BUSH: No, I'm not going to lose.

The video switches to John Kerry:

> TIM RUSSERT: You are both members of Skull & Bones.

JOHN KERRY: Not much because it's a secret. [Laughs heartily] Ha, ha.

TIM RUSSERT: Is there a handshake? Is there a secret code?

JOHN KERRY: I wish there were something secret I could manifest.

TIM RUSSERT: 322? A secret number?

JOHN KERRY: I know all kinds of secrets Tim, but one thing that's not a secret—I disagree with this president's direction that he is taking the country. We can do a better job and I intend to do it.

TIM RUSSERT: And we'll be watching. Be safe on the campaign trail. John Kerry, thanks for joining us. We'll be right back.

The next mainstream video I found was titled "Bohemian Grove Detailed Report 7 23 1982 NBC." I did not transcribe it, but you can find it by typing in the title in Google or YouTube or any other internet search engines. The video basically describes the people who were attending the Bohemian Grove, a place located in California where world leaders practice witchcraft in secret and engage in weird rituals in front of a very, very tall owl. Among the attendees that July of 1982 are George Schultz, Henry Kissinger, Chairman of General Motors and U.S. Steel, captain of industries, Gerald Ford, Helmut Schmidt, who was the Chancellor of West Germany, Ronald Reagan and Richard Nixon.

After viewing the video, I was interested in knowing whether or not there were other interviews which Tim Russert did on witchcraft. I found one titled "Jack Blood interviews Tim Russert." In this video, Tim specifically states that he had been invited to the Bohemian Grove, but turned down the invitation. *Hum, I wonder why he was assassinated!* He also said, "I think as I understand it the Bohemian Grove is pretty bipartisan: They have Republicans, Democrats, liberals, conservatives." This statement is very important, for it shows that there is an illusion that these political parties are different. They are not Republicans, Democrats, Conservatives, etc. They are all the same. They are only different on the surface. They produce the **same chaos** in the world. When one does the research one quickly understands that the same thing is true in England, Africa, and the rest of the world. These people are meeting in secret because their intent is malevolent. The next video shows exactly that.

I know that John F. Kennedy has his shortcomings (i.e., women), but I strongly believe that he was our last true defender of the Constitution of the United States and our freedom as Americans in general. This short version of the video is titled "JFK Reveals Skull and Bones society—zeitgeist—NOW."

JOHN F. KENNEDY: The very word "secrecy" is repugnant in a free and open society, and we are as a people inherently and historically opposed to secret societies, to secret oaths, and secret proceeding; for we are opposed around the world by a monolithic and ruthless conspiracy that relies primarily on covet means for expanding its sphere of influences; on infiltration instead of invasion, on subversion instead of elections, on intimidation instead of free choice. It is a system which has conscripted vast human and material resources into the building of tightly knit, highly efficient machine that combines military, diplomatic, intelligence, economic, scientific and political operations. Its preparations are concealed, not published. Its mistakes are buried not headlined. Its dissenters are silenced, not praised. No expenditure is questioned, no secret is revealed. That is why the Athenian law makers so decreed a crime for any citizen who shriek from controversy. I am asking your help in the tremendous task in informing and alerting the American people, confident with your help, man will be what he was born to be—free and independent.

Reader, I hope you have noticed the words "monolithic" and "system." JFK specifically said that the conspiracy is real, and is a single heavy unit that has penetrated every element of our social fabric. This was the president of the United States of America. It really boggles my mind when people brush away evidence and simply say "I do not believe in conspiracies." It is like they are in denial. The world is screwed up on purpose. It is not incompetency or a "conspiracy." It is being done **ON PURPOSE**. The assassination of JFK was no accident. Wars are no accidents. All of these things are orchestrated.

The next video transcript is titled "CIA Operations Secret Documents Made Public 6 24 2007 ABC" and shows just that.

LIZ MARLANTES: They are known as the "Family Jewels" document so secret and so potentially damaging that the CIA has fought to keep them occupied until now.

THOMAS BLANTON: The Family Jewels are a series of CIA officers going into the confessional and saying "forgive me father, for I have sinned.

LIZ MARLANTES: Then CIA director James Slechenger ordered the 700 page dossier in 1973, compiling decades of illegal activities by the agency. Many details were revealed by newspaper reports and congressional hearings. It is the stuff of spy novels. Among the abuses: assassination conspiracies against foreign leaders like Fidel Castro, the infiltration of anti-war groups and screening of private mail, including letters to actress and anti-war activist Jane Fonda. The CIA also put journalists under surveillance like columnist Jack Anderson and his then assistant Bret Hume.

MICHAEL GETLER [Former Washington Post Reporter] It was very spooky, very spooky. I mean this is America and you don't expect that.

LIZ MARLANTES: Former Washington Post Reporter Michael Getler was monitored by a team of agents 'round the clock.

The next video transcript is titled "Barack Obama Talking about the North American Union, Obama Town Hall Event CNN, Lancaster, PA. Reader, before you read the transcript and watch the video, keep in mind what JFK said about secret proceedings and meetings: They are ugly and undesirable in a free and open society. Meetings behind closed doors that involve world leaders in secret location is absolutely intended to do evil things: to control humanity. Reader, I want you to also recall that when Barack Obama was running for president, he kept using the word "transparency." There is absolutely no such thing when one meets in secret. This transcript is proof that Barack Obama is part of the negative control system. He is **not** a leader. The conversation begins with a man with a cap speaking:

MAN WEARING CAP: It's been reported that you and your wife are in the globalists CFR, which is the Council on Foreign Relations. Uhm, and uhm, I'd like to know if that is true and also I'd like to know where you stand on the North American Union, which has been confirmed recently in the Press. Ron Paul actually spoke about it and the Congress actually spent some money on it. This North American Union involves a union much like the European Union, only with Canada, Mexico and the United States and the possible merging of the money system into a piece called the Amero, uh which would actually strip the United States of its sovereignty and perhaps our rights. Where do you stand on that?

BARACK OBAMA: First of all, I'm not the,...the Council on Foreign Relations, I don't know if I am an official member. I've spoken there before. Uh, it's basically a forum where a bunch of people talk about foreign policy. There's no official membership. I don't have a card, or you know, a special handshake or anything like that. The, in terms of this North America Union; this has been something that Ron Paul has talked about and people have talked about. I have to say with all due respect, I see no evidence of this actually taking place. I think that this has been something that has been ginned up in certain blogs and the internet.

The video switches to Lou Dobbs.

LOU DOBBS: The Bush Administration is pushing, and pushing hard, a partnership between the U.S. and Mexico, and Canada with a goal of it call integration by 2010. This partnership among three nations is being discussed at the highest levels of the three governments at the urging of the largest multinational corporations, but it is barreling ahead with absolutely no congressional oversight, no voter approval, out of sight completely of the American people, and as far as we can determine without any constitutional authority whatsoever.

LOU DOBBS: Some uninformed people are suggesting that this isn't even happening. I saw a number of articles that say that this is a fiction, some wild conspiracy theory. Yet, it is absolutely documented. This administration continues to deny what's happening right in front of us, although it's happening with stealth and secrecy. It's happening.

So far we have seen how so accurate JFK was. Obama and multinational corporations seek to have more control over our freedom. Obama has admitted that he has partaken in secret proceedings. The control system wants more power, and is trying to do it through physical control of the human body.

The next video transcript is titled "Introduction of the Microchip." It was briefly shown in 2005, I believe. It is absolutely essential that you watch the video and read the transcript below.

PETER JENNINGS: Finally, from us this evening—technology on the cutting edge. We were interested today to hear that more than a hundred law enforcement officials in Mexico are having microchips implanted in their arms. The chip allows a person to be scanned, sort of like a cereal box at the supermarket check-out. In Mexico, this will be one more tool against crime.

JOHN MCKENZIE: You've seen it before.

VOICE ON FILM: These are the access codes microchip inside the body; a hidden high-tech identification tag. Now Mexico's attorney general and 160 of his deputies have had microchips implanted in their arms, to control access to the country's new criminal investigation center.

A.G. MACEDO DE LA CONCH: Es para acceso—

MCKENZIE: It is to provide access, said the attorney general, to the right people in exclusive areas, where there is valuable sensitive information. The microchip, the size of a grain of rice, is injected under the skin and gives off a low-frequency radio wave. A scanner reads each chip's identification number to verify an official security clearance.

SCOTT SILVERMAN [Applied Digital Solutions] The microchip is tamper-proof, it's secured; no one can take your microchip and use it to their advantage to gain access to your facility.

JOHN MCKENZIE: The chip, developed by Applied Digital Solutions, is similar to those used in the U.S. to identify and return runaway dogs. In humans, it can have several uses...the chip could also be programmed to carry medical information.

A picture of the microchip is shown.

JOHN MCKENZIE: The one in this patient details his blood type, allergies, and the fact that he has Alzheimer's disease. The chip is awaiting approval from the Food and Drug Administration. Some researchers are developing microchips for use in the home, so that wearing one turn on lights and open doors, hands free. The next step say researchers, is to develop an implantable chip with a global positioning system to track people miles away— whether kidnapped or lost—just as cars can now be traced: a kind of low-jack for the body. John McKenzie, ABC News, New York

PETER JENNINGS: That is our report on World News tonight. I am Peter Jennings. We hope you have a good evening. Good night.

A similar video that explains what the microchip is can be found under the titled "2017 Microchip New World Order Master Plan." This is also a mainstream video with a popular news reporter. It precisely states that Applied Digital Solutions wants to start implanting the microchips into human beings in 2017.

After reading and watching these videos about the microchip, I hope you were not fooled about the false benefits that the journalists presented. The microchip is not only dangerous, but will serve as a lethal weapon to controlling humanity in an unbelievable way. The ultimate goal is to limit our god-like awareness in this physical realm of existence so that we are caught in fear so that we suffer and radiate energy that negative inter-dimensional entities can feed on.

In order to fully appreciate the negative intent of the microchip, one must understand what the human body really is. Imagine having cable television. In order for you to have cable initially, the cable guy is obliged to come to your house to set up the system. Keep in mind that the key word here is "initially." He or she puts or connects a chip (a piece of an electronic device) to the television. Once the cable system is set up, the guy leaves. He or she returns to his company in some location far away from your home. The cable connection is set up and the customer is happy because he or she now has access to the cable network. However, consider this question: If a customer wants to add an additional station to his or her television system, does the cable guy have to come back to the house or apartment to add the channel? The answer is an absolute no. The cable guy does not have to return because he or she can now "add" the new channel from the "remote" station. How is this done? This is because a signal is sent to the customer's house or residence using a remote control system. The remote computer system is now able to connect with your television at your house.

Now, imagine how the internet works. I have a laptop computer. I can go to several locations such as Star Bucks, McDonald's and connect to it without wires. This is possible because my computer is connecting to a network: one computer to another. How is all this connected to the human body? As I said earlier, the human body is a biological computer. It can connect with other biological beings and physical computers. This is a fact. There are a handful of people who really understand this. They have admitted this in the videos I mentioned above.

Once the microchip is inside the human body, a person can be controlled and manipulated from a remote location. What these global corporations are seeking to do is to implant microchips that are the size of a grain of rice inside each human being, supposedly to store medical and financial information. Recall what I said earlier, if one could add an additional station to one's television system without the cable guy coming back to your house, the corporations can add and manipulate information on the microchip in the your body. They can determine how you feel emotionally, physically, and spiritually. This is because the human body is an electrical, magnetic being.

As I mentioned at the beginning of this book, the more *formally* "educated" a person is, the more likely it is that his or her soul exists in a dormant state. If you think that biologists, chemists, or doctors truly understand what the human body really is, then think again. There is a reason why the mainstream science says that we human beings use less 10 percent of our brain. Imagine someone standing in a big circle. Once in, the person only has access to ten percent of the entire circle at any particular time he or she moves within it. Now, do you really think that that person is aware of what is on the entire circle? No, of course not. Yet, this is the position that most people make their claims or base their knowledge on. If someone comes along and says something that seems different from that 10 percent mode of knowing, then that person is called crazy or is brushed aside without consideration. Yet, if one looks closely at that 10 percent norm-based knowledge one can sometimes find evidence that supports the "crazy" person's statements.

Let us briefly explore the five senses with an example. Yesterday, I spoke to one of my good-hearted colleagues about the microchip. He went to an Ivy-league university just like me. He teaches science and is very well-learned. I believe that his soul is very bright though I am thoroughly convinced that he does not know he has one and that it is inside his physical body. I kept this in mind when I walked into his classroom.

"What's new?" he asked me.

"Not much. I just finished the first draft of the book. I have to rework the conclusion," I answered. I read in his face that he did not know that I was working on a book.

"... The part about the human body is especially interesting. I am convinced that most people do not know what the physical body really is..."

Before I knew it, I was telling him about the microchip.

"They want to implant a microchip inside each person. The chip is awaiting FDA approval for 2017."

"It won't be approved."

"Even if people refuse it, I am sure they will find a way to sneak it into vaccines like flu shots."

"They can't make you do anything. There are a lot of redundant cells in the human body. The chip would be just one cell...They can make you sick. There is free will. No one can make you do anything."

I listened and thought about his words. They were making sense, but leaving out other elements of the puzzle. Microchips are not needed to convince our young men and women to go to war. They accept to do it mostly because they have been manipulated through the spoken word that they are really protecting their countries. Microchips are not needed to make people pay income taxes.

Let us return to what my colleague is not aware of. He is not considering the fact that there are hidden advanced technologies out there such as HAARP. HAARP can cause earthquakes. It has been briefly shown in the mainstream media. Lastly, there is the inter-dimensional element that my colleague would never consider. Inter-dimensional dark beings exist and are manipulating our world.

Given that it was past four o'clock in the afternoon and most teachers had already gone home, he suggested that we take the conversation to the photocopy machine room. I went there and was unsuccessfully trying to make copies for my French Beg.2 and 3H classes. The copier was jammed. He arrived less than a minute later. He was now at the left copy machine, and I was at the one at the right. After a little while, I began again.

"We cannot understand this whole thing if we only base it on the five senses."

"Let me say that I don't believe in the afterlife…I don't believe in things you can't prove," he said.

"Let me ask you a question about ultraviolet lights. I don't know when they were discovered—"

"They were discovered decades ago," he said.

"So, they were discovered very recently. There are things that exist that cannot be seen with the five senses without ultraviolet lights. They are invisible to the human eye. You need an instrument to see them. Now, if you lived in an era where there was no such instrument, would you have believed that such lights do not exist?"

He did not answer my question. I thought to myself: *There is a reason why our all time famous scientist Sir Isaac Newton's research into the spiritual world was kept from the norm of scientific community. There is a reason why Albert Einstein's God letter kept out of the norm of our educational institutions.*

Without realizing it, he said something even better.

"Just because you can't prove it does not mean that it doesn't exist."

"That's good enough for me," I said. I felt the conversation needed to come to an end, for I knew he would hold firm to his old paradigm even if I had given him more mainstream information for consideration. The conversation, however, allowed me to better verbalize the whole "prove it" or "nobody knows" crazy mentality. I decided to research two of the five senses: sight and hearing.

As I have alluded to earlier, the vast majority of human beings do not have full access to their five senses. Let us consider the sense of sight which I mentioned earlier in terms of ultraviolet lights. These lights cannot be seen with the naked eye without using an instrument, but yet they exist. Recall what my colleague said: "Just because you can't prove it does not mean that it doesn't exist."

Human beings' sense of hearing is also limited. Let us consider sound for example. A quick search on Wikipedia states the following about sound:

> Technically, sound is the propagation of longitudinal waves through matter. Sound waves involve longitudinal particle displacements in all kinds of matter—solid, liquid, or gaz. The wave motion of sound depends on the elasticity of the medium...Sound waves may have different frequencies and so form a spectrum similar to the electromagnetic spectrum. However, the sound

374

spectrum has much lower frequencies and is much simpler, with only three frequency regions. These regions are defined in terms of the audible range of human hearing, which is about 20 Hz to 20KHz and constitutes the audible region of the spectrum. Below the audible region is the infrasonic region, and above is the ultrasonic region. Waves in the infrasonic region, which humans cannot hear, are found in nature...Elephants and cattle have hearing response in the infrasonic region and may get advance warnings of earthquakes and weather disturbances...Sound is sometimes defined as those disturbances perceived by the human ear—this definition would omit a majority of the sound spectrum.

In other words, this scientific article is saying that if one were to focus solely on one portion of sound, one would be negating the other two-thirds of the spectrum. Hence, human beings only have access to *a **third*** of the actual total sound system. When you understand this, statements such as "You're hearings things" loses most of its negative connotation. One is then obliged to reconsider the fact that the person hearing "such things" may not be crazy after all. Well, unless one is in denial. I am not in any shape or form saying that one should automatically believe "the crazy" person. I am saying that it is foolish to rule out that person's claims or assertions without first carefully considering it.

My conclusion is as follows: It is a mistake to base everything on the limited five senses. We do not have full access to each of these five senses. Furthermore, the *norm* of human society is not technologically advanced enough to prove much of what it cannot see or hear. Despite this limitation, if the unaware or slightly aware person takes the time to analyze what the *norm* is hiding in the open, he or she at least will begin to connect the dots. He or she will begin to understand the bigger picture. He or she will see that our food supply is being poisoned, that the tax system is a fraud, that money is mostly just numbers on the computer screen, that there are hidden technologies such as HAARP that can cause earthquakes, that presidents and world leaders are part of secret societies, that there is a calculated purpose for war other than money or oil, that we cannot really own our own land or house in "developed" countries, that we have an education system that is based on the worship of the superficial (i.e., the mind or the intellect), that we are given a mostly-false science and religions, that there are "invisible" inter-dimensional entities who serve as the puppet masters, and that we are told that we have to bow down to a superior being called "God" because He "created" us. YES! One would be correct in saying that there is one God, but the minute *anyone or any being* says that "God" is superior, one is still stuck in "mind." There are layers of God, from the physical to the none-physical, the Most Light. There are layers of you—Reader. A piece of the none-physical part of God is literally inside your physical body vehicle. It is absolutely God. Not the child of God. You are literally God, a piece of God. Even animals, mammals, etc., are Gods. They have an essence in them that exits the biological physical animal body when they die.

I don't care who you are, where you are from, what your gender is, what your belief system is, you are literally God. Believe it or not, you need no permission to exist. You need not seek salvation. You already have it and will always have it. No exceptions! Even if you have killed someone like my stepfather did, you will not be "judged." You will give yourself and will be given a chance to learn (i.e., to become aware) again even if it means immense suffering. It is not punishment. It is taking responsibility for your purity.

Everybody and everything must eventually reach a state of awareness that is of the Most Light. A million Superman have absolutely nothing on you at the none-physical level. Death is a static perception or illusion. There is no death or birth. The Light Self enters the physical vehicle at the time of birth and sometimes a little earlier. Then, It leaves at the time of death. The perception of birth and death at the physical level is only a very small, minute perception of Infinity. There is no debate about it. Believe me or not, it is not a belief system or faith. It is what it is. You are beautiful beyond imagination. You are so beautiful that it still boggles my current state of mind. Unfortunately, billions of people are still not aware of this. They really need to start taking responsibility for what they do and sometimes what they do not do. You cannot reach this beauty if you are stuck in one perspective of seeing things. You cannot do this if you see only 10 percent of the 360 degree circle no matter how you turn. There is no master, or "superior God" or hierarchy. It only seems like that because you have not reached a state of awareness that allows you to *see* more of Infinity. The key is to become your own master, your own scientist, and to explore new ideas no matter where the source leads you. Often the bizarre is true and the accepted norm is only slightly true. Our goal is not to "believe" or simply be told what is. There is a lot of evidence out there. We have to stop being in denial and open up our minds. The world is screwed on purpose. It is not incompetency. It is not a conspiracy. It is happening now.

…The events of the last few months have shown me the importance of speaking out and not holding back the truth. Evil exists! By this, I mean a stubborn, deeply dark and raw selfishness. Evil hides *in* the human body. Though the base or essence of all souls is the same, no matter what planet,

377

galaxy, or dimension they come from, I must say that some extraterrestrials among us are just that—evil. Extraterrestrials and demons really do exist. On the surface, a typical human being seems human. However, there is no such thing. It is all about the Light body inside the human physical vehicle. Souls come in all sorts of colors. All human beings have some alien DNA in them. There are a lot of souls from other dimensions and star systems who have forgotten where they originated. They think they are human beings. Some are of the pure, brilliant Infinite light; while others come from very, very dark places in the universe. Barack Obama, Nicolas Sarkozy, the George Bush family, Hilary Clinton, the Pope, Tony Blair, and most world leaders who maintain and keep a hierarchical governing system, come from a very dark place. What we have here are global terrorists pretending to be good souls. Barack's soul is immensely dark and evil. There is a reason why he did not get permission from Congress before he started dropping bombs on Libya. There is a reason why he sent tens of thousands of troops to Afghanistan. He is worst than George W. Bush because he is slick like the fox. There is a reason why he is also his distant cousin. He knows how to sell lies better than him. The slow, complete fluttering of their eyes is not a lie.

There is no hierarchy![8] A society that is built on hierarchy in itself is ugly, repugnant, and is an insult to the luminosity of Infinity (i.e., God). Our current system was built on

---

[8] The words "hierarchy" and "superior" should not be confused. I am finding that a lot of people are confusing them. Just because I say that there is no hierarchy does not mean that the Source or God is not the ultimate power. It is, because clarity or Purity is ALWAYS more "powerful." Even the word powerful is not the right choice of word, but we are after all in the Third Dimension.

hierarchy. Presidents are the new versions of kings and queens of days of old. Only the names have changed. No politician is safe to vote for. *Stop feeding the beast by voting.* It only encourages the dark ones...**No!** Don't even think about it—Ron Paul is also a distraction. Anyone who props up such a system or keeps it going for even a month is preventing you from enjoying and literally feeling your Infinite freedom.

Reader, remember who you are! You are Infinity. Everything is a distraction: the poisonous Monsanto food that we eat, the house, the money, the fame, the fancy car, wars, gender bias, the voting system, the formal education system, Charles Darwin's racist theory of evolution, science, religion, reincarnation, too much focus on being an ET in a human body; and for the love of God, even the beautiful girl and red wine! When you refuse to join the army and to vote, you have already changed not only the world but the entire universe for the better. You are that powerful (i.e., Light).

What is at stake here is a lot more than just this planet. The battle goes all the way to Infinity. There are beautiful souls such as Mother Earth and Mother Ayahuasca in the South American Amazon who are helping us, but they cannot do it alone. I understand now why Mother Earth allows some earthquakes—the enormity of the negativity is too deep. Please stop destroying my Earth!

You are supposed to awaken to your God Self. Even if it takes a million years, you have to do it. Why can't you do it in this life time? What are you waiting for? Is it the mortgage? Losing your home? Money? Fear of being killed or assassinated? Fear of someone casting a spell on you? Enough of the mundane, superficial, fear-based answers! You are eternal and cannot die. Let the positivity of the brightest part of your Light shine. Your success is my success because there is really only one of us here. We are all soul mates. It is a win-win situation. We can make this world a paradise ***RIGHT NOW*** if we choose. We have to take ownership and more responsibility of who we really are beyond our dense, physical body. Like John F. Kennedy, I am asking your help in the tremendous task in helping, informing and alerting the world, confident with your help, we will be what we were born to be—free and independent. God speed!

Printed in Great Britain
by Amazon

74959420R10220